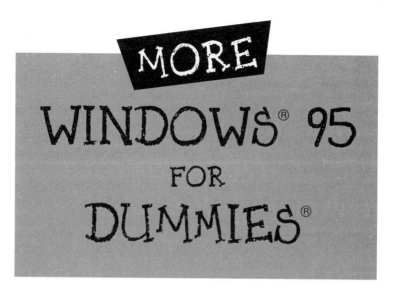

MORE WINDOWS® 95 FOR DUMMIES®

by Andy Rathbone

IDG Books Worldwide, Inc.
An International Data Group Company

Foster City, CA ♦ Chicago, IL ♦ Indianapolis, IN ♦ Southlake, TX

MORE Windows® 95 For Dummies®

Published by

IDG Books Worldwide, Inc.
An International Data Group Company
919 E. Hillsdale Blvd.
Suite 400
Foster City, CA 94404
www.dummies.com
www.idgbooks.com

Library of Congress Catalog Card No.: 96-76361

ISBN: 1-56884-607-X

Printed in the United States of America

10 9 8 7 6

1B/QX/QY/ZX/IN

Distributed in the United States by IDG Books Worldwide, Inc.

Distributed by Macmillan Canada for Canada; by Transworld Publishers Limited in the United Kingdom; by IDG Norge Books for Norway; by IDG Sweden Books for Sweden; by Woodslane Pty. Ltd. for Australia; by Woodslane Enterprises Ltd. for New Zealand; by Longman Singapore Publishers Ltd. for Singapore, Malaysia, Thailand, and Indonesia; by Simron Pty. Ltd. for South Africa; by Toppan Company Ltd. for Japan; by Distribuidora Cuspide for Argentina; by Livraria Cultura for Brazil; by Ediciencia S.A. for Ecuador; by Addison-Wesley Publishing Company for Korea; by Ediciones ZETA S.C.R. Ltda. for Peru; by WS Computer Publishing Corporation, Inc., for the Philippines; by Unalis Corporation for Taiwan; by Contemporanea de Ediciones for Venezuela; by Computer Book & Magazine Store for Puerto Rico; by Express Computer Distributors for the Caribbean and West Indies. Authorized Sales Agent: Anthony Rudkin Associates for the Middle East and North Africa.

For general information on IDG Books Worldwide's books in the U.S., please call our Consumer Customer Service department at 800-762-2974. For reseller information, including discounts and premium sales, please call our Reseller Customer Service department at 800-434-3422.

For information on where to purchase IDG Books Worldwide's books outside the U.S., please contact our International Sales department at 415-655-3200 or fax 415-655-3295.

For information on foreign language translations, please contact our Foreign & Subsidiary Rights department at 415-655-3021 or fax 415-655-3281.

For sales inquiries and special prices for bulk quantities, please contact our Sales department at 415-655-3200 or write to the address above.

For information on using IDG Books Worldwide's books in the classroom or for ordering examination copies, please contact our Educational Sales department at 800-434-2086 or fax 817-251-8174.

For press review copies, author interviews, or other publicity information, please contact our Public Relations department at 415-655-3000 or fax 415-655-3299.

For authorization to photocopy items for corporate, personal, or educational use, please contact Copyright Clearance Center, 222 Rosewood Drive, Danvers, MA 01923, or fax 508-750-4470.

Trademarks: All brand names and product names used in this book are trade names, service marks, trademarks, or registered trademarks of their respective owners. IDG Books Worldwide is not associated with any product or vendor mentioned in this book.

 is a trademark under exclusive license to IDG Books Worldwide, Inc., from International Data Group, Inc.

About the Author

Andy Rathbone started geeking around with computers in 1985 when he bought a boxy CP/M Kaypro 2X with lime-green letters. Like other budding nerds, he soon began playing with null-modem adapters, dialing up computer bulletin boards, and working part time at Radio Shack.

In between playing computer games, he served as editor of the *Daily Aztec* newspaper at San Diego State University. After graduating with a comparative literature degree, he went to work for a bizarre underground coffee-table magazine that sort of disappeared.

Andy began combining his two interests, words and computers, by selling articles to a local computer magazine. During the next few years, Rathbone started ghostwriting computer books for more-famous computer authors, as well as writing several hundred articles about computers for technoid publications like *Supercomputing Review, CompuServe, ID Systems, DataPro,* and *Shareware.*

In 1992, Andy and *DOS For Dummies* author/legend Dan Gookin teamed up to write *PCs For Dummies,* which was a runner-up in the Computer Press Association's 1993 awards. Andy subsequently wrote *Windows 95 For Dummies, OS/2 Warp For Dummies,* 2nd Edition, *Upgrading & Fixing PCs For Dummies,* 2nd Edition, and *Multimedia & CD-ROMs For Dummies.*

Andy is currently writing *Windows NT For Dummies,* as well as contributing regularly to *CompuServe,* a magazine mailed monthly to CompuServe members. (Feel free to drop him a line at 75300,1565.)

Andy lives with his most-excellent wife, Tina, and their cat in San Diego, California. When not writing, Rathbone fiddles with his MIDI synthesizer and tries to keep the cat off both keyboards.

ABOUT IDG BOOKS WORLDWIDE

Welcome to the world of IDG Books Worldwide.

IDG Books Worldwide, Inc., is a subsidiary of International Data Group, the world's largest publisher of computer-related information and the leading global provider of information services on information technology. IDG was founded more than 25 years ago and now employs more than 8,500 people worldwide. IDG publishes more than 275 computer publications in over 75 countries (see listing below). More than 60 million people read one or more IDG publications each month.

Launched in 1990, IDG Books Worldwide is today the #1 publisher of best-selling computer books in the United States. We are proud to have received eight awards from the Computer Press Association in recognition of editorial excellence and three from *Computer Currents'* First Annual Readers' Choice Awards. Our best-selling *...For Dummies®* series has more than 30 million copies in print with translations in 30 languages. IDG Books Worldwide, through a joint venture with IDG's Hi-Tech Beijing, became the first U.S. publisher to publish a computer book in the People's Republic of China. In record time, IDG Books Worldwide has become the first choice for millions of readers around the world who want to learn how to better manage their businesses.

Our mission is simple: Every one of our books is designed to bring extra value and skill-building instructions to the reader. Our books are written by experts who understand and care about our readers. The knowledge base of our editorial staff comes from years of experience in publishing, education, and journalism — experience we use to produce books for the '90s. In short, we care about books, so we attract the best people. We devote special attention to details such as audience, interior design, use of icons, and illustrations. And because we use an efficient process of authoring, editing, and desktop publishing our books electronically, we can spend more time ensuring superior content and spend less time on the technicalities of making books.

You can count on our commitment to deliver high-quality books at competitive prices on topics you want to read about. At IDG Books Worldwide, we continue in the IDG tradition of delivering quality for more than 25 years. You'll find no better book on a subject than one from IDG Books Worldwide.

IDG BOOKS WORLDWIDE

John Kilcullen
CEO
IDG Books Worldwide, Inc.

Steven Berkowitz
President and Publisher
IDG Books Worldwide, Inc.

Eighth Annual
Computer Press
Awards ≥1992

Ninth Annual
Computer Press
Awards ≥1993

Tenth Annual
Computer Press
Awards ≥1994

Eleventh Annual
Computer Press
Awards ≥1995

IDG Books Worldwide, Inc., is a subsidiary of International Data Group, the world's largest publisher of computer-related information and the leading global provider of information services on information technology. International Data Group publishes over 275 computer publications in over 75 countries. Sixty million people read one or more International Data Group publications each month. International Data Group's publications include: **ARGENTINA:** Buyer's Guide, Computerworld Argentina, PC World Argentina; **AUSTRALIA:** Australian Macworld, Australian PC World, Australian Reseller News, Computerworld, IT Casebook, Network World, Publish, Webmaster; **AUSTRIA:** Computerwelt Österreich, Networks Austria, PC Tip Austria; **BANGLADESH:** PC World Bangladesh; **BELARUS:** PC World Belarus; **BELGIUM:** Data News; **BRAZIL:** Annuário de Informática, Computerworld, Connections, Macworld, PC Player, PC World, Publish, Reseller News, Supergamepower; **BULGARIA:** Computerworld Bulgaria, Network World Bulgaria, PC & MacWorld Bulgaria; **CANADA:** CIO Canada, Client/Server World, ComputerWorld Canada, InfoWorld Canada, NetworkWorld Canada, WebWorld; **CHILE:** Computerworld Chile, PC World Chile; **COLOMBIA:** Computerworld Colombia, PC World Colombia; **COSTA RICA:** PC World Centro America; **THE CZECH AND SLOVAK REPUBLICS:** Computerworld Czechoslovakia, Macworld Czech Republic, PC World Czechoslovakia; **DENMARK:** Communications World Danmark, Computerworld Danmark, Macworld Danmark, PC World Danmark, Techworld Denmark; **DOMINICAN REPUBLIC:** PC World Republica Dominicana; **ECUADOR:** PC World Ecuador; **EGYPT:** Computerworld Middle East, PC World Middle East; **EL SALVADOR:** PC World Centro America; **FINLAND:** MikroPC, Tietoverkko, Tietoviikko; **FRANCE:** Distributique, Hebdo, Info PC, Le Monde Informatique, Macworld, Reseaux & Telecoms, WebMaster France; **GERMANY:** Computer Partner, Computerwoche, Computerwoche Extra, Computerwoche FOCUS, Global Online, Macwelt, PC Welt; **GREECE:** Amiga Computing, GamePro Greece, Multimedia World; **GUATEMALA:** PC World Centro America; **HONDURAS:** PC World Centro America; **HONG KONG:** Computerworld Hong Kong, PC World Hong Kong, Publish in Asia; **HUNGARY:** ABCD CD-ROM, Computerworld Szamitastechnika, Internetto online Magazine, PC World Hungary, PC-X Magazin Hungary; **ICELAND:** Tolvuheimur PC World Island; **INDIA:** Information Communications World, Information Systems Computerworld, PC World India, Publish in Asia; **INDONESIA:** InfoKomputer PC World, Komputek Computerworld, Publish in Asia; **IRELAND:** ComputerScope, PC Live!; **ISRAEL:** Macworld Israel, People & Computers/Computerworld; **ITALY:** Computerworld Italia, Macworld Italia, Networking Italia, PC World Italia; **JAPAN:** DTP World, Macworld Japan, Nikkei Personal Computing, OS/2 World Japan, SunWorld Japan, Windows NT World, Windows World Japan; **KENYA:** PC World East African; **KOREA:** Hi-Tech Information, Macworld Korea, PC World Korea; **MACEDONIA:** PC World Macedonia; **MALAYSIA:** Computerworld Malaysia, PC World Malaysia, Publish in Asia; **MALTA:** PC World Malta; **MEXICO:** Computerworld Mexico, PC World Mexico; **MYANMAR:** PC World Myanmar; **NETHERLANDS:** Computer! Totaal, LAN Internetworking Magazine, LAN World Buyers Guide, Macworld Netherlands, Net, WebWereld; **NEW ZEALAND:** Absolute Beginners Guide and Plain & Simple Series, Computer Buyer, Computer Industry Directory, Computerworld New Zealand, MTB, Network World, PC World New Zealand; **NICARAGUA:** PC World Centro America; **NORWAY:** Computerworld Norge, CW Rapport, Datamagasinet, Financial Rapport, Kursguide Norge, Macworld Norge, Multimediaworld Norge, PC World Ekspress Norge, PC World Nettverk, PC World Norge, PC World ProduktGuide Norge; **PAKISTAN:** Computerworld Pakistan; **PANAMA:** PC World Panama; **PEOPLE'S REPUBLIC OF CHINA:** China Computer Users, China Computerworld, China InfoWorld, China Telecom World Weekly, Computer & Communication, Electronic Design China, Electronics Today, Electronics Weekly, Game Software, PC World China, Popular Computer Week, Software Weekly, Software World, Telecom World; **PERU:** Computerworld Peru, PC World Profesional Peru, PC World SoHo Peru; **PHILIPPINES:** Click!, Computerworld Philippines, PC World Philippines, Publish in Asia; **POLAND:** Computerworld Poland, Computerworld Special Report Poland, Cyber, Macworld Poland, Networld Poland, PC World Komputer; **PORTUGAL:** Cerebro/PC World, Computerworld/Correio Informático, Dealer World Portugal, Mac*In/PC*In Portugal, Multimedia World; **PUERTO RICO:** PC World Puerto Rico; **ROMANIA:** Computerworld Romania, PC World Romania, Telecom Romania; **RUSSIA:** Computerworld Russia, Mir PK, Publish, Seti; **SINGAPORE:** Computerworld Singapore, PC World Singapore, Publish in Asia; **SLOVENIA:** Monitor; **SOUTH AFRICA:** Computing SA, Network World SA, Software World SA; **SPAIN:** Communicaciones World España, Computerworld España, Dealer World España, Macworld España, PC World España; **SRI LANKA:** Infolink PC World; **SWEDEN:** CAP&Design, Computer Sweden, Corporate Computing Sweden, Internetworld Sweden, it.branschen, Macworld Sweden, MaxiData Sweden, MikroDatorn, Nätverk & Kommunikation, PC World Sweden, PCaktiv, Windows World Sweden; **SWITZERLAND:** Computerworld Schweiz, Macworld Schweiz, PCtip; **TAIWAN:** Computerworld Taiwan, Macworld Taiwan, NEW ViSiON/Publish, PC World Taiwan, Windows World Taiwan; **THAILAND:** Publish in Asia, Thai Computerworld; **TURKEY:** Computerworld Turkiye, Macworld Turkiye, Network World Turkiye, PC World Turkiye; **UKRAINE:** Computerworld Kiev, Multimedia World Ukraine, PC World Ukraine; **UNITED KINGDOM:** Acorn User UK, Amiga Action UK, Amiga Computing UK, Apple Talk UK, Computing, Macworld, Parents and Computers UK, PC Advisor, PC Home, PSX Pro, The WEB; **UNITED STATES:** Cable in the Classroom, CIO Magazine, Computerworld, DOS World, Federal Computer Week, GamePro Magazine, InfoWorld, I-Way, Macworld, Network World, PC Games, PC World, Publish, Video Event, THE WEB Magazine, and WebMaster; online webzines: JavaWorld, NetscapeWorld, and SunWorld Online; **URUGUAY:** InfoWorld Uruguay; **VENEZUELA:** Computerworld Venezuela, PC World Venezuela; and **VIETNAM:** PC World Vietnam.   3/24/97

Dedication

To Windows users around the world.

Author's Acknowledgments

Special thanks to Tina Rathbone, Matt Wagner, Dan and Sandy Gookin, Mary Corder, Colleen Rainsberger, Suzanne Packer, and Gareth Hancock.

Publisher's Acknowledgments

We're proud of this book; please send us your comments about it by using the Reader Response Card at the back of the book or by e-mailing us at feedback/dummies@idgbooks.com. Some of the people who helped bring this book to market include the following:

Acquisitions, Development, and Editorial

Project Editor: Colleen Rainsberger

Assistant Acquisitions Editor: Gareth Hancock

Permissions Editor: Joyce Pepple

Copy Editors: Suzanne Packer, Kelly Ewing

Technical Reviewer: Rob Rubright

Editorial Manager: Mary C. Corder

Editorial Assistant: Chris H. Collins

Special Help

Mary Goodwin, Project Editor; Julie King; Stephanie Koutek, Proof Editor

Production

Associate Project Coordinator: Regina Snyder

Layout and Graphics: Brett Black, Cameron Booker, Cheryl Denski, Todd Klemme, Jane Martin, Kate Snell, Angela F. Hunckler, Brent Savage

Proofreaders: Jennifer K. Overmyer, Christine Meloy Beck, Rachel Garvey, Nancy Price, Dwight Ramsey, Robert Springer, Carrie Voorhis, Karen York

Indexer: Sharon Duffy

General and Administrative

IDG Books Worldwide, Inc.: John Kilcullen, CEO; Steven Berkowitz, President and Publisher

IDG Books Technology Publishing: Brenda McLaughlin, Senior Vice President and Group Publisher

Dummies Technology Press and Dummies Editorial: Diane Graves Steele, Vice President and Associate Publisher; Judith A. Taylor, Product Marketing Manager; Kristin A. Cocks, Editorial Director

Dummies Trade Press: Kathleen A. Welton, Vice President and Publisher

IDG Books Production for Dummies Press: Beth Jenkins, Production Director; Cindy L. Phipps, Supervisor of Project Coordination, Production Proofreading, and Indexing; Kathie S. Schutte, Supervisor of Page Layout; Shelley Lea, Supervisor of Graphics and Design; Debbie J. Gates, Production Systems Specialist; Tony Augsburger, Supervisor of Reprints and Bluelines; Leslie Popplewell, Media Archive Coordinator

Dummies Packaging and Book Design: Patti Sandez, Packaging Specialist; Lance Kayser, Packaging Assistant; Kavish + Kavish, Cover Design

♦

The publisher would like to give special thanks to Patrick J. McGovern, without whom this book would not have been possible.

♦

Contents at a Glance

Cartoons at a Glance

By Rich Tennant • Fax: 508-546-7747 • E-mail: the5wave@tiac.net

page 7

page 163

page 279

page 195

page 87

Table of Contents

Introduction

● ●

*W*elcome to *MORE Windows 95 For Dummies*, the book for people who find themselves doing more with Windows 95 than they ever wanted to.

The Windows *point-and-click* lifestyle never retires. No matter how long Windows has lived on your computer, it still tosses out fresh bits of confusion at regular intervals. You constantly find yourself needing to make Windows do just a little bit more than it did before. . . .

That's where this book comes in. Don't worry — it doesn't try to turn you into a card-carrying Windows 95 wizard. No, this book merely dishes out the information that you need to make Windows 95 do your bidding. And — if possible — to make Windows do it a little more quickly than before.

About This Book

Windows 95 isn't *new* anymore. Just like anything that's exposed to the weather, Windows 95 occasionally needs a little touching up. How do you make Windows 95 deal with your latest new programs, for example? And how do you get those programs off the floppy disks and onto the Start Menu?

Or perhaps you want to spark up a newsletter or report with a fun new *font*. How? Or maybe you upgraded your computer to make Windows 95 run faster and smoother — but now, unfortunately, Windows refuses to work at all. What do you do?

This book helps you tackle Windows 95 chores such as these:

- ✔ Installing a new program
- ✔ *Un*installing an old program
- ✔ Using those new Microsoft Plus! Windows 95 utilities
- ✔ Making the mouse work right
- ✔ Deciding which Windows 95 files you can get rid of
- ✔ Using Windows 95 on a laptop
- ✔ Calling other computers with HyperTerminal and Exchange
- ✔ Figuring out why everybody else's version of Windows 95 has more programs than yours

The information in this book is in easy-to-read packets that are just like the notes you got from that smart kid in math class with the big front teeth.

How to Use This Book

This book doesn't force you to *learn* anything about Windows 95. Save your brain cells for the important things in life. Instead, treat this book as your favorite reference. When you find yourself facing a particularly odious new Windows chore, find that subject in the Index or Table of Contents. Flip to the appropriate page and follow the step-by-step instructions. Done? Then close the book and finish your Windows work, most likely a little more quickly than before.

You — Yes, You

Chances are, you've been using Windows 95 for a little while — maybe a month or two. You've figured out how to make Windows 95 do *some* things. It may take all day, but you can usually convince Windows 95 to do more or less what you want. But you're getting a little less tolerant of how Windows 95 keeps tossing new obstacles in your path.

If *everything* about Windows 95 looks new and confusing, check out this book's parent, *Windows 95 For Dummies.* It explains how to start moving around in Windows 95 without breaking anything.

But if you're looking to solve those *new* problems that Windows 95 keeps bringing up, this book is for you.

How This Book Is Organized

Everything is easier to find when it's stored in its own well-marked bin, and the information in this book is no exception. This book contains five main parts, with each part divided into several chapters. You don't have to read Chapters 1 through 4, however, before you can figure out what's going on in Chapter 5.

So treat this book like the candy bins at the grocery store. Just reach straight in and grab the piece of information you want when you want it. You don't need to taste *everything* before you reach for the candy in the middle bin. In fact, the guy at the deli counter will yell if you even try.

Instead, just look up your particular problem and find the answer: a self-contained nugget that explains your particular situation and, what's more important, its particular solution.

Here are the book's main parts.

Part I: More on Everyday Stuff

Here you can find answers to those Windows 95 questions that pop up every day. Part I is stuffed with the information you didn't know you needed to know — until you'd been using Windows 95 for a while.

First-timers may want to check out Chapter 1, the *basics* chapter. It explains how to start Windows 95, push its menus around, and shut it down for the day. Chapter 1 is also a handy reference for Windows 95 users who suddenly realize that they need to know the difference between the Save command and the Save As command.

Part II: Making Windows 95 Do More

Sooner or later, you'll need to make Windows 95 do something new. For example, what's all that new modem and Internet stuff? How do you make Windows 95 work with that expensive new sound card? Can Windows *really* work on your new laptop? Part II answers these questions.

Plus, it tells you how to make HyperTerminal do more than simply sound ultra-depressing.

Part III: Getting More Out of Windows 95

Believe it or not, normal, everyday people like you have tricked Windows 95 into doing what they want it to do. Here you find Windows 95 desktops that were arranged by Windows 95 users. You see how they set up Windows 95 to solve their problems and learn what buttons you can push to make Windows 95 just as helpful to you.

Plus, you find clear-cut instructions on how to keep the mouse — and the rest of the computer — rolling down the right path.

Part IV: More Advanced Ugly Tasks Explained Carefully

Windows 95 eventually asks you to do something you'd just as soon not do. This part of the book tackles the most tortuous Windows tasks and turns them into simple, step-by-step procedures. Large signposts carefully mark all the areas that are most likely to collapse first. You even get information on how to use Windows 95 to create your own network.

Part V: More Shortcuts and Tips Galore

Finally, there's no sense in working harder than necessary. This part of the book explains the easiest ways to make Windows 95 do the most work — all with the least amount of effort on your part.

Icons Used in This Book

A picture is worth a thousand words. I'm being paid by the word for this book, so it has lots of *icons* — pictures that say "Look here!" Here's what the icons are saying:

This icon indicates a task or technique explained in step format.

Swerve past these signposts and don't bother slowing down. These icons point out boring pieces of extraneous technical information. (In fact, this technical stuff is only in the book so that your kids will have something to read.)

Keep an eye out for these icons. They point out a quick way of doing something. It's the kind of information that belongs on a note next to the monitor — if there's any room left.

When you need a friendly reminder to do something, you see this icon.

When you need a cautious tap on the shoulder to warn you not to do something, this icon is nearby.

Where to Go from Here

If you're looking for the most base-level Windows information, head for Chapter 1. If you're still stumped, head back to the bookstore for *Windows 95 For Dummies.*

But if you're looking for a just a little more information to get you through the day, you've got the right book right now. Grab it with both hands, and you're ready to start striking back with full force. Good luck!

Part I
More on Everyday Stuff

The 5th Wave   By Rich Tennant

"Hey Dad- guess how many Milk Duds fit inside your disk drive."

In this part . . .

This part of the book covers the stuff Windows 95 tosses at you every day: bunches of boxes that pile up on-screen like junk mail after a vacation. The first chapter explains how to shovel those boxes around so that you can find the good stuff.

The next few chapters talk about how to customize the World of Windows 95. You find out how to install new programs, add wallpaper, change fonts, install new screen savers, switch to new icons, record sounds, and use those other Windows 95 goodies that are flooding the market.

Finally, you learn the answer to that burning question: What the heck are all those other Windows versions supposed to do? Which is best? Should you be using Windows 3.1, Windows for Workgroups, Windows 95, Windows NT, or Windows with a View?

Chapter 1

A Bit o' the Basics

· ·

In This Chapter

▶ Understanding the Windows 95 routine

▶ Starting Windows 95

▶ Using a mouse

▶ Moving windows

▶ Starting a program

▶ Opening a file

▶ Saving a file

▶ Printing a file

▶ Exiting a program

▶ Exiting Windows 95

· ·

*N*ew to Windows 95 or need a refresher? Then you're ready for this chapter. If you've never used Windows 95, you should be reading *Windows 95 For Dummies*, not this sequel. But if you're an extremely fast learner, this chapter might be all that you need to get up to speed.

Here, you find out how to get some work done, despite the fancy *window* metaphor. You figure out how all those little menus are supposed to work and how you can make that little mouse arrow jump to the right places at the right times.

Finally, this chapter makes sure that *you* have the last word: You find out how to shoo Windows 95 off the screen when you've had enough pointing and clicking for one day.

The Windows 95 Computing Routine

Like government bureaucrats, computer users soon learn to follow the same steps over and over. That's the only way to make computers do your bidding.

Windows 95 expects — demands, in fact — that you complete each of the steps in the following list to accomplish just about anything. The rest of this chapter covers each of these steps in full gory detail.

1. **Start Windows.**

   After you flip the computer's on switch, Windows 95 jumps onto the computer screen. This task is called *starting, running,* or *loading* Windows. Luckily, Windows 95 loads itself automatically. (The lazy, earlier versions of Windows all had to be called to the screen by hand.)

2. **Create a new document.**

   In the old versions of Windows (if you're old enough to remember them), you opened a program and then created a file. Windows 95 now reverses matters. You first tell Windows 95 what *type* of file you'd like to create — a text file, a graphics file, spreadsheet, or other sort of file — and Windows 95 obediently loads the program you need for creating that particular file.

   Then you use that program to add your numbers, organize your words, deal your playing cards, or help you perform any other computing chores. (*Programs* — the files that store computerized instructions — are often called *software* or *applications.* The stuff you create — text, spreadsheets, and other goodies — is usually called *data.*)

3. **Name and save your file.**

   Done diddling with your data? Then tell the program to *save* your newly mingled mixture of numbers or words so that you can play with them another day. When you choose a name for your work, the program saves your creation in a computerized container called a *file.*

4. **Exit the program.**

   When you finish using a particular program, close it down. That process is called *exiting* a program. (It's different from *exciting* a program, which appeals only to a few eccentric programmers.)

5. **Exit Windows.**

   Finally, when you're done with Windows, you can make it leave — *exit* — the screen.

Don't just flip the computer's off switch when you're done working in Windows 95. You need to use the Start button's Sh<u>u</u>t Down command so that Windows 95 has time to pack its bags before you shut down the computer.

That's it! The rest of this chapter shows you how to perform those same five steps over and over again. Welcome to computers!

Start Here

Although some people claim that Windows 95 is easy to use, Windows 95 isn't listening. No, Windows 95 usually listens to only two things: the mouse and the keyboard. You can boss Windows 95 around by moving the mouse across your desk and pushing those little buttons on the mouse's back.

The first thing Windows 95 listens for, however, is the click of your computer's on switch, as described in the next section.

Starting Windows 95

This part's easy: Simply turn on your computer, and Windows 95 leaps to the screen. Unfortunately, a few exceptions occasionally occur, and they're described below.

If the screen is blank . . . If your computer and monitor are turned on, but Windows 95 isn't on the screen, try tapping your spacebar. Chances are, Windows 95 is up and running but has turned on its *screen saver* to keep from wearing out your monitor. Tapping the spacebar tells Windows that you've grabbed a Coke from the fridge, returned to the keyboard, and are ready to resume working.

If the screen says C:\> or something similar . . . The little C:\> symbol means that your computer is in MS-DOS mode — an antique method of using computers that some programs (and their users) still cling to. To bring Windows 95 back to the screen, type the word **exit** at the C:\> symbol, as shown below, and press the Enter key:

```
C:\> exit
```

Want to make Windows 95 load itself in a certain way — with your favorite programs already set up and running, for example? Then head for Chapter 17. It's loaded with ways to make Windows 95 start doing your bidding the instant it hits the screen.

Mouse mechanics

Nine out of ten German philosophers agree: Windows 95 prefers computers that are equipped with a mouse. Unlike the whiskered variety, a computer mouse looks like a little plastic bar of soap with a tail that plugs into the back of the computer.

When you nudge the mouse across your desk, Windows 95 responds by nudging a tiny arrow — officially called a mouse *pointer* — across the screen.

When the mouse's arrow points to a button on-screen, push one of the buttons on the mouse's back — usually the left one — to magically push the on-screen button.

  ✔ Don't pick up the mouse and point it at the screen. The little on-screen arrow won't budge, not even if you make spaceship noises. The mouse's belly needs to rub around on your desk.

  ✔ In fact, the mouse works best when it rolls around on a *mousepad,* a flat piece of rubber that looks like a child's place mat.

  ✔ If the mouse has reached the end of its rope and the arrow *still* isn't pointing at the right spot, lift the mouse off the desk. Then set it back down again, giving the cord some slack before nudging it around your desk again. In fact, picking up and repositioning a mouse is a major form of exercise for many computer aficionados.

  ✔ Sometimes, unfortunately, moving the mouse doesn't move the arrow. This heartbreaking predicament is solved in Chapter 10.

  ✔ A mouse has its own mouse language; the major terms are demystified in the following sections.

What's a click?

Pushing a button on the back of a mouse makes a clicking noise. So the engineers behind mouse movements dubbed the press of a button a *click.*

  ✔ You perform a click by pushing and quickly *releasing* the mouse button just as you use a button on a telephone. Pushing and *holding down* the mouse button is a completely different procedure. Computers and their mice take everything very literally.

  ✔ You'll find yourself clicking on lots of things in Windows 95 — buttons, icons, words, edges of squares — even Hovercraft in some of the latest Windows 95 games.

What's a double-click?

You perform a double-click by pushing and releasing the mouse button twice to make two clicks. But there's a catch to double-clicking: You have to press the mouse button *twice in rapid succession.*

If your clicks aren't fast enough, Windows 95 thinks you're just fooling around and making two single-clicks, not a bona fide double-click.

> ✔ After a little practice, you'll be able to double-click or click in the right place at the right time. After all, finding reverse gear the first time took a little practice, too.
>
> ✔ If Windows 95 has trouble telling the difference between your clicks and double-clicks, head for Chapter 10. That chapter shows how to fine-tune the Windows 95 *mouse click recognition* areas.

Which mouse button do I use?

Most mice have two buttons. Some have three, and some real chunky NASA models have a dozen or more. Windows 95 listens to only two mouse buttons — the left one and the right one.

> ✔ The button on the left is for immediate actions. Click or double-click the left button on icons or menus to highlight them or to make them jump into action.
>
> ✔ The button on the right, by contrast, performs more cautious acts. Click the right mouse button on an object — an icon, for example — and Windows 95 brings up a menu listing the things you can do to that object.
>
> ✔ Whenever you see the nonspecific phrase "click the mouse," click the left mouse button to remain safely above the high-water mark.
>
> ✔ If your right mouse button performs like your left mouse button should be performing, then see Chapter 10. Some left-hander may have swapped your mouse buttons.

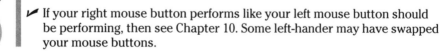

What's a drag 'n' drop?

The *point and click* concept stunned computer scientists with its inherent simplicity. So they took a vote and decided to complicate matters by adding the *drag and drop.*

Here's how it looks with your mouse on the dance floor:

1. Nudge the mouse on your desk until the on-screen arrow points at something on-screen that you want to move — an icon, for example.

2. **Hold down the left mouse button and** *don't* **release it. Then, while still holding down the button, subtly move the mouse.**

The object you point at glues itself to the mouse pointer. As you move the mouse, the pointer moves and *drags* the object along with it.

3. **Drag the object to a new position — a different place on the desktop, for example — and release the mouse button.**

The pointer subsequently lets go of the object and *drops* it in its new location.

- ✔ Dragging and dropping can be a quick way to move stuff around on the screen. If you're not using a mouse with Windows 95, however, you're left out — no dragging and dropping for you.

- ✔ Windows 95 doesn't tell you which things you can drag and drop. Some items drag willingly, but others hold on for dear life.

- ✔ You can drag most of the icons on your desktop, as well as the icons, filenames, and folders in the My Computer and Explorer programs.

- ✔ In Microsoft Word for Windows and some other programs, you can drag around words, paragraphs, and large chunks of text.

Window mechanics

The designers of Windows 95 had to know they were asking for trouble. How could anybody possibly work on a monitor-sized desktop that's smaller than one square foot?

When you work in Windows, everything piles up on top of everything else. You're not doing anything wrong — everything is supposed to pile up. So this section explains how to move extraneous windows out of the way and make the important ones rise to the top.

You also discover how to find that window that was there just a second ago. . . .

Finding a misplaced window

Windows 95 offers as many ways to retrieve windows as it does ways to lose them. To extract your favorite window from the on-screen pile, try these methods until one of 'em works:

- ✔ Can you see any part of the window that you're after? Then click on any part of it. The window instantly rises to the top. Whew!

- ✔ If the window is completely hidden, hold down Alt and press Tab. A little window pops up, as shown in Figure 1-1. Keep pressing Tab until a box surrounds the icon for your missing window and then let go of the Tab key. Your window rises to the top.

Figure 1-1:
Hold down
Alt and
press Tab to
see a list of
currently
open
windows
and
programs;
press Tab to
move from
window to
window.

FreeCell

✔ Click on a blank area of your desktop's *taskbar* — the bar that holds your Start button — and choose the <u>C</u>ascade button from the pop-up menu. Windows 95 deals all the open windows across the screen like playing cards.

✔ Or if you choose either of the Tile options from that same pop-up menu, Windows 95 will rearrange all your open windows across your desktop like tiles on a patio.

Almost any of the preceding techniques can round up and lasso runaway windows.

Changing a window's size or location

Open windows rarely appear on-screen in just the right size. Either they're too big and cover up everything else, or they're too small to play with.

To change a window's size, try any of the following tricks.

Double-click on the title bar

See the bar running across the top of the window in Figure 1-2? A window's title appears in that bar, which is why it's called the *title bar*.

Double-click on the title bar, and the window grows as big as it can. Or if the window *already* is as big as it can get, a deft double-click on the title bar shrinks it back down to normal size.

To move a window around on the screen, drag its title bar. The window turns into a little outline as you drag it around the screen with the mouse. When you like the window's new location, let go of the mouse button to drop the window in the new spot. (Windows that fill the entire screen can't be moved, however.)

Figure 1-2:
Double-click
on a
window's
title to
toggle a
window's
size from
large to
small.

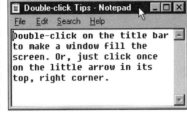

Drag its borders

For pinpoint accuracy in changing a window's size, drag its *borders* — the window's edges — in or out and drop them in their new location. The trick works like this:

1. **Move the mouse arrow until it points at the side or corner of a window, as shown in Figure 1-3.**

Figure 1-3:
A double-
headed
arrow
shows the
directions
you can
drag.

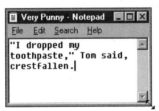

2. **While holding down the mouse button, nudge the mouse to move the window inward or outward (see Figure 1-4).**

Figure 1-4:
As you move
the mouse,
you move
the border.

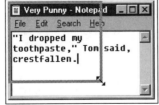

3. When the window is the size you want, release the mouse button.

The window snaps to fit its new size, as shown in Figure 1-5.

Figure 1-5:
Release the
mouse
button at the
window's
desired new
size.

You can change a window's size by dragging either its borders or its corners.

Click on the little corner symbols

You can shrink or expand a window by clicking on the little symbols in its upper-right corner (see Figure 1-6).

Figure 1-6:
Click on the
little box
symbol to
make the
window fill
the entire
screen.

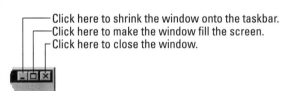

Click here to shrink the window onto the taskbar.
Click here to make the window fill the screen.
Click here to close the window.

After you click on the symbol containing the square, for example, the window grows as big as it can and covers up anything in its path — and the little square symbol turns into a symbol with two overlapping little squares. That symbol with the square is called the Maximize button because it maximizes the window.

✔ When a window fills the screen, click on the symbol in the upper-right corner — the one with two overlapping squares — to toggle back to the window's regular size. That symbol is called the Restore button.

✔ To shrink a window — turn it into a little icon at the bottom of the screen — click on the symbol with the little bar in the window's upper-right corner. That little symbol is called the Minimize button.

✔ Double-clicking on the window's title bar does the same thing as clicking on the symbol with the square in it — it toggles the window between full-screen and normal-sized.

Starting Your Work

You do all of your Windows 95 work in *programs*. The words *load, launch, start,* and *run* all describe the same thing: making a program come to the screen so that you can get some work done.

The programs appear on your computer's screen — your computerized *desktop* — while you move information around and get your work done.

Windows 95 offers several ways to start a program, and the following sections describe the least cumbersome.

Starting a program from the desktop

The best way to start a program is to simply grab it off the desktop. First, decide what type of file you want to create: a sound, a graphic, a simple text file, a more elaborate word-processed document, a spreadsheet, or other type of document.

Then follow these steps:

1. **Slide your mouse across the desktop until the little arrow points at a blank area.**

2. **Click on the right mouse button.**

   A menu pops up out of nowhere.

3. **Click on New from the menu, as shown in Figure 1-7.**

Figure 1-7:
Click on the
desktop with
your right
mouse
button,
choose
New, and
click on the
type of
document
that you'd
like to
create.

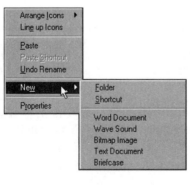

A menu pops up, listing all the types of new files Windows 95 lets you create. The menu is personalized — it's set up for the programs on your particular computer — so it looks different on different computers.

4. **Click on the type of file you want to create.**

The program that's responsible for creating that file comes to the screen, ready for you to work. If you choose Bitmap Image, for example, the Windows 95 Paint program appears, ready to create a picture.

- If this mouse *arrow* and *double-click* stuff sounds a little confusing, head for the "Mouse mechanics" section, earlier in this chapter.

- If this *basics* chapter seems like old hat, however, then skip it. All of the new stuff is in the later chapters.

- Although Microsoft may think Windows 95 is easy to use, most people don't think of the phrase *Bitmap Image* when they think of *picture.*

- If you don't see the type of file you'd like to create listed on the desktop's pop-up menu, then you might not have a program that's able to create that type of file. Time to head to the software store. Or if you're pretty sure that you have that program on your hard drive somewhere, move along to the next section, which explains how to load a program listed on your Start button.

- Do you see your program's icon sitting right on your desktop? If that icon has a little arrow embedded in its bottom left corner, then you've found your program's *shortcut.* Double-click on the shortcut, and the program comes to the screen. Shortcuts are an essential part of Windows 95, as you'll see throughout this book.

Starting a program from the Start button

An easy way to start a program is to launch it from the Start button, a button usually seen in the corner of your computer's taskbar. On most desktops, the Start button appears in the bottom left corner, as shown in Figure 1-8.

Figure 1-8:
Click on the
Start button
to see a
menu of
programs to
launch.

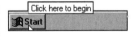
Click here to begin
Start

If you don't see the Start button immediately, it might be hiding: Move your mouse pointer slowly to all four edges of your monitor's screen. Eventually, the taskbar leaps out from one edge, revealing the Start button. Once you spot the Start button, follow these steps to launch a program.

1. Slide the mouse across your desk until the little arrow points at the Start button.

2. Click the left mouse button.

The Start menu appears, as shown in Figure 1-9.

Figure 1-9: Clicking on the Start button reveals a list of programs to launch.

3. Click on the word <u>P</u>rograms.

A new menu squirts out to the side, this time listing programs and types of programs.

4. Click on the name or type of program you'd like to use.

Windows 95 either loads the program you chose or delves deeper into its menus, displaying names of programs that match the types of programs you chose. Keep repeating Step 4 until your program appears on the screen.

• Want to reload a document you've used recently? Click on <u>D</u>ocuments — not <u>P</u>rograms — and the Start button will show you a list of the past 15 documents you've used. Click on the name of the document you want, and Windows 95 will obediently load that document into the program that created it and place them both on the screen for your perusal.

- Want to put an icon for a favorite program onto the Start button? Then forge ahead to Chapter 2. There, you also find out how to install a program — even if that program didn't come with a quick 'n' easy installation program.

Starting a program from My Computer

The My Computer icon — a picture of a computer as shown in Figure 1-10 — represents your computer and its contents. Double-click on the My Computer icon, and a window appears, listing various programs and *disk drives* — areas where your computer stores its files.

Figure 1-10:
The My
Computer
icon.

Starting a program from within My Computer works like starting a program from within the Start button: Keep moving from area to area until you spot the program's name and icon and then give the program's icon a double-click. The My Computer icon is a little harder to use than the Start button, however: My Computer displays nearly every file on your computer and doesn't bother filtering out extraneous files for easy viewing. Anyway, My Computer works like this:

1. **Slide the mouse across your desk until the little arrow points at the My Computer icon.**

   Double-click on the icon, and My Computer opens, revealing your computer's disk drives and a few other goodies.

2. **Double-click on the disk drive where your program lives.**

   You *do* know what disk drive your program lives on, don't you? If you don't, you'd best stick with the Start button method of launching programs.

   When you double-click on the disk drive, a new window reveals all the folders and programs living on that disk drive.

3. **Double-click on the program's name or the folder where it's located.**

If you double-click on the program's name, the program will come to life, ready for use. If you double-click on the folder, the folder will open to reveal its contents.

Because folders often contain more folders, you often have to double-click on several folders to get to the one containing your desired program.

Tired of double-clicking on folders to get to the program you're after? Make a shortcut to that program, as described in Chapter 16.

Starting a program from Explorer

Some folks don't like My Computer's window full of picture buttons. They prefer the more rectilinear Explorer program. Explorer lets you manipulate programs, files, and folders by pointing and clicking on their names.

Next to the names, you see miniature versions of the icons you spotted in My Computer, as well as minute details like file sizes, file types, and the dates the files were created. Figure 1-11 shows a picture of Explorer.

Figure 1-11: Explorer displays more detailed information about your computer's contents.

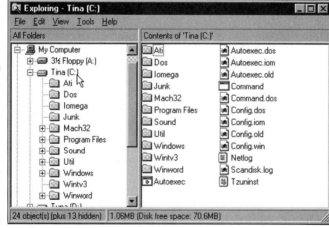

You start a program in the Explorer the same way that you start one in My Computer. Just follow these steps.

1. **Click on the Start button and choose Windows Explorer from the Programs menu.**

   Explorer rises to the screen, as seen earlier in Figure 1-11.

2. **Double-click on the disk drive where your program lives.**

   Like the My Computer program, Explorer requires that you already know what disk drive your program lives on. If you don't know, stick with the Start button method of launching programs.

   When you double-click on the disk drive, Explorer reveals folders and programs living on that disk drive. Or if Explorer was already showing all the goodies on that drive, it hides all the goodies, leaving more room on the screen for you to see other disk drives.

3. **Double-click on the program's name or the folder where the program is located.**

   If you double-click on the program's name, the program will come to life, ready for use. If you double-click on the folder, the folder will open to reveal its contents.

   Because folders often contain more folders, you often have to double-click on several folders to get to the one containing your desired program.

   ✔ Unlike My Computer, which usually displays one view of your computer's contents at a time, Explorer shows the contents of several disk drives at the same time. What are all those other files? Chapter 15 contains a handy chart to help you identify them.

   ✔ My Computer and Explorer can do much more than load programs. For example, you can use them to move files around on the hard drive. (Chapter 2 describes this chore.)

   ✔ Also, try pointing the mouse arrow at one of the filenames, programs, folders, or disk drives and clicking the right mouse button. The filename darkens, and a menu appears, listing all the things you can do to that object: change its name, make a copy of it, delete it, create a shortcut, or perform other computer-like activities.

   ✔ Confused about My Computer or Explorer? Then press the key labeled F1. (It's usually located near the keyboard's upper-left corner.) The Windows 95 Help program appears, ready to answer your questions. In fact, press F1 anytime Windows 95 leaves you rubbing your elbows in exasperation. The Help program pops up, usually bringing helpful information that pertains to your current dilemma.

Opening a File

A file is a computer's container for holding *data* — bits of important information — on disk. So whether you're trying to create something on a computer or touch up something that was created earlier, you need to snap open its container. That little chore is called *opening the file.*

TOOTORIAL

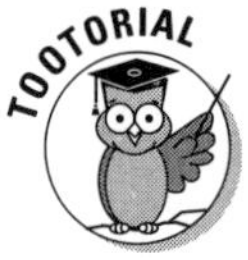

Opening a file from within a program

In a refreshing change of pace, all Windows 95 programs let you open a file by following the same steps:

1. Click on File in the program's menu bar, as shown in Figure 1-12.

Untitled - Notepad
File Edit Search Help
New
Open...
Save
Save As...
Page Setup...
Print
Exit

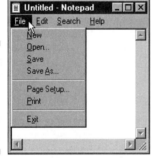

Figure 1-12: Click on File to expose a menu with file-oriented choices.

2. When the menu falls down, click on the word Open.

The Open box appears, as shown in Figure 1-13. By clicking on the words in this box, you can search for files in different locations.

Open
Look in:
Desktop
My Computer
Network Neighborhood
My Briefcase
Double-click Tips
Shortcut to 3½ Floppy (A)
Very Punny
File name:
*.txt
Files of type:
Text Documents
Open
Cancel

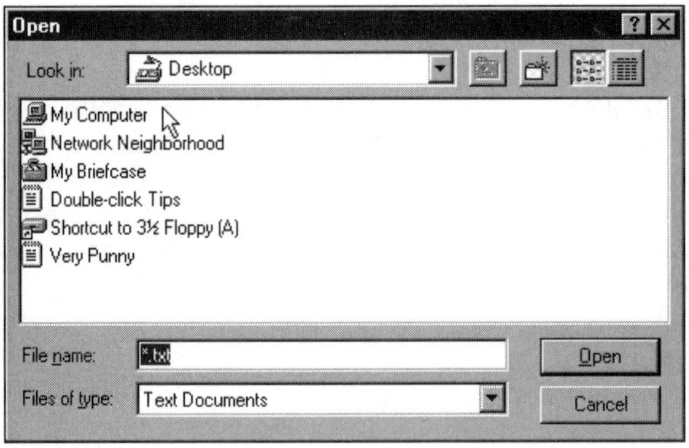

Figure 1-13: Clicking on various filenames, shortcuts, or disk drives in this box lets you find and choose the file that you want to open.

3. **If you see the name of the file you're after in the box, double-click on it.**

   You're lucky. The program immediately opens that file. If you don't see your file right off the bat, though, you have to do a little hunting — and that means moving to Step 4.

4. **Double-click the little My Computer icon listed in the Open box.**

   Don't confuse this with the big My Computer icon on your desktop; this is the little My Computer icon, seen earlier in Figure 1-13, that's mixed in with the filenames listed in your program's Open box.

   The program's Open box switches to a view of your computer's disk drives.

   Don't spot the My Computer icon in your program's Open box? Then click on the arrow next to the box marked Look in and choose My Computer from the menu that drops down. That also brings you to Step 5.

5. **Double-click on the disk drive where your desired file lives.**

   The Open window displays the folders stored on that particular disk drive. Spot your file? Double-click on it. Otherwise, move to Step 6.

6. **Double-click on the folder where your desired file lives.**

   The folder opens to reveal the files inside. Spot your file? Double-click on it to bring it to life. Otherwise, keep searching through your disk drives and folders until you find your file. Or if you don't know where the heck that file could be, you need to use the file finder program.

Viewing different types of files

Sometimes the Open file box doesn't display all the files in a particular folder or drive. For example, the Files of type box in the Open box (seen earlier in Figure 1-13) says it's currently displaying all Text Documents (files ending in TXT).

To see other types of files, click on the downward-pointing arrow in the List Files of type box. Then use the menu that drops down to choose a different type of file — or even *all* the files — that live in that folder.

  ✔ By looking in different directories and on different disk drives in the Open box, you eventually stumble across the file you're after.

  ✔ The Files of type box normally displays the types of files you're interested in. For example, when you try to open a file in Notepad, the box displays Text files. In Paint, the box displays Paint files.

✔ This Files of <u>t</u>ype stuff can be a little dizzying at first. To find out which Windows 95 program creates which type of file, head for Chapter 15.

✔ See how some words in a menu have an underlined letter, like the <u>F</u> in <u>F</u>ile and the <u>O</u> in <u>O</u>pen? That letter is a shortcut. You can press and release the Alt key and then press that underlined letter to trigger that menu item. For example, you press Alt, F, and O to make the File Open box pop up without any urging from the mouse.

Opening a file in Explorer or My Computer

Finally, something easy. The Explorer and My Computer programs can open a file the same way that they load a program, and they both work the same way: You just double-click on the name of the file that you're hungry for, and that file pops to the screen. It works like this:

1. **Find the name of the file that you want to open.**

2. **Move the mouse until the little arrow points at the filename.**

3. **Without moving the arrow away, double-click the mouse button.**

That's it. If you're working in Explorer, Explorer first loads the program that created the file you clicked on. Then Explorer loads the file into that program. For example, if you double-click on a file that you created in Windows 95 Notepad, Explorer first loads Notepad and then it loads the file into Notepad, leaving them both on-screen.

Opening a file in Explorer is easier than making a sandwich — especially if the mustard lid has dried closed.

Saving a File

Talk about lack of foresight. Even after you spend all morning painstakingly calculating the corporate cash flow, Windows 95 thinks you've been goofing around.

You see, computer programs don't know that you want to *save* your work. Unless you specifically tell the program to save it, the program just dumps it. And you can never retrieve unsaved files, not even with reinforced tongs.

To make a program save a file, do this:

1. Click on File from the program's menu bar.

A menu of file-oriented chores appears, the same menu you saw a few pages earlier in Figure 1-12.

2. After the menu falls down, click on Save.

A box pops up, looking much like the one you saw a bit earlier in Figure 1-13.

3. Type in a name for the newly created file.

If Windows 95 freaks out over the newly created file's name, you're probably trying to use one of the Forbidden Filename Characters that are described in Chapter 2.

4. Click on the folders in the Save As window until you open the folder where you want to store the file.

Want to create a new folder? Then click on the folder near the box's top that has the little sparkling star in its upper-right corner. Or if you want to save the file in a folder that's on a different drive, click on the little arrow in the Save in box to move to one of your computer's other drives.

5. Press Enter.

Typed in the name? Chosen the right folder and drive? Then press the Enter key, and the program saves the file using the name, folder, and disk drive that you've chosen.

- After you save a file for the first time, you won't have to repeat Steps 3-5. Instead, the program just saves the file, using the same name, folder and disk drive. Kind of anticlimactic, actually.

- If you want to use a different name or location to save a file, then choose the Save As option. That option comes in handy when you want to open a file, change a few numbers or paragraphs, and save the file under a new name or folder.

- The easiest way to save a file in any Windows 95 program is to press these three keys, one after the other: Alt, F, S. The little light on the hard drive blinks, and the program saves the file. Quick and easy, as long as you can remember Alt, F, S.

Printing a File

Printing a file works the same way as opening or saving one. Click on the right spots and grab the piece of paper as it slides out of the printer. If the printer is turned on and plugged in and the paper doesn't jam, you print a file this way:

1. **Click on File from the program's menu bar.**

   Once again, a menu of file-oriented chores appears, just as you saw in Figure 1-12.

2. **After the menu falls down, click on Print.**

   The program dutifully sends the information to the printer.

   - Some programs toss a Print box in your face, asking for more information. For example, Paint asks how many copies you want to print, and Word for Windows 95 asks whether you want to print all the pages or just a select few.

     Notepad, on the other hand, merely whisks the text straight to the printer. Whoosh! No stopping that program.

   - People with more than one printer might want to choose the Print Setup option instead. That option lets them choose which printer they want the information routed to. Then choose the program's Print command.

   - The quickest way to tell a program to print something is to press Alt, F, P. That method is faster than fumbling around with menus.

Done for the Day

When you've finished working, you haven't *really* finished working. No, the computer still demands a little more of your time. Before you can turn off the computer, you need to follow the steps described in the rest of this section.

Don't simply turn off the computer when Windows 95 is on-screen, no matter how frustrated you are. You must save your work and exit Windows 95 the right way. Doing anything else can cause problems.

Saving your work

As described in "Saving a File" earlier in this chapter, you save your work by telling the program to save it in a file so that you can return to it another day.

Exiting any running DOS programs

Are you running any DOS programs? You need to exit them before Windows 95 lets you leave. If you're running a DOS prompt (that little C:\> thing) in a window, type **exit** and press Enter:

```
C:\> exit
```

Some DOS programs make you press several keys before they'll disappear. Try pressing F10 and Alt+X or, if you're really stumped, check the program's manual. When you press the correct keys, the program shrivels up, disappears from the screen, and leaves you back at Windows.

Exiting any Windows 95 programs

Unlike DOS programs, Windows 95 programs shut themselves down automatically when you shut down Windows. They even ask whether you want to save your work. Still, you can use one of these methods to exit a Windows 95 program:

- Click on the little X in the program's upper-right corner, shown in Figure 1-14.

  The program disappears. If you haven't saved your work first, however, the program cautiously asks if you're *sure* you don't want to save your work.

- Hold down Alt and press F4 (known in Windows 95 parlance as pressing Alt+F4).

- Click on File in the menu bar and then click on Exit from the little menu that pops down.

- Press Alt, F, X, one after the other. That sequence quickly calls up the little File menu and presses the Exit button, all without the help of a mouse.

Figure 1-14:
Click on this
button to
close this
window or
program.

Exiting a program isn't a four-step procedure. You can use any of these methods to shut down a program.

Windows 95 offers bunches of ways to do the same thing. Some folks say that the alternatives offered by Windows 95 make it easier to use. Others say the alternatives just complicate matters.

Exiting Windows

Strangely enough, the way to stop using Windows 95 is to use the Start button. Click on the Start button and choose Shut Down, the option at the bottom of the menu. A menu pops up with four options, all described below.

✔ **Shut down the computer?**

Click here, and Windows 95 shuts itself down. Turn your computer off when a message appears on the screen saying it's okay, and you're ready to leave your desk and get some dinner.

✔ **Restart the computer?**

If your computer has been acting weird (or you've just installed some new software), choosing this option often comes into play. This option *reboots* your computer, making Windows 95 shut itself down and start itself back up from scratch.

✔ **Restart the computer in MS-DOS mode?**

Some picky MS-DOS programs prefer this mode, which leaves your computer with a C:\> prompt. (Type **exit** at the C:\> prompt and press Enter to return to Windows.)

✔ **Close all programs and log on as a different user?**

Windows 95 lets several people use the same computer, either through a network or a multiple users setup. Choose this feature, and the computer's other users can type in their name and password, making Windows 95 load the new user's customized desktop setup.

Chapter 2

How to Install New Software

In This Chapter

▶ Installing Windows 95 and DOS programs

▶ Using installation programs

▶ Working without installation programs

▶ Copying files

▶ Creating folders

▶ Adding programs to the Start button

*I*magine buying a toothbrush, opening the package, and finding a packet of loose little bristles plus instructions on fastening them to the brush's plastic handle. And you just wanted to brush your teeth!

A new Windows 95 program can bring similar complications. You don't always find the new program's icon waiting for you on the Start button. Instead, you find a floppy disk with a bunch of strange files on it. Which file does what? Where do they go?

Some programs come with an installation program that simplifies the whole process. Other programs leave it all up to you. To keep things simple, this chapter shows how to pry a program off a floppy disk, stick it on your computer's hard drive, and put its name and icon on the Start button menu where it belongs.

The Installation Nirvana

Windows 95 finally makes it easy to install programs — if the program's creator took advantage of these good graces. To find out if your new program's easy to install, just follow these steps:

1. **Click on the Start button, click on Settings, and choose Control Panel from the menu that appears.**

   The Control Panel appears, as shown in Figure 2-1, displaying a plethora of icons.

2. **Double-click on the Add/Remove Programs icon.**

3. **Click on the Install button at the top of the Add/Remove Programs Properties box.**

   Follow the instructions that appear in the following boxes. Windows 95 asks you to insert the disk containing your program. If Windows 95 can't find an installation program, however, and it sends out the box shown in Figure 2-2, you'll have to struggle through the rest of this chapter, unfortunately. The programmer took the easy way out.

Figure 2-1:
Double-click the Control Panel's Add/Remove Programs icon to install programs.

The Installation Headache

Programs are merely little bits of instructions for the computer, telling it to do different things at different times.

Unfortunately, most programs don't store those instructions in a single, easy-to-handle file. Instead, they're often spread out over several files — sometimes spread out over several floppy disks.

Figure 2-2:
This box
means
Windows 95
couldn't
find an
installation
program for
your pro-
gram, and
you'll have
to install the
program
yourself.

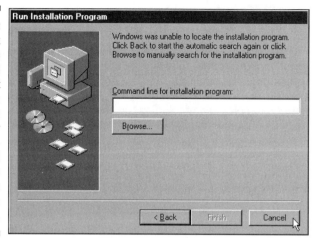

Regardless of what program you're installing, the basic idea behind installation is the same. You copy the program's files from the floppy disk onto the computer's hard drive. Then you place the program's "start-me button" — its icon — onto the Start button so that you can start using the program with a simple click.

- ✔ Programs come in two main types: DOS programs and Windows programs. Windows programs cause the fewest problems because they are designed to run under Windows 95.

- ✔ DOS programs, on the other hand, don't know anything about Windows 95. They're as helpless as a tourist who is visiting Disneyland on Labor Day and trying to find a bathroom without using a map.

- ✔ To help care for these confused DOS programs, Windows 95 often needs a *Properties* form — which works somewhat like a chart at the foot of a hospital patient's bed. The Properties form tells Windows 95 what that DOS program needs so that it can run most efficiently: memory limits, video expectations, and more trivia.

- ✔ Windows 95 recognizes some DOS programs when they're installed and fills out the Properties form automatically. Other DOS programs come with their Properties forms already filled out. Still other DOS programs make you handle the dirty details of filling out Properties forms. And some DOS programs run fine without a Properties form at all. If a DOS program causes you problems, check out the Properties form tips in Chapter 13.

- ✔ Windows 95 programs rarely need to have their Properties forms tweaked. They can automatically find the things that programs hold dear — sound cards, video cards, hard drives, and other treats.

What's an Installation Program?

Installing a program can be a long, tortuous process. So programmers handled the chore the best way they could. They wrote a second program designed specifically to install the first program.

Known as an *installation program,* it handles the chores of copying the program to the computer's innards and making sure that it gets along with Windows 95.

- ✔ Most programs sold in software stores come with an installation program.

- ✔ Some programmers were lazy, however, and didn't write an installation program. As a result, the installation chores are left squarely in your hands.

- ✔ Most shareware programs don't come with an installation program, so you have to tackle their installation yourself.

- ✔ The secret to a successful marriage is to know when to nod your head earnestly and say, "Gosh, you may be right, dear."

How to Install a Program

The steps that are described from here to the end of the chapter transform a disk or bundle of disks into a program that actually runs on your computer.

By following all of these steps, you'll install your new program, whether you like it or not. (And if you *don't* like it, head for Chapter 12 for instructions on how to *un*install it.)

If you're stumped by only a few installation procedures — putting a new program's name and icon on the Start button, for example — then jump ahead to that particular step. Pogo sticks are allowed here.

Finally, installing a program isn't as hard as it looks. This chapter describes every step in clinical detail — down to the last toe muscle twitch. After you install a program or two, you'll find that it's as easy as walking and chewing gum at the same time.

What's shareware?

In the early 1980s, an iconoclastic programmer named Jim Button startled the software industry by simply giving away his database program, PC-File. The catch? Button asked any satisfied PC-File users to mail him a check.

Much to the surprise of everybody, Button included, this honor system has since grossed millions of dollars. The shareware concept has matured into a healthy business.

By simply giving away their wares, shareware programmers can avoid the high costs of advertising, marketing, packaging, and distributing their products. They give away their programs on a trial basis, however. Users who discover a program, install it, and find it useful are obligated to mail the programmer a registration fee — usually somewhere between $5 and $30.

The price may be low, but the quality level usually is high. Only programs that really do the job convince new users to mail back that registration check.

If you only need a handrail while installing a new program, follow these steps:

1. **Find the program's disk.**
2. **Put the disk in the disk drive.**
3. **View the disk's contents in the My Computer program.**
4. **Find and load the installation program and read the README file.**

   No installation program? Then keep going:

5. **Create a new folder on the hard drive.**
6. **Copy the program's files to the new folder.**
7. **Put the program's name and icon on the Start button.**

Finding the installation disk

If your software came in a big box, start rooting around for the floppy disks. Look for one that's labeled *Disk 1*, *Setup*, *Installation*, or something similar. If your program only came on a compact disc, that's all you need — the installation program is usually on the disc.

While you're rummaging, look for a *cheat sheet*. Some companies offer a quick, one-page set of installation instructions. (Others hide the installation tips in the middle of the inch-thick manual.)

- ✔ If the software comes on a single disk, use that disk. The label doesn't matter.

- ✔ If you find a cheat sheet, give it a quick ogle. It may have some handy tips or pertinent warnings.

- ✔ If you find a registration card inside the box, fill it out and mail it in. Some companies make you register the program before they'll give you any technical support on the telephone. (Other companies just put you on a mailing list.)

Sliding a disk into the disk drive

If the disk doesn't fit inside your disk drives, troop back to the software store and ask to exchange your software for the *other* size of disk.

- ✔ Floppy disks slide into the drive with their label facing up. These disks have either a shiny metal edge or a small oval window — either way, slide that edge in first.

- ✔ Some disk drives make you slide down a little lever to hold the disk in place. Other drives swallow the disk with no special urging.

- ✔ The larger-sized floppy disks — a little over 5 inches wide — are quickly becoming obsolete. Better start counting your cash to buy a new disk drive that takes the smaller, more popular $3^{1}/_{2}$-inch disks. You won't find many programs still available on those older sizes.

- ✔ Some programs that come on compact discs have an "Autoplay" feature: As soon as you insert the disc, the installation program comes to the screen. If you're this lucky, just click on the Install or Setup program and the installation program will take over. You probably won't have to worry about the rest of the chapter.

Viewing a disk's contents in My Computer

Before working with a disk or CD-ROM, look at the files that live on it:

1. **Load the My Computer program by double-clicking on its little computer-shaped icon on your desktop.**

   My Computer's icon usually lives in the upper left corner of your screen; a double-click brings its window to life.

2. **Find the little pictures of disk drives in the My Computer window.**

3. **Double-click on the little picture of the drive where you put the disk.**

For example, if you put the floppy disk in drive A, double-click on the little picture of the drive labeled *(A:)*.

Or if you put the disk in drive B, double-click on the little drive labeled *(B:)*.

Or if you put the disc into your CD-ROM drive, double-click on your CD-ROM drive's icon.

Either way, My Computer shows the disk's contents (see Figure 2-3).

Finding a program's installation program

If you're lucky, your program came with a customized installation program that automatically handles the awkward migration from floppy disk to Start button. Here's how to tell for sure:

1. **After My Computer displays the disk's contents, look for a file named INSTALL.EXE, SETUP.EXE, or something similar.**

See anything that looks like the SETUP.EXE program listed in Figure 2-3? If so, you've found the installation program.

2. **Double-click on that particular filename.**

3. **Follow the instructions that the SETUP program tosses on-screen, and you're home free.**

The program copies itself to the hard drive and usually sticks its name and icon on the Start button's menu. (If it doesn't wind up on the Start button, you'll find instructions for putting it there yourself later in the chapter.)

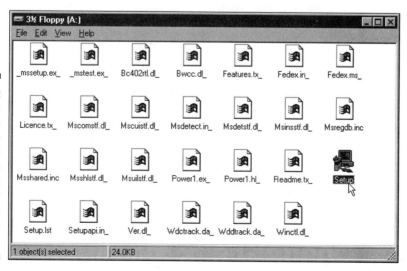

Figure 2-3:
Click on the icon for the drive where you inserted the program's disk, and My Computer displays that disk's contents.

Finding no installation program, however, means bad news: You have to handle all the installation grunt work yourself. So practice grunting earnestly a few times before you move to the next section.

Copying a program's files to a folder on the hard drive

If the lazy programmers didn't write an installation program for you, you have to install the program yourself. Following these steps should do the trick:

1. Create a new folder on your hard drive and name it after the program.

From within My Computer, create a new folder where you'd like the new program's files to live. In this example, we're installing the Tiny Elvis program into a Utility folder on drive C. So from within My Computer, open drive C by double-clicking on the drive C icon.

Next, from within the newly opened Drive C window, double-click on the Utility folder to open it. (Don't have a Utility folder? Then create one: Click on File, choose New from the drop-down menu, and then choose Folder.)

Then from within the Utility folder, create a new folder called Tiny Elvis. Your screen looks something like Figure 2-4.

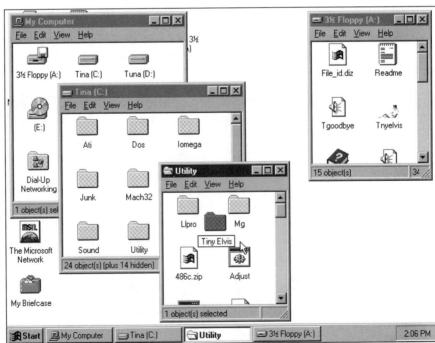

Figure 2-4:
When creating a new folder for a new program, try to "nest" it with similar programs; put the Tiny Elvis utility in the Utility folder, for example.

Try to keep your folders organized. For example, if you're installing the game Blasteroids onto drive C, create a folder called Games on drive C. Then create a folder called Blasteroids *inside* the Games folder. By keeping your games, utilities, and other types of programs grouped together, you can find programs easily when you need them.

2. **Move the program's file or files from its disk to its new folder.**

The new program — the one without an installation program — should be sitting in the My Computer's drive A window. The program's upcoming home, drive C, should be in another window on your desktop. You might need to rearrange all the windows on your desktop until you can see them both clearly, like you can in Figure 2-4.

Next, if you're installing the Tiny Elvis program from drive A, highlight all of its files. Then drag and drop those files onto the new Tiny Elvis folder in your Drive C's Utility folder, as shown in Figure 2-5.

Figure 2-5:
Drag and drop the highlighted files from the disk to their new folder on your hard drive.

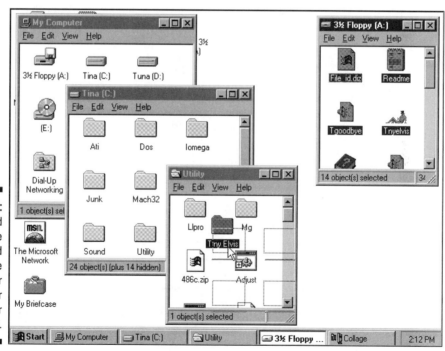

- ✔ A quick way to highlight a large number of files is to lasso them: Point the mouse adjacent to the corner, hold down the mouse button, and move the mouse to the other corner. A "lasso" appears, highlighting all the files in between the mouse movements. Let go of the mouse button, and the files and folders stay highlighted.

- ✔ An even *quicker* way to highlight all the files in a window is to click in the window once and press Ctrl+A.

- ✔ The My Computer program can make your desktop look awfully crowded when it leaves more than two windows open. If the desktop starts looking crowded, you can get rid of the windows you don't need. Just click in the little box in the upper left corner of each window that you don't want to see anymore. (The little box has an X in it.)

- ✔ You can use upper or lowercase letters when you name files and folders in Windows 95. This book uses uppercase letters so it's easier for you to see what to type.

- ✔ When peeling a clove of garlic, give it a deft twist with both hands to break the tough outer covering and make the skin easier to remove.

Reading README files

When programmers notice a goof in the software manual, they don't grab the correction fluid. Instead, they type a list of all the corrections and store them in a file called README.TXT, README, README.DOC, or something similar.

In fact, Figure 2-3 shows a file called README. To view that file, double-click on its name. The Windows 95 Notepad text editor pops up to show the README.TXT file's contents, and you learn which parts of the manual may trip you up.

Also, some README files contain quick, stick-to-the-point instructions on how the program expects you to install it. They're always worth at least a casual browse before you give up and move on.

Windows 95 can't digest these filenames

Windows 95 squirms uncomfortably if you try to use more than 255 letters or numbers in a filename or folder. (Earlier versions of Windows — and DOS — writhed in agony if you tried to use more than 8.) Windows 95 still won't let you use any of these forbidden characters, though:

$$" / \ : * | < > ?$$

The moral? Limit the names of files and folders to simple letters or numbers with no forbidden characters in between them.

Sometimes a disgruntled programmer names the README file README!.NOW or something even more obtuse. Because the file ends in letters unrecognizable to Windows 95, double-clicking on the file's name doesn't automatically bring up Notepad. The solution? Open Notepad to a window on your screen, and then drag the README!.NOW file's icon from the My Computer program and drop it into the Notepad program's window. Poof! Notepad reveals the file's contents.

Putting a program's name and icon in the Start button's menu

After a Windows 95 program moves onto the hard drive, it's ready to get its little button — or *icon* — and name placed in the Start button's menus. Windows 95 offers a bunch of ways to stick a new program's icon in the Start button's menus.

Here's the easiest way:

1. **Open the My Computer program.**

   It's that icon of a computer that usually rests in the upper left corner of your screen. Or if you've been installing a program throughout this chapter, My Computer is probably already open and waiting for action on your desktop.

2. **Move to the folder where you installed your new program.**

   In this chapter's example, for example, you'd point and click your way to the Tiny Elvis folder, which lives in the Utility folder of drive C.

3. **Drag and drop the program's icon to the Start button.**

   The program's name appears on the top of the Start menu for easy pointing and clicking. It's that easy — unless you want to place the program's name more strategically inside the Start button's menu, a process covered in the next section.

Putting a program's name in a specific section of the Start button's menu

The preceding section shows how to put a program's name at the top of the Start menu, where it's easy to reach. But if you want a more professional look, you'll want to be more organized. For example, you may want to list your newly installed program in the Applications section of the Start button's Programs menu. Here's how:

1. **Decide where you want the program's listing to appear.**

   For example, do you want the program to appear as a new item under the Start menu's Programs area? Do you want it listed as an Accessory under the Programs area?

2. **Click on the Start button with your right mouse button and choose Open.**

   The Start Menu window appears — looking suspiciously like the My Computer program. The icon called Programs stands for the Programs listing on the Start menu.

Figure 2-6:
Click on the
Start button
and choose
Open to
begin
adding
programs to
the menu.

3. **Double-click on the Programs icon.**

   Yet another window appears, this time revealing the items listed under the Start menu's Programs area: Accessories, Applications, Startup, and a few others.

4. **Open My Computer and open the folder where you installed your program.**

   If you want to move Tiny Elvis, for example, open the Tiny Elvis folder you created in the Utility folder of drive C.

5. **Drag and drop the program's icon into the appropriate icon in the Start menu's Programs window.**

   To move the Tiny Elvis program into the Applications section, drag and drop the Tiny Elvis program's icon into the Applications icon revealed in Step 3.

6. **Close down all the windows you opened for the previous five steps.**

   That's it; the next time you click on the Start button, you'll see the program waiting for you on the appropriate section of the Start button's Programs menu.

Dragging and dropping programs' icons into the Startup folder makes those programs load themselves automatically when you start Windows 95.

Putting a shortcut on the desktop

Find yourself using a program all the time? Then put an icon for the program right on your desktop, ready to be called into action with a double-click. Here's how to put one of those *shortcuts* onto your desktop.

1. **Open My Computer and open the folder where you've installed your program.**

   In this case, you want to open the Tiny Elvis folder you created in the Utility folder of drive C.

2. **With your right mouse button, drag and drop the Tiny Elvis program's icon onto your desktop.**

   After you let go of the mouse button, a menu pops up. Choose the Create Shortcut(s) Here option, and a shortcut to your program appears on the desktop. From then on, just double-click that shortcut icon, and Windows 95 pulls your program to the screen.

It Won't Install Right!

Occasionally, a widget falls into the wrong gear of the gatzoid, bringing everything to a resounding halt. Here are some of the more common problems that you can encounter while installing programs.

It's one big file ending in .ZIP!

If your file ends in .ZIP, like PICK.ZIP, you're holding a file that has been *zipped*. I'm not kidding.

The file has been compressed — shrunken like a dry sponge. You need an *unzipping* program to put water back into the sponge and turn the program into something you can use.

That unzipping program is called PKUNZIP, and it's shareware. You can find a description of shareware earlier in this chapter, and Chapter 11 tells you how to unzip a file.

When I loaded my new program, it exploded into a bunch of little files!

Sometimes you create a new folder for your new program, drag and drop the new program's file into the folder, and double-click the program's icon, expecting to start playing with the new program right away.

But instead of coming to the screen, the program's icon suddenly turns itself into a *bunch* of icons. What happened? Well, the program was probably in a *self-extracting compression program*. When you loaded it, it broke itself down into its *real* components.

So what do you do now? Well, look for an installation program, as described earlier in this chapter. If there's no installation program, just put the program's icon on your Start button menu, as mentioned previously in this chapter.

Then copy the big file — the one that contained all the little ones — to a diskette for safe-keeping and delete the original one from your hard drive to save space.

It keeps asking for some VBRUN thing!

Like ungracious dinner guests, some Windows programs keep shouting for *more*. Some of them start asking for a file called VBRUN300.DLL or something with a similarly vague name.

The solution? Find that VBRUN.DLL file. It doesn't come with Windows 95, however. Instead, you can *download* it — copy it onto your computer — from most computer bulletin boards or online services, such as CompuServe.

After you download it, copy it to the WINDOWS folder and ignore it. The program shuts up and runs.

✔ The program may ask for VBRUN100.DLL, VBRUN200.DLL, VBRUN300.DLL — you get the idea. The different numbers stand for different version numbers. Make sure that you download the same version that the program asks for.

✔ You need the specific version of VBRUN that the program asks for. You can't just get VBRUN300.DLL and expect it to satisfy older programs that ask for the earlier versions of VBRUN.

✔ A program that asks for VBRUN is written in a programming language called Visual Basic. Before the program can feel comfortable enough to run, it needs to find a special Visual Basic file, which is what the VBRUN100.DLL file is. Nothing really mysterious here.

My DOS program doesn't work!

DOS programs never expected to run under Windows 95. Some of them simply can't stand the lifestyle change.

It's as if somebody dropped you onto an ice-skating rink, and you were wearing slippery tennis shoes. You'd need ice skates to function normally.

A DOS program's ice skates come in the form of a *Properties form,* also discussed near the beginning of this chapter.

When you fill out the Properties form for a DOS program, Windows 95 knows how to treat it better, and it performs better. Unfortunately, filling out that form can be even harder than learning how to ice skate, so DOS Properties forms get their own chapter — Chapter 13.

There's no room on the hard disk!

Sometimes, Windows 95 stops copying files from the floppy disk to the hard disk because there's no room in the inn. The hard drive is full of files, with no room left for the stragglers.

You can install a bigger hard drive quickly. Or you can delete some of the files on the hard drive that you don't need. In fact, you can even delete some Windows 95 files that are on a hit list in Chapter 15.

Before installing a program, make sure that you have enough room. In My Computer, click on the drive's icon with your right mouse button and choose Properties from the menu. The Free Space area says how many megabytes you have left on your hard drive.

Chapter 3

Wallowing in Wallpaper, Screen Savers, Icons, Fonts, Sounds, and Drivers

In This Chapter

▶ Wallpaper

▶ Screen savers

▶ Icons

▶ Fonts

▶ Sounds

▶ Drivers

*Y*ou've probably seen a wild new screen saver on a co-worker's computer. Whenever she steps away from her computer for a few minutes, the screen turns black, and the little Grateful Dead bear starts kicking across the screen.

Or how about that guy down the street who uses all those weird fonts when he makes wild party fliers? Plus, he just upped his icon collection to 763 with that new Bart Simpson icon he found last week.

Or how about that guy whose computer lets loose with a different-sounding burp whenever he loads or exits Windows 95?

You can sprinkle hundreds of these little spices on the Windows 95 pie. Screen savers, icons, and sounds merely add new flavors. But the latest device drivers add necessary nourishment; Windows 95 probably can't work without them.

This chapter shows how to keep Windows 95 up to date by adding the new stuff and trimming off the old.

Where Can You Get These Things?

Windows 95 comes with a few screen savers, fonts, sounds, and icons. But where are people getting all their new goodies? Chances are, they're pulling them from some of the following pots.

Off the shelf

Most software stores carry boxes of Windows 95 add-ons. Look in the Windows 95 software section for packages of fonts, sounds, screen savers, icons — even movies.

- ✔ **Good news:** The stuff you can buy in the software store usually comes with an installation program, making it simpler to set up and put to work.

- ✔ **Bad news:** The stuff costs money; but software purchased by mail-order can sometimes be a tad cheaper. (Keep reading — you can even grab some of these goodies for free. . . .)

From the manufacturer

Sooner or later you need a new *driver* — software that enables Windows 95 to hold an intelligible conversation with a mouse, sound card, video card, or other part of your computer's hardware.

Windows 95 comes with drivers for many computer parts. However, drivers often need to be updated to perform at their peak. Your best bet for a new, custom-written driver is to go straight to the company that made the gadget. (Or you can sometimes get new drivers by calling Microsoft at 800-426-9400 and forking over about $20.)

If Windows 95 isn't working well with your sound or video card, try calling the tech support number of the company that made the card. Ask the techie who answers to send you the card's latest driver on a floppy disk. Some companies charge shipping costs, and others mail the drivers free of charge. Still other companies offer a third route: They let you grab the files through the phone lines.

Through the phone lines

This method may sound kind of wacky at first, but I'm not making it up. Some companies hook up a computer to their telephone lines. Then you connect your computer to your phone lines using a *modem*.

With the help of the modem and the Windows 95 HyperTerminal program (or any other modem program), you can dial up the company's computer and get copies of the latest Windows 95 goodies. In fact, Microsoft's BBS (bulletin board system) has the latest drivers for a huge assortment of printers, sound cards, video cards, and other toys.

Best yet, all that stuff is free for the taking (except for the long-distance charges that show up on your phone bill).

Some people call up CompuServe — a huge computer that's connected to a huge number of phone lines and charges huge fees. Well, actually it costs between $6 and $20 an hour, depending on how fast you're grabbing stuff. CompuServe carries bunches of icons, screen savers, wallpaper, and drivers and zillions of other software programs — all ready for the taking.

If you've bought a modem and want to put HyperTerminal to work, hop ahead to Chapter 7. It shows how to download the latest drivers from Microsoft's BBS for just the price of a long-distance call.

User groups

Some folks can't stop talking about their computers. So their spouses send them to local *user groups*. A user group is simply a club, just like a Saturday Sewing Club or '67 Corvette Lovers' Club. The members all meet, usually on a weekend or evening, and swap talk about the joy of computing.

If you're having trouble with Windows 95 or with locating some of its parts, ask your local computer store where the local Windows 95 User Group meets. Chances are, one of the folks at the meeting can come up with the Windows 95 goodie you're after.

From friends

Some charity-minded programmers give away their work for free (*freeware*). Knowing that people around the world are using their flying eyeball screen saver makes them feel all warm inside. Other programmers offer their programs as *shareware,* which is described in Chapter 2. You can try shareware programs for free; if you like them, you're obligated to mail the programmer a registration fee.

Many people swap these freeware and shareware programs with each other, and you'll find lots of shareware screen savers, wallpaper, and other goodies through online services like America Online and CompuServe.

> ✔ CompuServe probably has the best selection of files for downloading.
>
> ✔ Shareware and freeware are in a different legal realm than that of the boxed software that is sold in stores. That boxed software is known as *commercial* software, and giving copies of commercial software to friends can cause some big legal problems.
>
> In fact, making a copy of Windows 95 and giving it to a friend is illegal.
>
> ✔ Feel free to give away, or even sell, old copies of commercial software. Just be sure to include the manual and don't keep a copy of the software for yourself.

Wallowing in Wallpaper

Windows 95 *wallpaper* is the pretty pictures that you can stick to the back of the screen; the wallpaper becomes the coating for your desktop, and all your icons and windows ride on top of it. When you first install Windows 95, it looks pretty forlorn, with a boring gray/green backdrop. Windows 95 comes with several sheets of wallpaper to spruce things up, but those offerings can get old pretty fast.

So people start adding their own wallpaper, like the stuff in Figure 3-1.

Figure 3-1: Windows 95 lets you cover your desktop with your own personalized graphics.

Adding wallpaper is the easiest way to make Windows 95 reflect your own personal computer style.

What are wallpaper files?

Wallpaper is a picture that is stored in a special format known as a *bitmap* or *BMP* file. For easy identification, bitmap files have an icon of a little paintbrush painting some cubist oddities on a piece of paper. (You can spot one in Figure 3-2.)

Figure 3-2:
Files with this type of icon — bitmap files — can be used for wallpaper.

For example, Straw Mat and Black Thatch are some of the wallpaper files that are included with Windows 95. (And if you didn't get those with your copy of Windows 95, flip ahead to Chapter 16 for a solution.)

If you're tired of the wallpaper Windows 95 came with, create your own. You can use anything you draw in Windows 95 Paint as wallpaper.

✔ If somebody hands you a PCX file, you're stuck. Windows 95 can no longer handle that format. Sniff.

✔ For best results, use 256 color BMP files for wallpaper. Larger files can eat up memory, slowing Windows down.

Where to put wallpaper

Windows 95 looks for its wallpaper — bitmap files — in only one place: the computer's Windows folder. So if you have some wallpaper named Hand Smears on the floppy disk in drive A, copy the files from drive A into the hard drive's Windows folder. (Chapter 2 covers copying files from a floppy drive to a hard drive.)

How to display wallpaper

Follow these steps to display your new wallpaper (or any other wallpaper, for that matter):

1. **Click on a blank area of the desktop with your right mouse button and choose _P_roperties from the pop-up menu.**

   Yet another menu pops up, as shown in Figure 3-3. The window at the top of the box displays your current wallpaper; the box directly below it marked _W_allpaper lists the graphics files available.

2. **Click on the desired graphics file from the _W_allpaper box.**

   Windows 95 immediately shows a miniature view of what your choice looks like on the monitor.

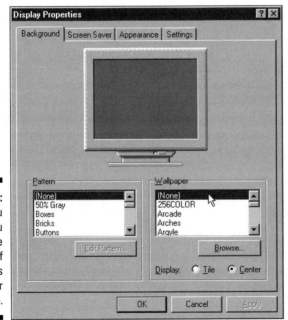

Figure 3-3: This menu lets you change the settings of all aspects of your desktop.

3. Click on the Apply button at the bottom of the box (optional).

To see what your choice looks like on the desktop itself, click on the Apply button. If you don't like it, head back to Step 2. When you finally find some wallpaper you like, move on to Step 4.

4. Satisfied with the choice? Click on the OK button.

The box disappears, and your new wallpaper selection coats your desktop.

- If you didn't like any of the selections, click on the Cancel button. That gets rid of the box and lets you get back to work. (You are left with either your original wallpaper or the last wallpaper you used the Apply button on.)

- In the Display area, choose the Tile button for small images to "tile" them across the screen. Choose the Center button to place one large image in the center of your screen.

- Don't bother with the Pattern button. The patterns are pretty ugly, and they only show up when you've selected None as your wallpaper.

- Created something fantastic in the Paint program? Save the file and choose one of the two Set As Wallpaper options from Paint's File menu. Your creation immediately appears on the desktop.

How to get rid of wallpaper

Wallpaper files consume a great deal of space on the hard drive, so excess wallpaper can fill up a hard disk fast.

To get rid of old wallpaper, follow these steps:

1. Choose Files and Folders from the Start button's Find menu.

The handy Windows 95 file finder comes to the screen, ready to prowl.

2. Type *.bmp in the Named box, type c:\windows in the Look in box, and click in the Include subfolders box to make the check mark disappear.

The screen looks like Figure 3-4.

3. Click on the Find Now button.

The file finder program finds all the Bitmap files living in your Windows folder, which is the home of all your wallpaper files.

4. With your right mouse button, click on the name of a file that you don't want anymore and choose Quick View from the menu.

The Quick View window pops up, showing you what the file looks like. No Quick View option on the menu? Troop ahead to Chapter 16 to find out how to add this valuable weapon to your Windows 95 arsenal.

Figure 3-4:
Fill out the
dialog box
to make the
Windows 95
file finder
seek out
all the
wallpaper
files living
on your hard
drive.

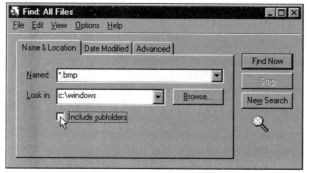

5. Drag and drop the files that you don't want to the Recycle Bin.

The Recycle Bin erases those files from the hard drive. (If it asks permission first, click on the Yes button.)

6. Continue to drag and drop files to the Quick View window for quick viewing and continue to drag and drop them to the Recycle Bin, if they're no longer needed.

By dragging and dropping the filenames to the Quick View window, you can tell if you want to keep them or not. Then just drag the rejects to the Recycle Bin.

What's the hard part?

Changing wallpaper or adding new wallpaper is pretty easy. You shouldn't go wild, though, for two reasons.

✔ First, huge, ornate wallpaper files take up a lotta memory, which can slow Windows 95 down. If Windows 95 starts running sluggishly, stick with the boring gray backdrop. Or use a tiny piece of wallpaper and tile it across the screen.

✔ Second, huge wallpaper files take up a lotta space on a hard drive. Don't fill up the hard drive with frivolous wallpaper that you'll never use. When bitmaps get boring, delete them or copy them to a floppy disk to trade with friends.

✔ If you can't remember what a bitmap file looks like, click on its name with your right mouse button from within My Computer or Explorer. Choose Quick View from the menu, and you can see the picture.

Adding or Changing a Screen Saver

If you've seen a dusty old monitor peering from the shelves at the Salvation Army store, you've probably seen WordPerfect, too. The popular word processor's faint outline still appears on many old monitors, even when they're turned off.

In the old days, frequently used programs burned an image of themselves onto the monitor's face. So to save the screens, a programmer invented a *screen saver*. When the computer's keyboard hasn't been touched for a few minutes, the screen saver kicks in and turns the screen black to give the monitor a rest.

Burn-in isn't really a problem with today's color monitors, but screen savers persist — mainly because they're fun. Plus, turning on a screen saver when you go get a cup of coffee keeps other people from seeing what you're really doing on the computer.

What are screen saver files?

Screen savers aren't as simple as the files you use for wallpaper. You need to be a programmer to build a Windows 95 screen saver. A screen saver is a miniature program. Two of the screen savers that are included with Windows 95 are called Flying Windows and Scrolling Marquee.

Windows 95 doesn't normally reveal a file's *extension* — three letters tacked onto a file's name that identify its purpose. However, bitmap files end in BMP (that's why you told the file finder program to search for files ending in BMP in the wallpaper example earlier); screen saver files end in SCR.

Where to put screen savers

Just like wallpaper files, screen savers have to live in the Windows folder. So if you have a Grateful Dead Bear screen saver named DBEAR.SCR on the floppy disk in drive A, copy DBEAR.SCR from drive A onto the hard drive's Windows folder. Chapter 2 covers copying files from a floppy drive to the hard drive.

How to use screen savers

To try out a new screen saver, follow these steps:

1. Copy the new screen saver to your Windows folder.

   Some screen savers come with installation programs that put them in the right place. If you just have a single screen saver file, copy it to your Windows folder. (That folder is almost always on drive C.)

Or if you just want to see what screen savers are currently on your system, move to Step 2.

2. Click on a blank area of the desktop with your right mouse button and choose Properties from the pop-up menu.

The desktop's Properties dialog box pops up, the same one you saw in Figure 3-3 when changing wallpaper.

3. Click on the tab marked Screen Saver along the top of the box.

As shown in Figure 3-5, Windows 95 immediately shows a miniature view of what your currently selected screen saver choice looks like. If you don't have a screen saver set up, the miniature view will be blank.

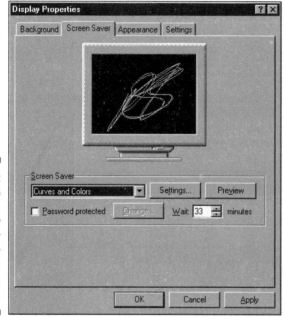

Figure 3-5:
Windows 95 provides a preview of your currently selected screen saver.

4. Click on the downward pointing arrow in the box that says Screen Saver.

A menu drops down, revealing your current choices of screen savers.

5. Click on one of the listed screen savers.

A miniature view of that new screen saver appears on the monitor inside the box.

6. Click on the Preview button (optional).

To see what your choice will look like on the desktop itself, click on the Preview button. If you don't like it, press the spacebar to return to the desktop and head back to Step 3. When you finally find a screen saver you like, move on to Step 7.

7. Satisfied with the choice? Click on the OK button.

The box disappears, and your new screen saver selection starts counting down the minutes until it's set to kick in. (The number of minutes you choose in the Wait box determine how long the screen saver waits before kicking in.)

- Different screen savers have different settings — the speed the bears dance across the screen and so on. To change these settings, click on the Settings button.

- Click on the Password protected box if you want your screen saver to stay put until somebody types the right password. (If you forget the password, though, you're out of luck.)

- Some monitors can turn themselves off or go into "low-power" mode if they haven't been used for awhile. If your monitor falls into one of these categories, you can fill out the Energy saving features of monitor box. The minutes you type into the first box determine how long the monitor waits before going blank; the second box decides how long the monitor stays powered up.

How to get rid of screen savers

When you're sick of the same old screen savers, delete the old ones to keep the hard drive from filling up.

To get rid of old screen savers, follow these steps:

1. Choose Files and Folders from the Start button's Find menu.

The handy Windows 95 file finder comes to the screen, ready to prowl.

2. Type *.scr in the Named box, type c:\windows in the Look in box, and click in the Include subfolders box to make the check mark disappear.

The screen looks like Figure 3-6.

3. Click on the Find Now button.

Figure 3-6:
Fill out the
dialog box
like this to
make the
Windows 95
file finder
seek out all
the screen
saver files
living on
your hard
drive.

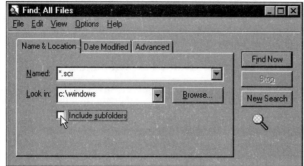

The file finder program finds all the screen saver files living in your Windows folder, which is also the home of all your wallpaper files. The files with the little screen saver icons all contain little screen saver programs.

4. With your right mouse button, click on the name of a file that you don't want anymore and choose Test from the menu.

The screen saver takes over the screen, showing you what the file looks like. (Wiggle the mouse slightly to get the screen saver off the screen.)

5. Drag and drop the files you don't want to the Recycle Bin.

The Recycle Bin erases those files from the hard drive. (If it asks permission first, click on the Yes button.)

6. Continue to test files for quick viewing, if needed, and then drag and drop them to the Recycle Bin if you don't want them any longer.

By testing the files, you can tell if you want to keep them or not. Then just drag the rejects to the Recycle Bin.

What's the hard part?

Don't let too many screen savers pile up in your Windows 95 folder; they hog space, just as wallpaper does.

Finding decent screen savers can be hard because creating them takes some work. A programmer needs to sit down and create one, preferably while in a good mood. Expect to find a lot more wallpaper and icons floating around than screen savers.

All about Icons

Soon after Windows 95 hits a computer, the icon urge sets in. Face it, icons are cute. Pointing and clicking at a little picture of the Mona Lisa is a lot more fun than the old DOS computing method of typing C:\UTILITY\PAINT\ART.EXE into a box and pressing Enter.

If you've ever collected anything — stamps, seashells, bubble-gum wrappers — you'll be tempted to start adding "just a few more" icons to your current crop.

What are icon files?

Icons — those little pictures you point at and click on — come embedded inside just about every Windows 95 program. Windows 95 reaches inside the program, grabs its embedded icon, and sticks the icon on its menus.

But DOS programs are too boring to come with any embedded icons. So Windows 95 uses the same generic MS-DOS icon to represent all DOS programs.

Luckily, Windows 95 can jazz things up. You can assign any icon to any program, whether its ancestry is DOS or Windows 95.

A single icon comes packaged in a small file that ends in .ICO, such as BART.ICO or FLAVOR.ICO. A group of icons also can come packaged as a program — a file ending in .EXE. Some files ending in .DLL also contain icons. (Windows 95 usually hides extensions like EXE, ICO, DLL, and others, so you won't be able to see them, though.)

Windows 95 can mix and match any icon to any program — if you tickle the icon and program files in the right places.

Although wallpaper files and icon files both contain pictures, the two types of files aren't interchangeable. Their goods are stored in completely different formats.

Where to put icons

Although Windows 95 is picky about the location of its wallpaper and screen savers, icons can live anywhere on the hard drive. To stay organized, however, try to keep all the icon files in their own folder.

For example, create an Icons folder that's nestled in the Windows folder by following the instructions in Chapter 2. Then when you come across any new icons, copy their files into the new Icons folder for easy access. (Chapter 2 also contains instructions for copying files onto a hard disk.)

Finally, Windows 95 doesn't let you create your own icons; you need to find a program to do that. Also, Windows 95 won't let you change every icon on your desktop. You'll have the best luck if you stick to fiddling with Shortcut and program icons.

How to change an icon in Windows 95

To change the icon of a Shortcut or program in Windows 95, follow these steps:

1. Click on the program's icon with your right mouse button and choose Properties from the pop-up menu.

The program's Properties form appears.

2. Click on the tab marked Shortcut or Program.

If you're changing the icon on a Shortcut, click on the Shortcut tab; likewise, click on the Program tab if you're changing a program's icon.

3. Click on the Change Icon button.

As shown in Figure 3-7, Windows 95 displays the icons available in the file currently displayed in the Properties or File Name box.

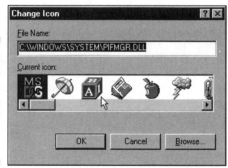

Figure 3-7:
Windows 95 displays the icons currently available to the file.

But here's the catch: The filename currently displayed in the File Name box isn't always the name of the program that you're fiddling with. Yep — Windows 95 can reach inside other files and assign the icons from those other files to your current shortcut or program.

4. Spot an icon you like? Double-click on the icon you like and choose OK.

Your newly chosen icon subsequently replaces your old icon. (Press F5 to refresh the screen if the new icon doesn't show up right away.) If you want to steal an icon from a different source, head for Step 5.

5. **Click on the Browse button, double-click on any of the icons you like in any of the folders, and click on the OK button.**

   Feel free to double-click on any of the folders throughout your hard drive. You can rob any icons you spot by simply double-clicking on them. Still don't find any icons you like? Head to Step 6.

   If you've copied a file full of icons into a folder on your hard drive — an Icon folder in your Windows folder, for example — move to that folder, and those icons will appear in the window, ready to be selected.

6. **Type the name of an icon file in the File Name box and click on the OK button.**

   Here are a few files full of icons that you'll find in Windows 95. Type any of these four names into the filename box, just as they appear below:

   ```
   Pifmgr.dll
   Moricons.dll
   Explorer.exe
   Shell32.dll
   ```

   After you click on the OK button, the screen clears and you find some jazzy new icons to choose from.

How to get rid of dorky icons

After you start collecting icons, the little guys come on fast and furiously. Finding them packaged in groups of thousands is not uncommon.

When you find yourself with icons coming out of your ears, delete the yucky ones this way:

1. **Decide which icons to delete.**

   Write down the filenames of the icons you no longer need. (If you need help finding the files, see the instructions in the preceding section for finding excess wallpaper and screen saver files — you can use the Windows 95 file finder to search your hard drive for *.ICO files.)

2. **Drag the boring icons to the Recycle Bin.**

   Repeat these steps for each icon that you want to delete.

   - Yes, it's laborious. If all of the icon files are in a single folder, however, Explorer or My Computer can wipe out the entire folder at once.

- Be careful when you delete files. To stay on high ground, just delete files that end in .ICO. If you're deleting a file that ends in .DLL, make sure that it's the file that contains the icons you want to get rid of. Many other programs use .DLL files — they don't all contain icons.

- Dozens of shareware packages make creating icons, deleting icons, and assigning icons to programs easy. Check out CompuServe and computer bulletin boards, which are discussed in Chapter 7, for some icon programs.

What's the hard part?

You can't make your own Windows 95 icons. Paint can't handle it. And trying to rename your BART.BMP file to BART.ICO won't fool Windows 95, either.

The solution? Pick up an icon management program. Some of them enable you to create your own icons; you can use others to see the icons inside your icon files. And you can still use others to create animated icons that throw spitballs at each other and make splat sounds.

A Font of Font Wisdom

Different fonts project different images.

- ✔ People with large mahogany desks and antique clocks that play Winchester chimes like the traditional **Bookman Old Style** look.

- ✔ The arty types who like to buy clothes at thrift shops have probably experimented with the **Impact** look.

- ✔ People who like gothic novels can't resist AGaramond.

The key here is the *font* — the shape and style of the letters. Windows 95 comes with a mere handful of fonts. Hundreds of additional fonts fill the store shelves, however, and you can find even more fonts on CompuServe or other online services.

Windows 95 uses several types of fonts, but the most popular by far is a breed of fonts called *TrueType*. TrueType is a fancy name for fonts that look the same on-screen as they do when you print them. Before TrueType fonts, fonts didn't look as good. In fact, a headline that looked smooth on-screen had jagged edges when you printed it out.

Fonts versus typeface

Traditional printers wipe the black off their fingers with thick towels and mutter, "The shape of the letters is called their *typeface*, not their *font.*"

Computer users retort, "So what? Language is changing, and desktop publishing is putting you guys out of business, anyway."

Technically speaking, and that's why this stuff is down here in the small print, a *font* refers to a collection of letters that are all of the same size and style.

A *typeface,* on the other hand, simply refers to the style of the letters.

Most computer users merely shrug and wipe their hands of the whole controversy.

What are font files?

The file names for TrueType fonts end with the letters TTF. But who cares? Windows 95 comes with an installation program that handles all those loose ends, so you don't need to know what the filenames are called.

Where to put fonts

Just put the floppy disk in the disk drive. Windows 95 handles the rest.

How to install fonts

Windows 95 controls the font installation process through its Control Panel. Just follow these steps to font nirvana:

1. **From within the Start menu, choose Settings and click on the Control Panel.**

   The Control Panel hops to the screen.

2. **Double-click on the Control Panel's Fonts folder to see your computer's collection of fonts, shown in Figure 3-8.**

   The Fonts box appears, as shown in Figure 3-8, and shows your current selection of fonts. Double-click on a font's name to see what it looks like; a window opens, revealing its contents. (Click on the Done button to close the window; click on the Print button to see what the font looks like on your printer.)

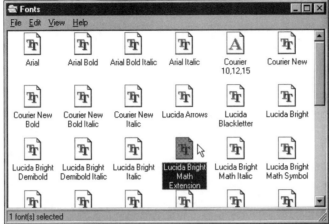

3. Choose File and choose Install New Font.

The Add Fonts box shown in Figure 3-9 appears, eager to bring new fonts into the fold. But where are they? You need to tell Windows 95 where those fonts are lurking, so move to Step 4.

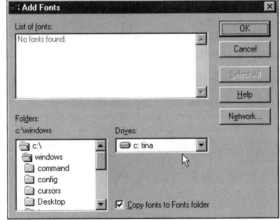

4. Click on the letter of the drive or folder that contains the new fonts you want to install.

Are the fonts on a disk? Then click on the little arrow by the Drives box and choose the disk drive where you've placed the disk. (First make sure that you've put the disk in the correct drive and closed the little latch.)

Or if the fonts are already on the hard disk, click on the appropriate folder in the Folders box.

After you click on the folder or drive where the new fonts live, their names appear in the List of fonts box.

If a little X isn't in the Copy fonts to fonts folder box, click in the box. You *want* Windows 95 to copy the new fonts to its own folder.

Windows 95 copies incoming new fonts to the Fonts folder in your Windows folder, but discussing that setup makes for exceptionally dry conversation in hotel lobbies.

5. Select the fonts you want.

You probably want to install all the fonts on the disk, so just click on the Select All button. Or if you're in a picky mood, click on the names of the individual fonts you're after.

6. Click on the OK button.

A moment after you click on the OK button, Windows 95 adds the new fonts to the list, one by one.

7. Click on the Cancel button to close the window.

That's it! The next time you open the word processor, the new fonts will be on the list, waiting to be used.

How to get rid of fonts

The fonts that came with Windows 95 should stay with Windows 95. Only delete fonts that you *know* you have added. Many programs need Windows 95 fonts to survive. In fact, Windows 95 uses some of those fonts for its menus.

Getting rid of fonts is even easier than installing them:

1. From within the Start button's menu, choose Control Panel from the Settings option.

The Control Panel hops to the screen.

2. Double-click on the Control Panel's Fonts folder.

The Fonts box pops to the screen, seen earlier in Figure 3-8, showing the fonts currently installed on your computer.

3. Click on the name of the font you're sick of.

If you're not absolutely sure which font you're sick of, double-click on the font's icon — the font appears on the screen so you can make sure that you've chosen the one you want to delete.

4. Choose Delete from the File menu.

Windows 95 asks whether you're sure you want to delete the font, as shown in Figure 3-10. If you're *really* sure, click on the Yes button. If you want to remove more fonts, back up to Step 3. Otherwise, move to Step 5.

Figure 3-10:
Click on Yes
if you're
sure that
you want
to delete
the font.

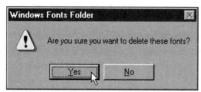

5. Close the Fonts box.

That's it. You're back at the Control Panel, and the font has been erased from the hard drive.

What's the hard part?

The hardest part of fonts comes from the language. Table 3-1 explains some of the weirdness.

✔ If you're not using a program called *Adobe Type Manager*, choose TrueType fonts whenever they're offered in Windows 95. They're much more hassle free and usually look better than the other fonts.

✔ In fact, you should almost always use TrueType fonts — except for use in professional-level desktop publishing, where PostScript fonts are more popular.

Table 3-1	Types of Fonts
These Fonts . . .	*. . . Do This*
Screen fonts	Windows 95 uses these fonts to display letters on your screen.
Printer fonts	Your printer uses these fonts to create letters and stick them on the printed page. (Some say the word *Plotter.*) Any printer fonts in a menu have a little picture of a printer next to them.

These Fonts . . .	. . . Do This
TrueType fonts	These fonts were introduced with Windows 3.1. Screen fonts and printer fonts are combined in one package to make fonts look the same on-screen as they do on the printed page. A little pair of *Ts* appear next to any TrueType fonts that are listed in a menu.
PostScript	An older type of font that is popular with professional-level desktop publishers. To use PostScript fonts in Windows, you need to have Adobe Type Manager (ATM).

Adding or Changing Sounds

For years, the howls of anguished computer users provided the only sounds at the computer desktop. Today, however, Windows 95 can wail with the best of them.

But there's one big problem. Windows 95 can't make any sounds until you attach a sound card and some speakers. Medium-range sound cards usually cost about $50 – $200.

What are sound files?

Windows 95 can play two popular types of sound files. The first type of files, known as *WAV* files, contain real sounds — a duck quacking or the sound of a tree falling in a forest (if somebody was there to record it). Windows 95 comes with several of these recorded sounds: Chord, Chimes, and, if you bought the compact disc version, the ultra-hip "Microsoft Sound" composed by Brian Eno.

MIDI files are the second type of sound files. They aren't actual recordings. Rather, they're instructions for a synthesizer to play certain musical tones. Whereas the WAV files usually contain short recorded sounds, MIDI files usually contain songs. In fact, Windows 95 comes with a MIDI file named Canyon. It's a pleasant jingle, the kind you hear while put on hold by a computerized answering machine.

Because WAV files contain actual recorded sounds, they can be huge. A ten-second sound can fill a floppy disk. MIDI files, in contrast, contain synthesizer instructions — not the sounds — so their size is smaller.

The MOD Squad

Okay, Windows 95 can play a third type of sound file — a MOD file. A mixture of WAV and MIDI, MOD files contain actual sounds, plus instructions to play them in sequence. They sound sort of like MIDI files, but with real instruments.

The problem? To keep space to a minimum, most of the sounds are repeats — the same drumbeat, the same guitar riff, the same hand clap, ad nauseam. Most MOD files sound rather robotic. But, hey, add a few strobe lights and pretend you're in the '70s again.

Windows 95 doesn't come with a MOD player or MOD files, but wherever you find MOD files, a MOD player shouldn't be far behind.

Some MIDI programs save MIDI files in different formats that end with different extensions than MIDI. Windows 95, however, prefers the MIDI format that ends in MIDI. Similarly, some sound cards come with sounds that are stored in an SND format. Windows 95 can't play those files, but the sound card may come with its own sound-playing program that can play them.

You can find plenty more help with sound files in the multimedia chapter, Chapter 8.

Where to put sound files

MIDI files can live anywhere on the hard drive. Chances are, the software included with your sound card contains a few MIDI files. Feel free to toss a few more MIDI files in the same directories.

WAV files can live anywhere on the hard drive, too. If you want to assign any sounds to events — hear a duck quack whenever you start Windows 95, for example — then copy those particular sounds to the Windows folder (the same place where you've been keeping wallpaper, as described previously in this chapter).

Chapter 2 explains how to create a folder on a hard drive and copy files to it from a floppy disk.

How to listen to sounds

After the sound card is hooked up and the driver is installed (described in the section "Adding or Changing Drivers" later in this chapter), listening to sounds is a snap.

✔ From My Computer or Explorer, double-click on the file's name.

✔ If you double-click on a MIDI file, the Windows 95 Media Player leaps to the screen and begins playing it. Simple.

✔ If you double-click on a WAV file, the Windows 95 Sound Recorder leaps to the screen and starts playing it.

✔ Here's a quick way to listen to sounds: Load the Windows 95 Media Player; then place the Explorer or My Computer program next to it. To hear a sound, drag a WAV or MIDI file from the Explorer or My Computer window and drop it onto the Media Player window. The sound plays immediately. (Never dragged and dropped? Chapter 1 has a refresher course.)

How to assign sounds to events

Windows 95 can let loose with different sounds at different times. Better yet, Windows 95 lets *you* decide what sound it should play and when.

To assign different sounds to different events, follow these steps:

1. **From within the Start button menu, choose the <u>C</u>ontrol Panel from the <u>S</u>ettings area.**

   The Control Panel hops to the screen.

2. **Double-click on the Control Panel's Sounds icon.**

   The Sounds Properties box, shown in Figure 3-11, appears on-screen. It lists the sounds that are currently assigned to Windows 95 events.

   If you haven't set up and installed a sound card, you can't play with the settings. The sounds look grayed out — dimmer than the rest of the text — and you can't click on them.

3. **Click on an event and then click on the sound that you want Windows 95 to play when that event occurs.**

   Windows 95 is rather vague about what words in the <u>E</u>vents box are supposed to mean. An event is usually a box that pops up on-screen. For example, the message in Figure 3-12 occasionally pops up on-screen. See the exclamation point in the left side of the box? Windows 95 considers that box an "Exclamation" event.

Figure 3-11:
The Sounds
Properties
box lets
you tell
Windows 95
what sounds
to play
during
which
events.

Figure 3-12:
The
exclamation
point in this
box means
Windows 95
considers
this to be an
"Exclamation"
event.

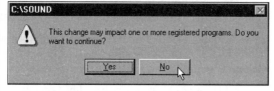

Now look at the sound files listed in the Events box that is shown earlier in Figure 3-11. When you click on Exclamation, the Chord sound is highlighted to indicate that Windows 95 plays the Chord sound whenever the box with the Exclamation point pops up.

Table 3-2 explains the events that you can assign sounds to.

The Sounds Properties Name box lists all the sounds in the Windows folder. To see sounds in other directories, click on the Browse button.

4. Click on the Preview button.

Windows 95 dutifully trumpets the sound you selected. If you like it, click on the OK button, and you're done. If you don't like it, however, head back to Step 3 and click on a different sound.

Don't like any of the sounds? Then record your own! Head to Chapter 8 for the details.

Table 3-2   Windows 95 Sound Events and Their Causes

This Event or Picture . . .		. . . Plays a Sound Because of This
Asterisk/Information	(i)	A box has appeared on-screen, offering more information about your current situation.
Critical Stop	(X)	An urgent box warns of dire consequences if you proceed — but lets you click on the OK button to keep going, anyway.
Default Beep		The most common event; this means you've clicked outside a dialog box or done something equally harmless.
Exclamation	(!)	This box urges caution, to a slightly less degree than the Critical Stop warning.
Question	(?)	A box is asking you to choose between a variety of choices.
Exit Windows		Plays when you shut down Windows 95
Start Windows		Plays when you load Windows 95

How to get rid of sounds

MIDI files don't take up too much room in the hard disk closet, but WAV files are clunkier than a cast-iron Hoover vacuum cleaner.

To get rid of sound files, head for the Start button's file finder program.

1. Click on Find from the Start button and choose Files or Folders.

2. Type *.WAV into the Named box and click on the Find Now button.

Although sound files can be scattered throughout your hard drive, the ones assigned to your events usually live in the Media folder, which is tucked inside your Windows folder.

3. Double-click on the name of the dorky sound file.

Windows 95 plays the file, so keep your ears ready. Is that *really* the dorky one? Then move to Step 4. Otherwise, keep double-clicking on the names of the listed sound files until you find the boring one.

4. Drag the dorky sound file to the Recycle Bin.

That gets rid of the sound file.

What's the hard part?

The hard part of using sound in Windows 95 comes from the computer's sound card. If the sound card is installed correctly, with the right drivers, everything should work pretty smoothly. But until that sound card is set up right, things can be pretty ugly.

You're better off sticking with name-brand sound cards, like the ones made by Creative Labs or Turtle Beach. Some of the really cheap ones can cause some awful headaches.

Adding or Changing Drivers

Even after you wrestle with the tiny screws on the back of the computer's case, slide in the new sound card, extract the tiny screws from the shag carpet, and reattach the computer's case, you're not through.

After you install a new gadget in the computer, you need to tell Windows 95 how to use it. Those instructions come in the form of a *driver* — a piece of software that teaches Windows 95 how to make that new gadget work.

Most gadgets — things like sound cards, video cards, and CD-ROM players — come with a driver on a floppy disk. Some gadgets can use the drivers that came with Windows 95. In fact, Windows 95 uses a concept called *plug and play:* After you've installed the new computer part, Windows 95 automatically sniffs it out, installs the correct driver, and makes everything work right.

But if your gadget is not working right under Windows 95, chances are it needs a new driver.

What are driver files?

Driver files end in DRV, but you can promptly forget that bit of information. The Control Panel handles all the driver installation chores, sparing you the trouble of searching for individual files, moving them around, or trying to delete them.

Where to put drivers

Drivers come on floppy disks. The Control Panel handles the installation chores, so merely put the disk in the disk drive and close the latch.

How to install drivers

Don't try to add a driver until you've installed the new mouse, keyboard, video card, or whatever else you have. (If you've added a monitor, however, skip ahead to the tip at the end of this section.) Next, add the driver by following these steps:

1. **Shut down all your programs, leaving Windows 95 bare on the screen.**

   If something goes wrong, you don't want any programs running in the background.

2. **Click on the Control Panel from the Start button's Settings area.**

   The Control Panel appears on-screen.

3. **Double-click on the Add New Hardware icon.**

   A box appears, as shown in Figure 3-13.

Figure 3-13:
Windows 95 can automatically set up most pieces of hardware you add to your system.

4. **Click on the Next button.**

   Windows 95 asks if you want it to automatically detect your new piece of hardware. Why should you work any harder than necessary? Make sure that the Yes button is checked, and Windows 95 will seek out and set up your new part.

   The only reason you'd want to check the No button is if Windows 95 can't detect your new part — either you've tried it before, or Windows 95 won't run with your new part installed, forcing you to tell it in advance what you're about to install.

5. **Click on the Next button, read the message, and then click on the next button again.**

   After warning you that the search might take a few minutes, Windows 95 begins rummaging through your hard drive, looking for the new part. After huffing and puffing, it reveals what it found in Step 6.

6. **If Windows 95 says it didn't find your new part, you'll have to click on the Next button and pick it out of a list.**

   ✔ If Windows 95 says it found your part, it asks whether the new part came with a disk. If so, insert the disk into the drive and you're off; otherwise, Windows 95 uses one of its drivers. Either way, your new part should be up and running.

   ✔ Windows 95 can't detect monitors, so they're not installed this way. Instead, click on a blank part of your desktop with your right mouse button and choose Properties from the menu. Click on the Settings tab and choose Change Display Type from the bottom of the box. Finally, click on the Change button next to Monitor Type and choose your new monitor from the list. Not listed? Choose the closest one you find. (Usually Standard VGA or one of the SuperVGA types.)

   ✔ Sometimes Windows 95 says it already has a driver for a gadget. Then it asks whether it should use the current driver (the one already installed) or the new one (the one on your floppy disk). Choose the new one.

Ugly IRQs

Sometimes new computer gadgets — sound cards, for example — upset other parts of the computer. They argue over things such as *interrupts*, which are also known as *IRQs*. When you set up the card so it works right, remember its settings. For example, if the sound card says that it uses *IRQ 7* and *Port 220*, write that information

down — no matter how technodork it sounds. Chances are, Windows 95 asks you for the same numbers.

If the gadget doesn't work right, check out the book, *Upgrading & Fixing PCs For Dummies*, 2nd Edition (published by IDG Books Worldwide, Inc.). It may be able to give you a hand.

How to get rid of drivers

You only need to get rid of drivers under two circumstances:

- ✔ You're installing a new driver and you want to get rid of the old driver first.
- ✔ You've sold your gadget or you've stopped using it for some other reason, and you don't want the driver installed anymore.

In either case, follow the bouncing ball to delete your driver:

1. **Load the Control Panel from the Start button's Settings area.**

   The Control Panel hops to the screen.

2. **Double-click on the System icon and click on the Device Manager tab.**

   As shown in Figure 3-14, the Device Manager box lists the currently installed gadgets and drivers on your system.

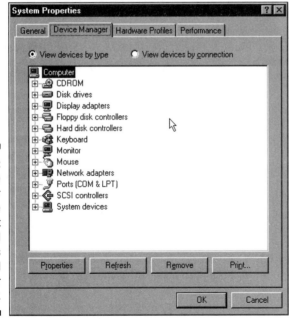

Figure 3-14: The Device Manager box lists the current gadgets and drivers installed on your computer.

3. **Double-click on the name of the gadget you no longer have installed on your computer and click on the <u>R</u>emove button.**

   Windows 95 asks whether you're sure you want to get rid of that driver. If you are sure, click on the <u>Y</u>es button, and Windows 95 sweeps it from the hard drive.

   You're through!

Make sure that you really don't need a driver before you remove it, however; its gadget can't work without it.

What's the hard part?

The hardest part of working with drivers is getting the gadget set up right in the first place. Once drivers are up and running, though, they'll usually work well. Always keep your eye out for an updated driver, though. Manufacturers usually release new versions every few months in order to fix the problems found in the old ones.

Always keep a copy of your old driver as a backup before installing a new version of that driver. You never can tell when a new driver might cause more problems than the old one.

Chapter 4

Uh, Which Version of Windows Does What?

· ·

In This Chapter

▶ Finding out which version of Windows you have

▶ Windows Versions 1.0 and 2.0

▶ Windows Version 3.0

▶ Windows Version 3.1

▶ Windows Version 3.11 (Windows for Workgroups)

▶ Windows NT

▶ Windows 95

▶ Windows NT 4.0

▶ Windows for Pens

· ·

*F*or the past several years, PC users lined up into two distinct rows. One group loved Windows. Everybody else stuck with plain ol' DOS. And unless the two groups tried to compute while they were in the same room, nobody hurled food at anybody else.

It's not that simple anymore, though. That single row of Windows users now has more than six split ends.

Which version of Windows does what? Which one is best? Which version do you have? And are you using the right one?

This chapter rounds up all the different types of Windows — antique, modern, and the upcoming versions that are peeking right around the corner.

Which Version of Windows Do You Have?

Don't know which version of Windows you're using? Check the front of the Windows box; that's the easiest clue. No box? Then check the labels on the Windows floppy disks.

If all that stuff fell off the pickup truck during the last move, try this: Click on the My Computer icon with your right mouse button and choose Properties. You should see a box like Figure 4-1.

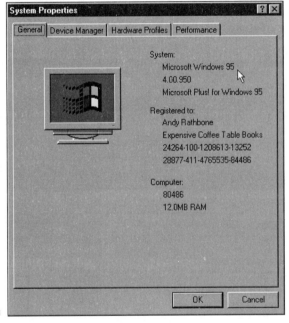

Figure 4-1:
Click on
the My
Computer
icon with
your right
mouse
button and
choose
Properties
to see which
version of
Windows
you're using.

In this case, we're using Windows 95. No My Computer icon? Then load the Help menu of one of your programs: Click on <u>H</u>elp from the menu bar and then click on <u>A</u>bout when the little menu drops down.

A box like the one shown in Figure 4-2 lists the version number.

✔ Chances are, you're using Windows 95. More than a few holdouts are still using Windows 3.1. A few groups of people who are clustered in offices use Windows for Workgroups, also known as Windows 3.11.

✔ If you're using Windows 95, you can still run almost all of your old Windows programs. But if you're still using Windows 3.1 or anything earlier, you won't be able to run any Windows 95 programs.

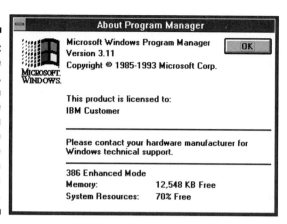

Figure 4-2:
In some programs, you can click on the Help menu and choose About to see which version you are using.

✔ If you're still using Versions 1.0 or 2.0 of Windows, your computer probably won't run *any* of the Windows programs that are on the market today.

✔ To see what sneaky little cartoons Microsoft snuck into that innocent-looking About Program Manager box, sneak ahead to Chapter 21.

✔ The rest of this chapter describes all the versions of Windows that you might come across at the computer store, bundled with a PC, or on the shelf at the Salvation Army. Most important, it says what you can do with them and whether you should upgrade.

Windows Versions 1.0 and 2.0

Era: Announced in 1983, Windows 1.0 finally hit the shelves in November 1985. Windows 2.0 followed in December 1987.

Required hardware: Windows 1.0 required 256K of memory and two floppy drives. Anybody who wanted to do more than watch the mouse pointer turn into a perpetual hourglass needed a hard drive and a least 1MB of RAM.

Reason for living: Microsoft was trying to get rid of the computer's *typewriter look*. With DOS, people typed letters and numbers into the computer. The computer listened and then typed letters and numbers back at them.

It worked well — after people struggled through all the manuals. But it was, well, boring. A lot more boring than that "fun" Macintosh. Programmers designed DOS for other programmers, who thrived on elusive strings of techno-gibberish.

So to camouflage DOS's shortcomings, Microsoft released Windows 1.0. Windows enabled people to boss around their computers much more pleasantly. They'd slide a mouse around on the desk, pointing at buttons on the screen and clicking a button on the mouse.

Major features: Everybody hated Windows 1.0. The colors were awful. They looked as if they'd been chosen by a snooty interior decorator who was trying to make a *statement.* Windows wanted every window to be the same awkward size, and they couldn't overlap. To fine-tune the concept and attract new users, Windows 2.01 added *Dynamic Data Exchange (DDE),* a dramatic marketing term for a simple concept — letting programs share information.

For example, the golf scores in the spreadsheet could be *hot-wired* to the club newsletter in the word processor. When somebody typed the latest golf scores into the spreadsheet, the spreadsheet automatically updated the golf scores in the newsletter.

For the first time, club members actually volunteered to serve as the newsletter editor.

Verdict: Like the first microwave oven, Windows offered something dramatically new — and dramatically frightening. Most people simply ignored it. The final straw? Windows required an expensive, powerhouse computer, and back then, tiny little XT computers ruled the desktops.

Interest in Windows 2.0 picked up a little, mainly because of IBM's new AT computer. The AT's rocking 286 chip could open and shut windows much faster than the XT.

✔ Windows 1.0 and 2.0 are brittle antiques. Ninety-nine percent of today's software can't run on any version of Windows older than Windows 3.0. Hang on to those old versions only as appreciating collectibles, like the Marvel Comics X-Men series.

✔ Even as Windows 1.0 and 2.0 sat on the shelves, Microsoft's programmers toiled in the background, cranking out a few other special versions of Windows. They released Windows 286, for the new AT computers, and Windows 386, for those super-new 386 computers. Yawn.

✔ Windows 386 could finally run a DOS program in a little on-screen window, instead of forcing it to hog the whole screen. These in-between versions were practice efforts for the upcoming Windows 3.0 version; neither can run most of the Windows software that is sold today.

Windows 3.0

Era: Born in May 1990.

Required hardware: Although the box said that Windows 3.0 worked on XTs, ATs, and 386s, it crawled on anything but a 386.

Reason for living: Windows finally grew up with this release. The powerful computers of the day could finally handle it, and Microsoft had sanded off the rough edges that plagued earlier versions.

Major features: Compared to the earlier Windows versions, Windows 3.0 took off like a cat stepping on a hot waffle iron. Cosmetically, Windows 3.0 *looked* better than earlier versions; plus, users could maneuver on-screen windows much more easily. Finally, it did a much better job of insulating users from ugly DOS mechanics; people could *point and click* their way through boring file-management tasks.

Windows 3.0 could handle networks for the first time (see the section "Windows for Workgroups," later in this chapter), and it did everything a lot faster.

Verdict: Most Windows software still runs under Windows 3.0. In fact, a few people still use Windows 3.0, — although they're always muttering under their breath about upgrading "real soon now."

What mode are you?

Windows 3.0 brought three new Windows *modes* along with it.

Real: By loading Windows 3.0 in Real mode, users could still run some of the older Windows software that was written for Windows 2.0. Unfortunately, Real mode meant that Windows worked *Real slow.* But it was the only mode that XT computers could handle.

Standard: In Standard mode, Windows programs could run at their quickest, but DOS programs suffered. DOS programs couldn't run in little on-screen windows; they had to fill the whole screen. And although several DOS programs could run at the same time, only the currently running DOS program could show up on-screen. The rest had to lurk in the background, frozen as icons.

386-Enhanced: Designed specifically for the 386 chip (as well as any 286 chips), this mode let several DOS programs run simultaneously in their own on-screen windows. It also let Windows grab a chunk of the hard disk and pretend that it was memory, swapping information back and forth when *real* memory was too full to handle any more. (More swap file facts live in Chapter 5.)

Windows 3.1 dumped Real mode, but it still runs in the other two modes.

Windows 3.1

Era: Born in April 1992.

Required hardware: A 386SX or faster computer, at least 2MB of RAM, and at least 10MB of space on the hard drive. For best results, however, look for at least 4MB of RAM and at least an 80MB hard drive.

Reason for living: Ninety percent of Windows 3.1 is the same as Windows 3.0. That new ten percent, however, makes quite a difference. Windows 3.1 got rid of those ugly jagged fonts and added sound support so that people can play with multimedia programs. It carries on the evolution toward making computers easier to use, as well as more fun.

Major features: Windows 3.1 continues the success of Windows 3.0. It adds a revamped, more efficient File Manager, easy-to-use TrueType fonts, more drag-and-drop features, and sound.

Verdict: Because more than 70 million people have been using Windows 3.1, it will remain popular for many years to come.

Windows 3.11 (Windows for Workgroups)

Era: Born in 1992.

Hardware requirements: Same as Windows 3.1, but toss in an extra megabyte or two of RAM.

Reason for living: For years, Steve printed out the spreadsheet and handed it to Jackie. Today, though, Jackie wants to read Steve's spreadsheet from her own computer. She needs a *network* — a way to link all the computers in the office so that everybody can share the same information.

Software Development Kits

A Windows Software Development Kit (dubbed SDK by highly paid marketing workers) helps programmers make little windows and menus pop onto the screen at the touch of a button.

An SDK, therefore, contains a bunch of weird code words to help programmers write Windows programs. Normal people find the SDK pretty useless.

You're not missing much, though; SDKs can cost about five times as much as Windows.

Windows for Workgroups looks pretty much like plain old Windows. But Windows for Workgroups has all the networking stuff built into it. It comes with an enhanced version of Windows software, long cables, and special cards that plug into a computer's guts. Stringing cables from computer to computer enables everybody to share spreadsheets and Solitaire scores — and to send their party fliers to the same printer, as well.

Major features: In addition to linking all the computers, this version of Windows has a special mail and scheduling system. Without leaving their desks, workers can decide where to meet for lunch *twice* as quickly as people without a network.

Verdict: Windows 3.11 moved right onto the desktops like Windows 3.1. It's still out there. People are still using it. Some people just don't like Windows 95.

Windows NT

Era: Born in 1993.

Required hardware: Back then, you needed a fast (at least 25 MHz) 386 computer or a 486. You also needed at least 12MB of RAM and about 75MB of free hard drive space.

Reason for living: Windows 3.1 didn't replace DOS; it rode on top of it, like a shiny new camper shell on a rusty old pickup truck. And DOS, designed for computers that were created more than ten years ago, simply couldn't take advantage of powerful computers. So Microsoft stuck its programmers in the closet for two years and came up with Windows NT.

Major features: The first versions of Windows NT looked like plain old Windows 3.1, but they were designed specifically for speedy computers. They could run bunches of programs at the same time without falling down and dropping everything. Big corporations liked it.

Verdict: Although Windows 95 currently rules, Windows NT may be the next big thing. However, it's expensive and requires an expensive machine. Windows NT seems to work best when it's at the heart of a big network and is pumping files up and down cables into other computers. It's a little too fat for today's average desktop PC.

Windows 95

Born: August 24,1995.

Required hardware: At least a 386DX, with 8MB of memory.

Major features: Windows 95 finally combined DOS and Windows into one operating system. Plus, it finally lets you use filenames that are more than eight characters long — and you only had to wait 15 years!

Reason for living: Microsoft's Windows NT is too chunky for most people's desktops, and Windows 3.11 was getting too old. So Microsoft spruced up Windows again and released Windows 95.

Verdict: Here's a little secret. Lots of people don't like Windows 95, and it hasn't been the overwhelming sales success that Microsoft expected. Corporations aren't snapping it up, either. But Bill Gates doesn't care, and here's why: Gates forced all programmers to make their "Official" Windows 95 programs compatible with the new version of Windows NT.

Since all programmers want their programs to be labeled "Official," they're setting up the programs to work with both Windows 95 and Windows NT. That means that when a new version of Windows NT hits the shelves in late 1996, Windows 95 users will still be able to run their Windows 95 programs while they're making the transition to Windows NT. Since everybody will want to use their same programs for awhile, they'll simply migrate painlessly from one Microsoft operating system to another. There won't be any room for a competing operating system to muscle in, and Windows NT programs will be everywhere! Sneaky, eh?

Finally, don't look for a new version of Windows 95 in 1996. No, if there is even going to be another version, it won't be out until late 1997. (Historically, Microsoft takes about 2 years to build each version of Windows.) Instead, you'll see a few updates issued to fix mechanical problems as they arise.

Windows NT 4.0

Era: Late 1996.

Required hardware: Probably a 486 or Pentium with at least 16MB.

Reason for living: Instead of looking like Windows 3.1, this updated version of Windows NT will sport the flashy new Windows 95 interface.

Major features: Microsoft is mum.

Verdict: Your neighborhood grocer knows as much as anybody else.

Microsoft Windows for Pens

Era: 1992.

Required hardware: A pen-driven computer, like the ones advertised in fancy computer magazines. A pen-driven computer looks like an expensive Etch-A-Sketch without the little white knobs. (A product called PenDirect for Windows, from another company, lets you wipe a pen across a plain old desktop monitor and doesn't require a mouse or fancy Etch-A-Sketch.)

Reason for living: After years of technical research, programmers discovered that laps disappear when a person stands up. A few nerds experimented by wearing their laptops on trays like those worn by cigarette sales girls in casinos, but others turned to pen-driven computers. Mobile users can now poke Windows' on-screen buttons with a plastic pen rather than a mouse. Because using a pen-driven computer is like writing on a notepad, inventory crews can count cases of canned asparagus without sitting down and struggling with a laptop.

Major features: Windows for Pens is really Windows 3.1, with a special pen-like device that you use to *write* directly onto the computer's screen. Windows looks at the scribbles and translates them into words, letter by letter. (Yes, it's that slow.) Windows for Pens comes pre-installed on several pen-driven computers; you can't buy it separately.

Verdict: Those little pen tablets are somewhat pricey for everybody but supermarket chains that are trying to inventory their vegetables. In a few years, however, pen computers may be built into cars so that drivers can find out how far ahead their next Slurpee lies.

So, Which Windows Is for What?

In a nutshell, Microsoft is doing three things:

1. Trying to push Windows 95 onto as many computers as possible.
2. Trying to make people buy as many Windows 95 programs as possible.

3. Trying to make people buy Windows NT 4.0 when it arrives, so they can run all their Windows 95 programs a little bit more efficiently.

✔ If you're happy with your current version of Windows, stick with it. There's no rule that says you have to automatically buy the latest version.

✔ To Microsoft, however, all the older versions of Windows are just tiny fish in the huge Windows sea. They're a dying breed, as is plain old DOS. You won't find as many new programs written for these older operating systems, nor will it be easy to find technical support for them.

✔ Solitaire is a *lot* easier to play with a pen than with a mouse, says Windows for Pens user Brian Bates. "What could be easier than picking up the Jack of Hearts and setting it on top of the Queen of Spades in one fluid pen movement?" Bates reports. "There's no hunt for the mouse pointer. Just put the pen on the Jack of Hearts, and it's ready to move."

Part II
Making Windows 95 Do More

The 5th Wave   By Rich Tennant

"WELL, RIGHT OFF, THE RESPONSE TIME SEEMS A BIT SLOW."

In this part . . .

*B*y now, you probably have figured out the Windows 95 basics: Click here to make something appear; double-click there to make it disappear. Ho hum.

To keep things moving, this part of the book shows you how to handle those *new* things you need to make Windows 95 accomplish.

You read about how to dust off the Windows HyperTerminal program, dial up Microsoft's Driver library, and pull the latest drivers off the shelf (as well as grab those special programs that Microsoft left off the floppy disk version of Windows 95).

Another chapter in this part shows you how to cram all those Windows programs onto that new laptop. Finally, you find out how to put all that flashy Windows multimedia stuff to work. Groovy!

Chapter 5

Stuffing Windows onto a Laptop

. . . .

In This Chapter

▶ Installing Windows on a laptop

▶ Stuffing the Briefcase

▶ Making Windows easier to see

▶ Working with a mouse or trackball

▶ Making Windows run better on a laptop

. . . .

*F*or years, nobody bothered trying to run Windows on a laptop. Windows was simply too big and too clumsy, and the laptops of the day were too small to digest it.

Windows 95 is bigger than ever. But today's laptops are much more powerful than before: Most of 'em can digest Windows 95 without even chewing. This chapter shows the *right* way to feed Windows 95 to a laptop, as well as some things to try if the laptop tries to burp Windows back up.

Installing Windows 95 on a Laptop

A laptop is a completely different organism than a desktop computer, so stuffing Windows 95 onto a laptop takes a few extra tricks. To make sure that Windows knows it is heading for a laptop's hard drive, you have to push a few different buttons while installing Windows.

In fact, if you *already* have installed Windows on your laptop, head for the chapter's later sections. There, you'll find information about Briefcase, a program that simplifies the chore of moving files between your laptop and desktop. You'll also find tips on ways to make laptopping less awkward.

If you're getting ready to install Windows 95 on your laptop right now, however, keep a wary eye on the next few sections.

Reinstall Windows 95; don't LapLink it over

A program by Traveling Software called LapLink can be a lifesaver. By installing LapLink on both your laptop and your desktop computer — and then stringing a cable between the serial or parallel ports of the two computers — you can quickly copy or move files back and forth between the two computers.

In fact, Windows 95 comes with a Direct Cable Connection that lets you perform many of the same tasks. (Direct Cable Connection is covered later in this chapter.) However, *don't* use either LapLink or Direct Cable Connection to copy Windows 95 from your desktop computer to your laptop. It won't work.

- ✔ And don't use DOS 6 *Interlink*, a LapLink clone, to copy Windows 95 over to your laptop, either. Sure, that would be the quickest way to install Windows 95. But even though Windows 95 files would be located on your laptop, the Windows 95 program would still think it was living on your desktop. It wouldn't be able to find its favorite files, and you may not be able to see it on your laptop's temperamental liquid crystal screen.

- ✔ Although it takes more time, install Windows 95 onto your laptop the old-fashioned way: by inserting the disks into the floppy drive, one at a time. (Or if your laptop has a CD-ROM drive, you lucky dog, install Windows 95 from the CD.)

- ✔ When laptopping in a hot-air balloon, don't bother wearing a heavy jacket. All that hot air overhead keeps you surprisingly warm in that little dangling basket.

Choose the Portable option when installing Windows 95

When installing Windows 95 on a laptop, choose the Portable option, not the Typical option. By choosing Portable, you tell Windows 95 to include files that come in handy for laptop users.

Specifically, you get the following laptop-based goodies:

- ✔ A program called Briefcase, described later in this chapter, makes it easier to keep track of which files are the most up-to-date when you start moving files between your laptop and desktop computer.

- ✔ A Direct Cable Connection program lets you squirt files back and forth between your laptop and desktop computer through a serial or parallel cable.

✔ Microsoft Exchange, described in Chapter 6, lets you keep in touch with your e-mail while on the road. Plus, a fax program lets you send and receive faxes — if your laptop's modem can handle faxes, that is.

✔ Advanced Power Management lets you customize your laptop's battery usage and suspend levels to save the most power.

If you didn't select these options when installing Windows on your laptop, check out the Windows Setup tab of the Control Panel's Add/Remove Programs icon.

Stuffing the Briefcase

Have you already installed Briefcase onto your computer? You can tell by clicking on a blank part of your desktop with your right mouse button and looking for Briefcase under the New menu. *If the word Briefcase isn't listed,* head for the Windows Setup tab under the Control Panel's Add/Remove Programs icon.

After you install Briefcase, here's how to make it work.

1. **Click on a blank part of the desktop with your right mouse button and choose Briefcase from the New menu.**

   A little briefcase icon appears on your desktop.

2. **Decide what files you want to work on while on the road with your laptop.**

   For example, decide what letters, spreadsheets, reports, or other files you need to complete.

   Briefcase only moves the data files, not the programs required to edit those data files. When copying files to your Briefcase, make sure that your other computer has the appropriate programs available to open and edit your files. For example, you need a copy of Microsoft Word for Windows on your laptop *and* your desktop computer in order to edit the Word files in your Briefcase.

3. **Drag and drop those files to your newly created Briefcase icon.**

   Windows 95 creates shortcuts to those documents in the Briefcase folder, keeping track of where the original files are located on your hard drive, as well as the file's current time and date.

   In fact, you see that information, shown in Figure 5-1, if you double-click on the Briefcase icon.

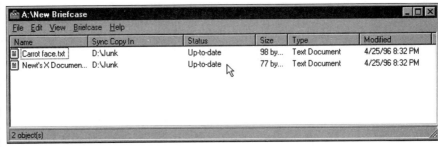

Figure 5-1:
Briefcase
makes sure
that you're
always
working on
the most
current file.

4. **Close the Briefcase window and drag and drop the Briefcase icon onto a floppy disk. (Or transfer the Briefcase using a cable link or the Direct Cable Connection, as described later in this chapter.)**

   The Briefcase icon disappears from your desktop as it's transferred onto the floppy disk.

   If you're copying the Briefcase to a floppy disk, make sure that all the files fit onto a single floppy. If you try to copy too many files, you'll have to use more than one disk, and Briefcase won't be able to keep track of which files belong where. (Direct Cable Connection worshippers don't have this worry.)

5. **Insert the floppy disk into your laptop or other computer and double-click on the disk's Briefcase icon.**

   The Briefcase opens up, showing you the files you placed inside it from your desktop computer.

6. **Drag and drop the files from inside the floppy's Briefcase onto your laptop's desktop.**

   Actually, you don't have to do this; you could edit the other files while they're still on the floppy disk. Floppy disks are a lot slower than hard disks, though, and they consume more battery power on laptops.

   Don't copy the Briefcase icon from the floppy disk to the hard disk, though, because Briefcase gets thoroughly confused. Just copy the files over from inside the Briefcase onto your desktop.

7. **Edit your files.**

   Do that "work on the road stuff" work, pretending the guy next to you on the plane isn't watching everything you type. (But you know he is because he has nothing else to do, and somebody else has already done the inflight magazine's crossword puzzle.)

8. Open the Briefcase on the floppy disk.

At this point, Briefcase hasn't done anything but serve as a glorified folder with an icon that looks like a briefcase. But the next few steps show you its magic.

9. Choose Update All from the Briefcase menu.

Briefcase peeks at the files on the floppy disk and your laptop, decides which ones are most up-to-date, and shows you a cool chart to make sure that it's copying the right files to the right place, as shown in Figure 5-2.

10. Click on the Update button.

Briefcase copies the appropriate files back into your Briefcase.

11. Close the Briefcase and put the floppy disk into your desktop computer.

12. Open the Briefcase on your floppy disk.

See how the Briefcase lists the files that need to be updated in Figure 5-3?

13. Choose Update All from the Briefcase menu.

Once again, Briefcase shows you the cool chart and asks permission to copy the updated files to your hard drive, effectively replacing the older ones you started with in Step 1.

Figure 5-2:
Briefcase
tells you
which files
are out
of date
and asks
permission
to update
them.

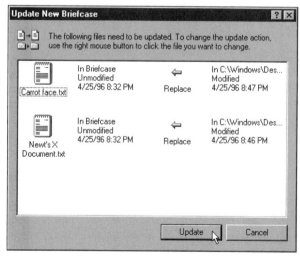

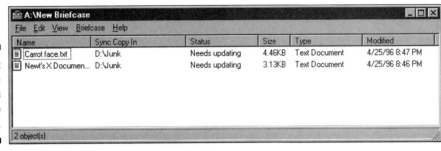

Figure 5-3:
Briefcase
lists the files
that need to
be updated.

✔ When using Briefcase, you can edit either the files from within their hard drive folders or directly from inside Briefcase. Because Briefcase only contains shortcuts, the two icons actually point to the same file. Just remember to leave the Briefcase on the floppy disk — it can't be moved around like the files can.

✔ When deciding which is the most up-to-date of two files, Briefcase looks at the time and date the file was last edited. So be sure to keep your computer's clock set to the correct time, or Briefcase won't know which file is really the most recent. Don't let daylight saving time wipe out your last hour of work.

Transferring Files with a Direct Cable Connection

You can transfer files between your laptop and your desktop computer the old-fashioned way: You can copy the files onto floppy disks and move them from one drive to another.

Or you can go the high-speed route of connecting the computers with a cable. This route is called Direct Cable Connection, and it works like this:

✔ Buy a *null modem* serial or parallel cable. (Or if you already have a spare cable lying around that's *normal,* buy a *null modem* adapter to convert it into a null modem serial or parallel cable.)

✔ If you installed Windows 95 with the Portable option, you already have the Direct Cable Connection software installed on your computer. (It's listed in the Accessories area of your Start menu's Programs area.) Not listed? Then install it through the Control Panel's Add/Remove Programs icon. (Double-click on that icon, click on the Windows Setup tab, and you find the cable stuff listed under Communications.)

After you've installed the cable program, here's how to set it up.

1. **Connect a port from your desktop computer to a port of your laptop computer.**

   Use a null modem serial or parallel cable. Then make sure that you're connecting the same type of ports on both computers. (You can't connect a serial to a parallel port. You can connect your serial cable to COM1 on one computer and COM2 on the other, however.)

2. **On your desktop computer, load Direct Cable Connection from the Accessories area of the Start menu's Programs area.**

   The configuration screen appears, as shown in Figure 5-4.

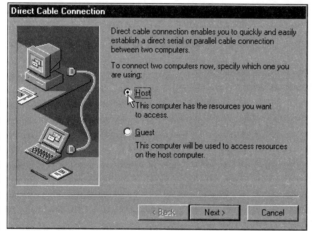

Figure 5-4: Set up one of your computers as Host and the other as Guest.

3. **Choose Host and click on Next.**

   Because you'll be grabbing files off your desktop computer and putting them onto your laptop, your desktop computer will be Host.

4. **Click on the File and Print Sharing button.**

   Because you want the computers to share files, you need to create a sort of *mini-network*. So the Network page appears, as shown in Figure 5-5.

5. **Click on the Identification tab and make sure that a name is typed in for your computer.**

   Type in an individual name for your computer; each computer must have its own name. Both of the linked computers need to have the same name listed under Workgroup, though.

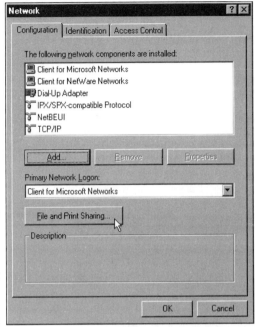

Figure 5-5:
Click on the
File and
Print
Sharing
button.

6. **Click on the File and Print Sharing button.**

   Yep, this is the second time you've clicked on a File and Print Sharing button.

7. **Click on the I want to be able to give others access to my files box and then click on OK.**

   Feel free to click in the box that lets people access your printer, too, if you want the laptop to be able to print through this mini-network.

8. **Click on the OK button.**

9. **Click on the OK button to let Windows restart the computer.**

   Be sure to close down any open files. When the computer comes back up, your mini-network should be in place.

10. **Load Direct Cable Connection from the Accessories area, just as you did in Step 2.**

11. **Select the port you want to use and click on Next.**

   Choose the port you've plugged your cable into, as shown in Figure 5-6. (The ports are often marked on the back of your computer, luckily.)

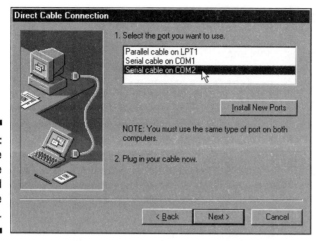

Figure 5-6:
Select the
port you've
plugged
your cable
into.

12. **On your desktop computer's screen, use your right mouse button to click on the folders that you want the laptop to be able to grab.**

13. **Choose the S̲haring option from the pop-up menu.**

14. **Click on the Shared As button and click on OK.**

15. **Click on the Next button in the Direct Cable Connection box.**

16. **Set up your laptop computer as Guest, using the proper port, and click on Finish.**

    Choose Guest from the Direct Cable Connection box and choose the port you've connected your cable to on your laptop computer.

    The laptop computer tries to connect to your desktop computer. And if nothing went wrong, you should be able to access the folder that you set up as shared on your desktop computer.

    ✔ If something does go wrong, however, click on a blank part of your desktop, press F1, click on the Contents tab, and double-click on the Troubleshooting option. Double-click on If you have trouble using a Direct Cable Connection, and Windows 95 takes you through a step-by-step list of things to check.

    ✔ Those nifty cables from LapLink software don't work with the Direct Cable Connection software. Sniff.

Making Windows Easier to See

One of the biggest problems with running Windows 95 on a laptop, especially an older model, becomes apparent when you look at the screen: It's hard to see what's going on. Some of the boxes have funny lines running up and down the screen, the mouse pointer often disappears at the worst possible moment, and your finger can get a workout adjusting the laptop's contrast or brightness knobs.

Unfortunately, there's no sure-fire cure. Unlike desktop computers, laptops find themselves under various lighting conditions. Working beneath a tree in an Amtrak station calls for a slightly different screen setup than working under the little swiveling overhead light on an airplane.

Here are some lighting weapons to keep in your armament bag; keep trying them until you find the one that works for your particular situation.

Wallpaper may look cool on a desktop computer, but take it easy on a laptop. Most wallpaper just gives the mouse pointer another place to hide.

Adjusting the contrast knobs

Your first line of defense comes from the little contrast knob found on nearly every laptop, either along one edge or near the screen.

Whenever the laptop's screen looks a little washed out, try giving the knob a quick turn to control the light source.

Changing your display

Windows comes with several settings that are custom designed to stand out on a laptop's display. When you first install Windows on your laptop, try out each setting until you find the one that makes Windows 95 show up most clearly.

Or if you have already installed Windows 95, follow the steps in this section to change the colors to something a little more appealing.

Feel free to test each color scheme in Windows until you find the one that looks best for your particular laptop:

1. **Click on a blank part of the desktop with your right mouse button and choose Properties from the pop-up menu.**

2. **Click on the Appearance tab.**

   The Appearance box, as shown in Figure 5-7, lets you change Windows' colors. Unless you are using an expensive color-screen laptop, everything on-screen is a mottled-gray color. Your mission: To choose the *clearest* shade of mottled gray.

3. **Click in the Scheme box and then click on a new scheme.**

   Click on the Scheme box, and a menu drops. Each time you click on a different scheme from the menu, Windows offers a preview of what the color scheme looks like.

Some manufacturers toss in a floppy disk containing video drivers designed especially for their laptop's screen. These special pieces of software often let you see Windows 95 more easily on your laptop's screen. (Refer to Chapter 3 if you're not sure how to get those drivers off the disk and onto your hard drive.)

Laptoppers should try out the High Contrast Black and High Contrast White, all in various sizes.

Figure 5-7:
If you're using an older laptop, the Display Properties all look gray and washed out.

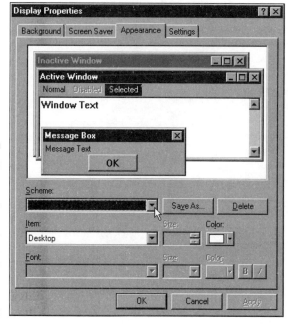

Changing to a better mouse pointer

Even when the laptop's screen is easy to read, your troubles aren't over. The mouse pointer on a laptop sometimes disappears when it's moved — the screens simply can't update themselves quickly enough to reflect the movement on the screen. And because the mouse pointer is moving about 90 percent of the time, a disappearing mouse pointer can be a problem on older laptops.

Here's one way to make the pointer easier to spot:

1. **From the Start menu's Settings area, click on the Control Panel icon.**

2. **Double-click on the Mouse icon.**

   The Mouse Properties control box appears.

3. **Click on the Motion tab.**

4. **Click in the box next to Show pointer trails.**

   As soon as a check mark appears in the Show pointer trails box, your mouse begins leaving mouse droppings all over your screen (see Figure 5-8).

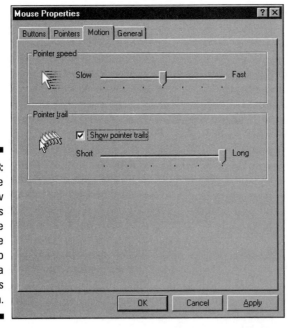

Figure 5-8:
Choose Show pointer trails to make your mouse easier to see on a laptop's screen.

✔ Some mice or trackballs come with software that makes their pointers easier to spot. For example, Microsoft's clip-on trackball comes with a special Control Panel that makes the mouse pointer as big and black as a Happy Hour meatball.

✔ Several shareware and public domain programs also can make mouse pointers easier to spot. Turn to Chapter 7 for tips on downloading those programs.

The letters are all too small!

A laptop's screen is nearly always smaller than a desktop monitor. Text often looks smaller than the ingredients list on a package of Hostess Chocodiles. Luckily, fonts are easy to enlarge in both DOS and Windows programs.

Windows programs: When using Windows word processors, spreadsheets, or other Windows programs with text, tell the program to use larger fonts. Usually the program's Format menu contains a Font or Size option.

If you're using Word for Windows or another word processor that uses *style sheets*, change your Normal style to something big and easy to read, such as 14-point Arial. This adjustment causes the word processor to display your text in a larger, more visible font.

DOS programs: Windows can enlarge the fonts used by DOS programs, but only while the program runs in an on-screen window and doesn't use any fancy graphics. To enlarge the fonts, click on the little box in the DOS window's upper-left corner (or press Alt+spacebar) and choose Fonts from the menu that drops down. Click on the 10 x 18 option to make the window larger and easier to see.

The DOS window's new larger size probably keeps it from fitting completely on-screen, but Windows automatically shifts your point of view, keeping the cursor in sight.

If the DOS program looks too small when run in an on-screen window, press Alt+Enter. The DOS program fills the screen, making it much easier to see. Press Alt+Enter again to return it to its own window.

Playing with a Mouse on the Airline Tray

A mouse makes Windows easier to use on a desktop computer, but it often gets in the way on a laptop. Luckily, there are a few alternatives.

Trackballs: These little guys look like tiny upside-down mice that clip to the side of your laptop. Some laptops come with a trackball built in near the screen. Just give the ball a deft spin with your thumb, and the mouse pointer stumbles across the screen. Definitely give yourself a few days to get used to it.

Trackballs work on desktop computers as well as laptops. To get used to the trackball's different feel, clip it to your desktop computer's keyboard. After giving it a whirl for a few days, you will feel more confident thumbing a trackball when you are on the road.

Keyboard: Some laptops let you move the mouse pointer by pressing a special function key and tapping the arrow keys. It's as awkward as it sounds, but arrow keys are better than the last alternative, described next.

Memorizing keystrokes: Windows can be controlled exclusively through the keyboard. See those underlined letters on the menus of just about any Windows program? Press and release Alt and then press one of those underlined letters, which activates the command. For example, press Alt, F while you are in Program Manager, and the File menu drops down.

✔ Ever tried to change a window's size by using a trackball? Grabbing a window's border is like trying to pick up a toothpick with salad tongs. The border is just too skinny to get a grip on.

To enlarge the border, head for the Appearance portion of the Display Properties box. Then under Scheme, change the Active Window Border to 5 and click on OK. If the border is still hard to grab, increase the number to 6 and try again.

✔ Don't have much space to move your mouse on the airplane's fold-down tray? Head for the Control Panel's Mouse icon, click on the Motion tab and change the Pointer speed to fast. A subtle push then sends the mouse flying across the screen. Keep fine-tuning until you have the speed adjusted the way you like it.

Plain Old Windows/Laptop Tips

Here's a grab bag of tips for running Windows 95 on a laptop. Test them over to see which ones fit in best with your sort of work.

- ✔ When traveling, don't forget to change your laptop's internal clock to match the time zone in your current location. Double-click on the Date/Time icon in the Control Panel and type the new time in the little box.

- ✔ Do you frequently change your laptop's time? Then drag the Date/Time icon from the Control Panel to a corner of your desktop. That creates a shortcut so that you can change your laptop's time or date with a simple double-click.

- ✔ When using Solitaire, click on Game, choose Options from the menu, and click on the Outline dragging option. That makes the cards a *lot* easier to see.

Testing before Traveling

Did you just buy a new laptop for that upcoming business trip? Then copy all your programs onto it and use it exclusively for two or three days before you leave. By trying out your laptop beforehand, you can determine which programs you forgot to copy — before it's too late to take them with you. Plus, you can decide which pages of the Help manual you should photocopy and stick in your laptop bag!

Chapter 6

The Internet Explorer, Exchange, and Minor Bits of World Wide Webbery

*M*icrosoft grabbed the operating system market years ago and never let go. Today, Bill Gates is the richest man in the United States of America. What's he doing with all that cash? He's trying to predict the future so that he can become the richest man in the galaxy.

Gates has his eyes set on the *Internet* — a collection of computers strung together throughout the world. Some people use the Internet for sending electronic mail (e-mail). Others prefer to create or browse Web pages — picturesque electronic bulletin boards where you find everything from battery replacement charts to live-action videos of Hawaiian surf.

This chapter shows how to connect to the Internet, as well as how to use Microsoft Exchange, the program for automatically sending and receiving your electronic mail.

But be forewarned: These connections are some of the most difficult things to figure out in Windows 95. Some of them can take hours to set up, and some can't be set up at all.

If this chapter doesn't delve deeply enough into the Internet for you, consider checking out *Windows 95 SECRETS,* by Brian Livingston and Davis Straub (published by IDG Books Worldwide, Inc.).

Connecting to the Internet with Windows 95

You need a computer and a modem to connect to the Internet. Those are the basics. After that, you need two more things. First, you need an *Internet provider* — that's the service that gives you a phone number to dial and a bill each month. The best Internet provider charges the cheapest rates, gives you the fewest busy signals, and has the fastest modems.

Some companies, such as CompuServe and America Online, run their own online services but offer Internet access on the side — if you pay extra.

Second, you need *software* for accessing the Internet. With Internet software, you can dial up your Internet provider and connect to the Internet. The best software works the quickest and can handle the most advanced sound and graphics.

There are a wide variety of ways to connect to the Internet, but Microsoft broke them down into two groups: Microsoft's way and everybody else's way. (Guess which method Microsoft made the easiest?)

Which method is *really* the best? Right now, most people prefer using software called *Netscape* for connecting to the Internet and exploring the World Wide Web. If you're serious about Web-surfing, you'll probably want to use that program. But this section of the book shows how to make the best of whatever you might already have so you won't have to buy something else.

The easy, ten-step Microsoft way of connecting to the Internet

Microsoft prefers you to use this method to connect to the Internet. It's quick, easy, and puts the most money in Microsoft's pocket. Just follow the steps below, clicking on the Next button after you make your choice.

However, this method forces you to use Microsoft as your Internet provider (you have to pay Microsoft a monthly fee); it also makes you use Microsoft's Internet Explorer software to explore the Internet's World Wide Web.

1. **Buy and install a copy of Microsoft Plus!**

   The program places an icon called The Internet on your desktop, as well as several other Internet utilities that lurk in the background.

2. **Double-click on The Internet icon.**

   When the Internet Setup Wizard box comes up, as shown in Figure 6-1, click on the Next button.

Figure 6-1:
Microsoft's
Wizard
automates
the process
of connecting
you to the
Internet.

3. Choose The Microsoft Network as your Internet provider.

If you don't have an Internet provider, click on The Microsoft Network. If you already have an Internet provider, such as CompuServe, stop right now and jump to the next section.

4. Choose whether or not you're already a Microsoft Network member.

If you're not already a member — and you probably aren't — click on the button that signs you up. The Microsoft Network sign-up box appears, as shown in Figure 6-2.

Figure 6-2:
Choosing
The
Microsoft
Network is
probably the
easiest
(but not
necessarily
the best)
way to join
the Internet.

5. Click on the OK button.

A new box appears, and Microsoft Network asks for information about your modem setup.

6. Type in the first three digits of your phone number and click on OK.

A box appears, saying that Microsoft will tell your modem to call The Microsoft Network for the first time.

7. Click on the Connect button to make your modem call The Microsoft Network.

The computer dials, the modems shriek at each other, the sound stops, and The Microsoft Network begins dumping information into your computer. Eventually, a form appears, as shown in Figure 6-3.

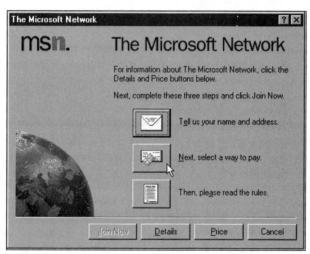

Figure 6-3:
To access the Internet, you need to pay, as The Microsoft Network reminds you on its opening screen.

8. Fill out your name, choose your pricing scheme, read the rules, and click on the Join Now button.

9. Click on the Connect button.

Your modem calls back Microsoft's computers to give them your credit card number and other information on the form you filled out.

10. Fill in a name and password.

Type in a name and password. Why can't everybody simply use their *real* name? Because a lot of Bill Smiths are out there, and the computer can get confused.

Please don't use the word *password* as your password. That's the first word that nasty people try out when they're breaking into your account.

After connecting, The Microsoft Network (MSN) tells you the phone number it's using, and it places its Microsoft Network icon on your desktop for future use. You're through!

- ✔ To connect to MSN from here, just double-click on The Microsoft Network icon and type your member name and password into the form, as shown in Figure 6-4.

- ✔ After you've connected to MSN, you can connect to the Internet. However, the version of Internet Explorer that came with your version of Microsoft Plus! might be out of date. (Microsoft updates Internet Explorer pretty quickly.) If your version is out of date, MSN will tell you about it and let you download the latest copy for free. (Downloading the copy took about a half hour the last time I tried, and I used a fast modem.)

Figure 6-4:
After you've signed up for an account on The Microsoft Network, just type your member name and password to connect.

The more difficult, non-Microsoft way of connecting to the Internet

Some people choose to skip The Microsoft Network and sign on to the World Wide Web through their own Internet provider, like CompuServe, America Online, Prodigy, or a "dedicated Internet provider" that provides access to the Internet only.

In fact, a lot of these people are also using *Netscape* — a Web browser that's a lot more popular than the Internet Explorer. Microsoft is beginning to realize that it can't force everybody to use The Microsoft Network, but it is still pushing Internet Explorer as the Web surfboard of choice.

You can set up Windows 95 to use your own, non-Microsoft brand of Internet provider, as well as your own non-Microsoft Web browser, but it's usually not as easy to do as the Microsoft method described earlier. Depending on your computer's setup, you might find yourself wearing some pretty heavy gloves.

For example, here's how to use Internets Explorer with the Internet provider of your choice. Start by grabbing a copy of Internet Explorer. (Microsoft's giving it away for free on its Web page at www.msn.com.)

1. Find a copy of Internet Explorer.

Look for at least Version 2; Version 3 is better.

2. Double-click on the Internet Explorer's Install program icon.

The program probably tells you what version of itself it's about to install, and then it asks you to click on the I Agree button after you've read the boring licensing agreement. Then the program installs itself.

3. When prompted, restart your computer.

Whenever Windows 95 makes changes to its most sensitive internal organs, it asks you to reboot the computer. Then, after it comes back to life, it can read its new settings without having to worry about having some of its old settings rolling around in its memory.

So save all your work, close down your programs, pull any floppy disk out of drive A, and choose the Restart the computer option from the Start menu's Shut down option.

4. Click on the Start button and choose the Internet Setup Wizard.

The Internet Setup Wizard is buried deep within the Start button's menus, living in the Internet Tools area of the Accessories area (which lives in the Programs area, of course).

The Internet Setup Wizard comes to the screen (refer to Figure 6-1).

5. Click on the Next button and choose the different service provider option.

Tell Mr. Wizard that you'd like to connect to the Internet using your own provider, thank you (as shown in Figure 6-5).

6. Choose No for Microsoft Exchange and click on the Next button.

Microsoft Exchange, described in the next section, works like an electronic mail carrier. It can automatically log on to your mail box, grab any mail, and notify you if you've gotten anything good. It sends mail automatically too, all in the background.

Some people find Microsoft Exchange incredibly handy. Others think that it's incredibly distracting. Because it can always be installed later, you can read the last section in this chapter and decide for yourself then.

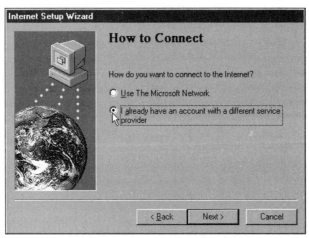

Figure 6-5:
The Internet
Explorer can
connect to
other
Internet
providers
besides The
Microsoft
Network.

7. **Type in the name of your Internet Service Provider and click on the Next button.**

Here's where Microsoft makes things a little sticky. First, it tosses out language like *Point-to-Point Protocol* (PPP). Actually, PPP is a format supported by almost all the main service providers, so don't let the weird words worry you.

The name you type in this box isn't as important as the number that goes in the upcoming boxes. After all, your mail still gets to your house if your name's spelled wrong — it's the street number that makes the difference.

8. **Type in the phone number of your service provider and click on the Next button.**

Whether you use CompuServe, America Online, or a dedicated Internet provider, type in the phone number your modem dials in order to reach the provider.

You probably don't need to click in the Bring up terminal window after dialing box unless you're having problems connecting and you want to watch the action on your screen as the modems talk.

9. **Type the user name and password that you use to log on to your service and then click on the Next button.**

10. **Fill in the IP Address Form and click on the Next button.**

See how things are getting stickier? You have to ask your Internet provider about this one. Some Internet providers automatically assign you an IP Address, but others make you fill in the form.

Pssst. I've got an account on CompuServe, so I know that CompuServe automatically assigns you an IP Address.

11. Fill in the DNS Server Address (Domain Name Server) form and click on the Next button.

How come this ugly stuff never came up when people used The Microsoft Network? Anyway, you have to ask your Internet provider for the right numbers to plug into this form, as shown in Figure 6-6. Try calling your Internet provider's customer service number for help.

For CompuServe, you can enter 149.174.211.5 and 149.174.213.5 as your DNS Server and Alternate DNS Server numbers

Figure 6-6:
These numbers work when connecting to CompuServe's Internet service.

12. Click on the Finish button.

Now you can test the thing and hope it works. If you have a dedicated Internet provider, Internet Explorer might be able to log on without problems. If you have an online service, Internet Explorer probably won't work on the first try.

- Online services like CompuServe usually need a special "script" written in a modem-like programming language. The script tells the Internet Explorer how to log on to the Internet side of the online service.

- To get to the script, you need to install the Dial-Up Scripting Tool, sometimes found in the Accessories area of the Start menu's Programs section.

- Not there? Then you'll find the script program in the Dscript folder of your Windows 95 CD. (That folder is in the Apptools folder, which is in the Admin folder.) The installation directions are in the Dscript file.

- In short, you can probably count on staying up a night or two trying to get Internet Explorer to work with other Internet providers besides The Microsoft Network.

Microsoft Exchange and the Inbox

Microsoft Exchange lets you send and receive messages on your computer, automatically grabbing them from all your online services, accounts, and networks, and placing them into one convenient Inbox.

When you've gotten around to answering the e-mail that isn't junk, Exchange distributes your responses back to the appropriate parties.

If Microsoft Exchange isn't already on your Start menu, double-click on the Control Panel's Add/Programs icon, click on the Windows Setup tab, double-click on the Communications section, and click on Microsoft Exchange.

To set up Exchange for the first time, follow the steps below.

1. Load Exchange from the Start menu.

The Inbox Setup Wizard jumps in, as shown in Figure 6-7, to help configure the program.

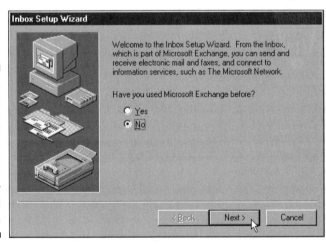

Figure 6-7:
The Inbox
Setup
Wizard
can help
configure
Exchange to
meet your
own e-mail
setup.

2. Click on the No button and then click on Next.

If you haven't configured Exchange, click on the No button.

3. Click in the boxes next to the information services that you'd like Exchange to monitor and then click on Next.

For example, if you want Exchange to grab your mail from CompuServe as well as an Internet provider, click on the Internet Mail and CompuServe Mail options, as shown in Figure 6-8.

Figure 6-8:
Click on the e-mail services you'd like Exchange to monitor.

4. **Provide information about your information service.**

   This step differs on different computers. If you want Microsoft Exchange to grab your Internet mail, for instance, you need to tell it how you connect to the Internet: The program, your user name, password, and the phone number.

5. **Enter a name for your new Address Book and then click on Next.**

   Go ahead and accept the default choice so that the program doesn't get confused.

6. **Enter a name for your new file folder and then click on Next.**

   Do the same here; just click on Next.

7. **To make Exchange run automatically during the day, click on Add Inbox to the Startup group.**

   If you want Exchange to monitor your mail box constantly, choose the Add Inbox to the Startup group. That loads Microsoft Exchange when you turn on your computer for the day.

   If you prefer to get your e-mail manually, don't check this option.

8. **Click on the Finish button.**

   You're through! Microsoft Exchange appears on-screen, ready to roll.

Using Microsoft Exchange

Once Microsoft Exchange is hooked up to your mail service, be it a local network or an online service like America Online, Exchange automatically checks your accounts, grabs any waiting messages, and puts them into your Inbox. Whether you're sending or receiving mail, the program works like this:

1. Double-click on the Inbox icon.

Double-click on the Inbox icon — the little globe resting behind an inbox full of envelopes — to bring Microsoft Exchange to the screen, as shown in Figure 6-9. Each envelope stands for a message waiting in your Inbox. After you read the message, you can delete it or copy it to another folder.

To use Exchange effectively, put it in your Start menu's Startup folder, so that it starts automatically whenever you load Windows.

Figure 6-9:
Feel free to
minimize
Exchange
unless
you're
currently
sending or
receiving
messages; it
works in the
background.

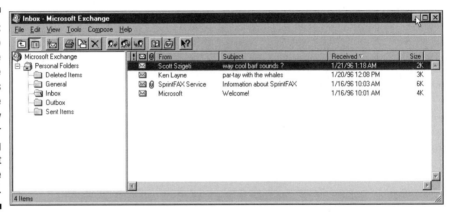

2. Minimize the Exchange program.

Keep Exchange minimized, lurking on the bottom of your screen. It searches the online services it's been assigned to, looking for new messages as often as you've specified.

3. Click on the little envelope in the screen's bottom, right corner.

After somebody sends you a message — and Exchange retrieves it and places it into your Inbox — you see a minuscule envelope waiting for you in the taskbar next to the clock. A click on the envelope brings Exchange to the screen, listing your newly retrieved message at the top of its list.

4. Double-click on your newly retrieved message.

The letter appears, as shown in Figure 6-10.

5. Click on the first little head icon in the upper-left corner to respond to the message.

When the window appears, type your responding message, as shown in Figure 6-11.

6. Click on the little "send" icon that's shaped like an envelope.

Click on the little envelope next to the mouse pointer in Figure 6-11, and Exchange tosses your reply into its Outbox folder, ready to be mailed during its next round of mail deliveries.

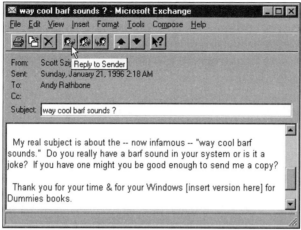

Figure 6-10:
Click on the
first little
head — the
one next to
the mouse
pointer — to
respond
to the
message.

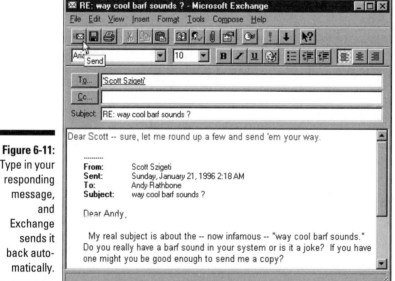

Figure 6-11:
Type in your
responding
message,
and
Exchange
sends it
back auto-
matically.

Exchange can be terribly difficult to figure out, much less set up. Don't try to set it up yourself unless you're reasonably familiar with computers, networks, or online services.

Rest your mouse pointer over an icon in Exchange, and a box appears to tell you about that icon's purpose.

Sending a message in Exchange

Sending messages in Exchange is relatively easy, except for one problem: You need the e-mail address of the person you're about to send the message to. If you have the e-mail address, here's how it works.

1. **Choose New Message from the Compose menu.**

   A window appears for you to type your message.

2. **Click on the To button.**

   This brings up the list of people you have addresses for.

3. **Double-click on the name of the person that you'd like to send mail to and then click on the OK button.**

4. **Fill out your message.**

5. **Click on the little "send" icon that resembles an envelope, just as you did in the last step of the previous lesson.**

   Once again, Exchange places your message into your Outbox, ready to be delivered when it makes its next round.

Exchange can also send and receive faxes, if your computer's modem can handle them.

Chapter 7

Dialing Up Other Computers with HyperTerminal

*E*very once in a while, the newspapers expose some sneaky kids who have used a modem to hook up their computers to the phone lines.

With the modem, they can order a pizza, charge it to somebody else's bank account, and have the pepperoni-and-mushroom, crispy crust delivered during their social studies class.

Those kids probably didn't do all that sneaky stuff with HyperTerminal, the built-in telecommunications program that comes with Windows 95. HyperTerminal is a bare-bones operation, lacking most of the fancy features cherished by devious computer nerds. It can't browse the World Wide Web, even if you know what the World Wide Web is.

HyperTerminal is a relatively simple program, but it's not particularly easy to use. In fact, HyperTerminal is one of the most unfriendly programs packaged with Windows 95.

This chapter shows how you can pry something useful from that grim HyperTerminal screen. (You won't find any tips on prying a pizza out of it, however.)

Why Bother with HyperTerminal?

Some people are afraid to fly. If you want to get from point A to point B without wearing out a few pairs of tennis shoes, however, an airplane is the best tool for the job.

The same holds true for HyperTerminal and a *modem* — the gizmo with a scary reputation that hooks your computer up to the phone line. With a modem connected to your computer, HyperTerminal can handle all the tasks described in the following sections.

HyperTerminal might not be the best program for bossing modems around, but hey, it's free. Besides, *all* modem programs are unfriendly, and HyperTerminal's no exception.

Calling Microsoft's BBS to grab the latest drivers

Sooner or later, Windows 95 starts asking for new *drivers* — special pieces of software that let Windows 95 talk to different parts of your computer. But where do you get those drivers? A few nice companies mail them to you on a floppy disk — if you mail them a check.

But the quickest way to find a driver is to grab it directly off Microsoft's own computer. Yep, by using HyperTerminal, you can tell your computer's modem to call up Microsoft's computer. When Microsoft's computer answers the phone, you tell HyperTerminal to grab the driver. Got the driver? Then you're done. Hang up and put that new driver to use.

Best of all, you're only paying for a few minutes of long-distance charges.

Sure, all this HyperTerminal stuff sounds kind of nerdy. It *is* nerdy. But it's also the fastest and cheapest way to shut up Windows 95 when it starts asking for new drivers.

- ✔ After you have grabbed the new drivers, review Chapter 3 for the dance steps required to install them.

- ✔ Just buy a new video card? Chances are, the video drivers on Microsoft's BBS are more up-to-date than the video drivers that came with your new card.

✔ Microsoft's computer — called a *Bulletin Board System,* or *BBS* — offers drivers and helpful information about Windows 95, DOS, Word, Excel, Works, and a few other Microsoft products. You may even find some goodies for your friend's Macintosh.

Call CompuServe for Microsoft's help forums

Is Windows 95 giving you some grief? And you don't want to wait on hold for Microsoft's Tech Support folks to help fix the problem? Then use HyperTerminal to join CompuServe. Unlike Microsoft's BBS, CompuServe runs on H&R Block's gargantuan income-tax computers, and thousands of people can call in at the same time.

Using HyperTerminal, you can call CompuServe and type a question for Microsoft's Technical Support staff. Windows 95 Technical Support people then read your question and type an answer.

If you're leery of typing messages into a strange computer, browse through the messages other confused people have already typed into CompuServe. Chances are, somebody before you has had the same question, and the answer may be waiting for you to read and hastily scribble onto a sticky note.

✔ The bad news? CompuServe costs money, charged by the hour. Most of the online services, including Prodigy, America Online, and The Microsoft Network, charge a fee of some sort.

✔ For more information about CompuServe (including the current hourly rates), call 1-800-848-8990. After you have signed up for the service, type **go mswin** to reach the forum where Microsoft's helpful technical folks hang out.

✔ You can find support for many Windows 95 programs on CompuServe. Type **find windows 95** at the CompuServe prompt for an up-to-date list of helpful Windows 95 topics.

✔ CompuServe isn't just about Windows 95. CompuServe attracts more than one million callers who meet in various forums to discuss everything from politics to which vintages of Cabernet Sauvignon turn your teeth red.

Finding wacky shareware programs

Where do your friends get all those cool new icons? All that fun wallpaper? Those wild screen savers that make winged zucchini flap across your screen?

Chances are, they found all that stuff on online services like CompuServe and America Online, or on any of the thousands of other computers set up for callers around the world. Some online services, like CompuServe, are set up by big corporations who charge big hourly rates. Other services are plain ol' PCs — just like yours — set up by nerds in their living rooms. Other people find programs on computers linked together through the Internet and the World Wide Web.

And best of all, most of those programs you can grab from these computers are either free or cost just a few dollars.

- ✔ Don't know what a shareware program is? Trot back to Chapter 2 for a quick refresher.

- ✔ Oh, and in case your new shareware programs start asking for some weird VBRUN thing, you can find an explanation of that in Chapter 2 as well.

- ✔ Can't see your mouse pointer very well? Explore CompuServe's Windows 95 Shareware Forum for some shareware mouse pointer enlargers. (Flip ahead to Chapter 10 first, though.)

- ✔ To see what some of these shareware programs look like, sneak a peek at Chapter 9.

Making HyperTerminal Call Another Computer

No doubt about it, computers are downright hostile to their users. Computers are even *more* hostile when they're dealing with other computers. Consequently, the whole world of *telecommunications* — making computers talk to each other over the phone lines — can be pretty stressful. Too many things can go wrong.

First, your modem may be having a bad data day. Or the cable connecting it to the phone jack might have a few fibers out of place. Or HyperTerminal might not be set up correctly to talk to your particular modem.

The problem might even be out of your reach: The phone lines could be crackling, or the *other* computer's modem may be turned off. The problem might even be that the other computer is out of commission or its software isn't properly set up.

The next few sections cover all the hoops you can jump through in your quest to get HyperTerminal up and running. If you have called up other computers before but just want a quick refresher on a particular area, jump ahead to the section that's got you stumped; otherwise, read each section in order for the whole scoop on how to have your computer make that first phone call.

Plugging a modem into your computer

HyperTerminal's main purpose is to talk to a modem — that gadget that attaches to your computer and hooks up to the phone line. Modems come in two basic models:

- *Internal* modems come on a *card* that lives inside your computer, hidden from sight.

- *External* modems come in a little box that sits next to your computer. A cable runs between the modem and a little plug on the back of your computer called a *serial, or COM,* port.

The biggest problem? Your computer can talk to the modem through one of *four* different COM ports. Unless Windows 95 knows which COM port your modem is connected to, nothing exciting happens.

- Internal modems grab a COM port from their bunk inside the computer. No need for connector cables, on/off switches, or power cables.

- External modems grab a COM port through a cable that plugs into the back of your computer. External modems also need power, which is usually supplied by an AC adapter that plugs into the wall.

- Most internal and external modems come with two phone jacks. Look for a little picture of a telephone by one jack; that's where the cord from your normal telephone plugs in. Plug a phone cord into the second jack (often labeled "line"), with the other end plugging into the phone jack in your wall.

- COM ports are little pathways that your computer uses to send and receive information. Although your computer can talk through four COM ports, it can only use two of those ports at the same time. So if your mouse plugs into one COM port, your modem has to grab the other COM port. If they both try to grab the same port, they'll bicker like rude neighbors on a party line, and neither will work.

- If you have an external modem, look to see where its cable plugs into the back of your computer. Does it fit into a plug that is about $1/2$-inch long? That's probably COM1. If it fits into a plug that's a little longer than 1 inch, it's probably COM2.

- You don't really need to keep track of which COM port the modem's using; Windows 95 can figure it out for itself. Just load the <u>C</u>ontrol Panel from the Start button's <u>S</u>ettings area and then double-click the Add New Hardware button.

- Having trouble installing your modem? Check out *Modems For Dummies* by Tina Rathbone (published by IDG Books Worldwide, Inc.). It offers a guiding hand to help tame a squiggling octopus of problems.

Loading HyperTerminal

Loading HyperTerminal is the easiest part of the entire process. Click on Programs from the Start button menu, click on Accessories, and click on HyperTerminal from the menu. A folder containing HyperTerminal hops to the screen, as shown in Figure 7-1.

Figure 7-1:
Loading
HyperTerminal
from the
Start button
menu brings
up a folder
containing
the
HyperTerminal
program, as
well as
previously
set-up
places
to call.

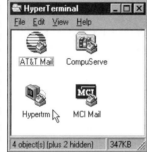

Double-click on the HyperTrm icon, and the program pops to the screen.

✔ Although HyperTerminal is a program, its Start menu icon looks like a plain old folder. That's not only confusing, it's boring.

✔ If you or somebody else has loaded HyperTerminal before, you'll see little icons inside the folder. The icon labeled HyperTerminal is the actual program. The other icons also launch HyperTerminal, but they launch the program with the settings it needs to dial another computer.

✔ In fact, if you've called another computer with HyperTerminal before, just double-click on the icon that represents that other computer. HyperTerminal leaps to the screen, ready to call the other computer.

Getting HyperTerminal ready to call another computer for the first time

After you bring HyperTerminal to the screen, you must tell the program a few facts about the computer you are trying to call.

First, you must know the other computer's *phone number*. For example, the phone number for Microsoft's BBS is 206-637-9009. (Don't worry about the long distance stuff — Windows 95 is smart enough to know whether or not it needs to add a 1 or an area code to the phone number.)

1. **Fill out the Connection Description box with a name, choose an icon, and click the OK button.**

   The first time you load HyperTerminal — or make a call to a new place — the Connection Description dialog box pops up and asks you to enter a name and choose an icon for the place you're calling, as shown in Figure 7-2. If you're calling Microsoft's BBS, for example, type **Microsoft BBS** into the Name box and click on any icon that catches your eye in the Icon box.

Figure 7-2: Choose an icon for the BBS and type a name for the connection.

2. **Fill in the phone number your modem needs to dial and click the OK button.**

   When the Phone Number dialog box appears, fill in the number your modem needs to dial, as shown in Figure 7-3. To enter the number for Microsoft, for example, enter **206** in the Area code box and **637-9009** in the Phone number box.

Feel free to add the little hyphen between numbers if you think it looks better. Or leave the hyphen out — HyperTerminal doesn't care either way. (Just don't try to put the area code in parentheses, or you'll get into big trouble.)

You probably won't need to mess with the other parts of the form, unless you're dialing another country or you have more than one modem connected to your system.

3. Click the Dial button.

If you're not calling while on the road with a laptop computer, you're probably calling from your immobile desktop computer — your *Default Location*. Similarly, you probably won't need to click the Modify button unless you goofed when entering the phone number.

Your modem will call the other BBS and, hopefully, shake hands and begin a successful relationship.

✔ Busy? A dialog box pops up, ready for you to click the Dial Now button. Still busy? A dialog box pops up, ready for you to click the Dial Now button. Still busy? Click that button. Yep, there's no way to make the modem dial automatically until it finally connects.

✔ If HyperTerminal didn't connect, a few things may have happened. The phone line might be busy: Somebody else's modem may have beat you to it. Wait a few minutes and try again.

✔ If things still seem awry, head for the end of this chapter for some troubleshooting tips. Unfortunately, it may be time to call in a computer guru.

✔ After you dial the Microsoft BBS, as with most other computers you dial, you have to type your name, your city, and your state. That invasion of privacy is called *logging on*.

✔ When other computers begin sending information over the phone lines, HyperTerminal's screen looks like a strange new program, complete with menus.

✔ If you are calling a new computer for the first time, you might want to capture everything that flows by to a text file (described in an upcoming section). Then when the stress level isn't so high, you can review exactly what transpired while you were online.

To make the modem dial numbers faster, load the settings for the place you want to call and choose Properties from the File menu. Click the Configure button to see the modem's properties, and choose the Connection tab at the box's top. Click the Advanced button. Huff, puff. Finally, type **ats11=55** into the Extra settings box and click on the OK button. Return to the main menu, and your modem will henceforth dial more quickly.

✔ Using a laptop while on the road? Then set up as many different locations as you want by clicking on the Dialing Properties button from the Connect box (the box that has the Dial button on it). From there, click the New button, fill out a new "Where am I calling from" box, and save the settings under a new name. Then you can simply call up that name when you return to that city, and you'll be ready to call.

Capturing Something from the Screen

After you are connected to another computer, the fun begins. HyperTerminal's window fills up with information sent by the computer on the other end of the phone line.

See anything interesting? Tell HyperTerminal to grab it right off the screen. For example, to grab a few interesting paragraphs off the screen, follow these steps:

1. Find the paragraphs you want to grab.

If the interesting paragraph has already scrolled off the top of HyperTerminal's screen, it's not gone for good. Bring it back from the dead by clicking on HyperTerminal's scroll bar — the long skinny thing along the right edge (see Figure 7-4). Keep clicking near the top of the scroll bar until the information slides back onto the screen.

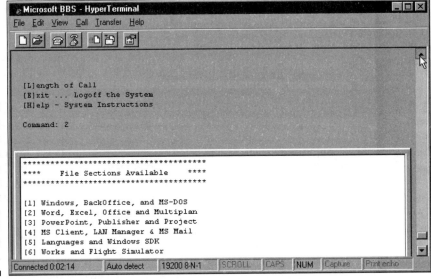

2. Hold down the mouse button and slide the pointer over the information.

Point to the beginning of the first word you want to grab. Then while holding down the left mouse button, slide the mouse until it points to the end of the last word you want to grab. The stuff you want to grab changes color, or becomes *highlighted*.

3. From HyperTerminal's Edit menu, click on Copy or press Ctrl+C.

When you choose Copy or press Ctrl+C (see Figure 7-5), the highlighted information you grabbed is sent to the Windows 95 Clipboard.

4. Paste the information into Notepad or some other program.

To save the information quickly, call up Notepad from the Accessories area of the Start button's Programs section and choose Paste from Notepad's Edit menu. The Clipboard dumps your newly grabbed information into Notepad, and then you can save it to a file.

Actually, you can paste the information into any program; Notepad just makes a nice place to store it for a while.

✔ Sometimes the information goes by too quickly to grab. To keep that from happening, make HyperTerminal hold on to as big a chunk of information as possible. Choose Properties from HyperTerminal's File menu. Then click on the Settings tab along the top. Finally, type **500** in the Backscroll buffer lines box. Now you can scroll back to read the preceding 500 lines.

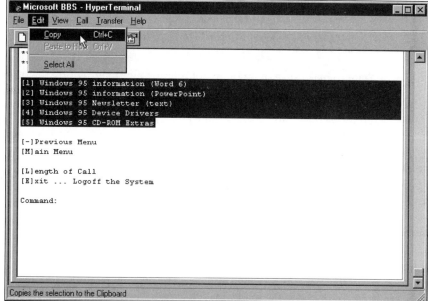

Figure 7-5:
Highlight
information
and choose
Copy from
the File
menu to
copy it to
the Clipboard
for later
pasting into
Notepad or
another file.

✔ If Ctrl+C makes the other computer act weird — and HyperTerminal refuses to grab the information — here's the fix: Choose HyperTerminal Preferences from the File menu. Then make sure that there's a check mark in the Function, arrow, and ctrl keys act as Terminal keys button.

✔ If you grabbed a horrendously huge chunk of information, Notepad won't be able to handle it. Notepad is not a big enough program to handle files of more than about 50K. Dump the information into WordPad instead.

✔ Called someplace with HyperTerminal but forgot to grab something that scrolled off the screen? HyperTerminal keeps the scroll buffer hanging around from your last session. So double-click on the icon of the place you called and click the scroll bars. Your information might still be there, waiting to be grabbed.

Capturing Everything from the Other Computer

Want to make sure that you're not missing anything sent by the other computer? Then capture *everything* that flows across HyperTerminal's screen.

With this technique, if something has flown past too quickly to see, you still have the information stored in a file. After you *log off* — hang up and disconnect from the other computer — you can read the file at your leisure.

Here's how to make HyperTerminal stuff everything that flows by into a file of your choosing:

1. **From HyperTerminal's Transfer menu, choose Capture Text.**

2. **Enter the name of the file in which you want to store the information and click on the OK button.**

   If you just type a filename, Windows 95 will store that file in your HyperTerminal folder (which lives in the Accessories folder, which lives in your Windows folder). Feel free to click on the Browse button if you'd like HyperTerminal to store that incoming text somewhere else. Done? Click on the OK button.

From that point on, HyperTerminal stores everything that goes by in the file you specified.

 ✔ Tell HyperTerminal to begin "receiving its text file" *before* you call the other computer. This technique gives you a copy of everything that flows by, even during that scary moment of first typing in your name and location.

 ✔ Want to use a single file as a storage pot for everything? Then don't keep entering a new filename. Instead, set up one file using the Capture Text button and then use its Pause setting to turn your captures on and off.

 ✔ When you call a particular computer for the first time, it's a good idea to capture everything. That way you can always print out that computer's help menu for later reference.

Downloading a File

Now it's time to start grabbing some files from the other computer. Believe it or not, you're not stealing. Those other computers are set up so that people can grab files from them.

Here are the official file-grabbing procedures:

1. **Find the file you want to grab.**

   Before you get to the name of the file you want to grab, you may want to spend a few minutes navigating the menus on the other computer. Check the menus for the words *file library* or *download area*.

   For example, pressing 2 on Microsoft's BBS brings the File Index to the screen, as shown in Figure 7-6. That's where all the files are stored.

2. **Tell the other computer what file you want and how it should send that particular file.**

   Did you find the file you were after? Then look on the other computer's menu for a *download* option. Choose the download option from the menu and type the name of the file you want to grab.

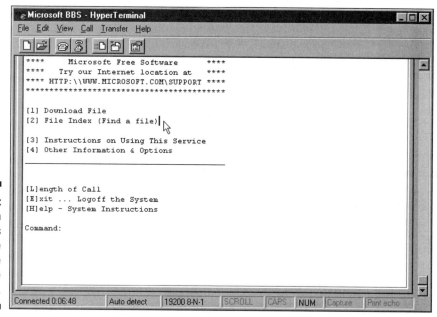

Figure 7-6: Press 2 on Microsoft's BBS to see where the files are stored.

Next, tell the other computer what *protocol* to use when it sends the file. Choosing the protocol is easier than you might think: Always choose ZMODEM when using HyperTerminal. The other computer will immediately say it's starting to send the file, and HyperTerminal will immediately start grabbing it, as shown in Figure 7-7. You're done! No sense reading any further in this section.

If the other computer *doesn't* offer ZMODEM on its menu, unfortunately, you'll have to struggle along with XMODEM. Choose the 1K XMODEM option, and the other computer will tell you it's ready to send the file.

Then after the other computer has gotten ready to send the file, you have to tell HyperTerminal to start receiving it.

3. From HyperTerminal's Transfer menu, choose Receive File.

After you have told the other computer to send a file using 1K XMODEM, it's time to tell HyperTerminal to receive that incoming file.

Click the arrow on the Use receiving protocol box and select 1K Xmodem. (Some computers use uppercase letters for XMODEM; others stick with lowercase.)

4. Click the Receive button, type the name of the file, and click on the OK button.

When you click the Receive button, HyperTerminal makes *you* type in the name of the incoming file. (Yep, computers can be pretty dumb sometimes.)

You can watch the progress of the download in a window similar to the one shown in Figure 7-7, or you can double-click on the little modem next to the clock on your taskbar. That brings up a window that describes how fast your modem is sucking information, as shown in Figure 7-8.

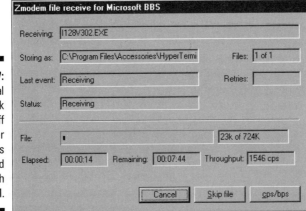

Figure 7-7:
HyperTerminal can suck files off other computers quickly and easily with ZMODEM.

Figure 7-8:
Double-click
on the little
modem on
your taskbar
to see how
fast your
modem is
transporting
information.

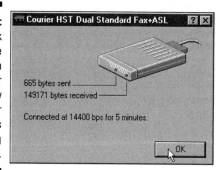

When the messages and boxes disappear, HyperTerminal has finished grabbing the file. Press Enter, and the other computer wakes up and starts sending menus again.

5. **Choose Exit from the other computer's menu.**

   When you are done using the other computer, don't just tell HyperTerminal to hang up. Always let the other computer hang up first. Look for the words Exit, Off, or Log Off from the other computer's menu.

6. **Move to your download folder in My Computer or Explorer.**

   Unless you've specifically told it to do otherwise, HyperTerminal stores downloaded files in the HyperTerminal folder (which lives in the Accessories folder, which lives in the Program Files folder, which is usually on drive C).

7. **Click on the file with the right mouse button, choose Properties, and look at the file's MS-DOS name.**

   Take a look at the last three letters in the file's name — known as the file's *extension* — and look at the chart below to see what to do.

These Letters . . .	Mean to Do This
.ZIP or .ARC	Head for Chapter 11. You must *unzip* or *de-archive* the file before you can do anything with it.
.EXE or .COM	Make a new folder on your desktop called Trash, copy the file into that folder, and double-click on the file. Two things could happen: If the program simply comes to life, you're safe. Create a permanent folder for your new program, close it from the screen, and drag and drop its files into it from the Trash folder to its new folder. If the program explodes into a bunch of little files, see the "When I loaded my new program, it exploded into a bunch of little files!" section of Chapter 2.

These Letters . . .	Mean to Do This
.DRV	You've downloaded a new driver, so turn to Chapter 3 for tips on installing it. *Hint:* When Windows 95 asks you to insert a disk containing the driver, click on the <u>B</u>rowse button; then click on the HyperTerminal folder where you downloaded your new driver.

✔ HyperTerminal lists two ways to *download,* or transfer, information. To capture information as it flows across the screen, choose the <u>C</u>apture Text method. To download a particular file, choose <u>R</u>eceive File.

✔ Want to send a file? Follow the same steps: Make sure that the other computer is ready to receive your file and then send it. Click on the <u>S</u>end File option instead of the <u>R</u>eceive File option just described.

When you're done calling the other computer for the first time — and you're about to exit HyperTerminal — be sure to click the Save button so that HyperTerminal will save the phone number and settings for the other computer. To call up that computer again, just double-click on its icon in the HyperTerminal folder.

Uh, It Doesn't Work Right

Sometimes only part of HyperTerminal works. Here are a few places you can prod when HyperTerminal doesn't walk the straight and narrow.

I don't know where to start!

Windows 95 has gotten much friendlier in helping its users solve problems. If your modem or HyperTerminal is just plain acting weird, try putting the computerized gurus included with Windows 95 on the problem.

Call up the Control Panel from the Start button's <u>S</u>ettings area and double-click the modem icon. Click the Diagnostics tab from along the top of the window and then click on the <u>H</u>elp button.

The HyperTerminal Help screen jumps into action, as shown in Figure 7-9.

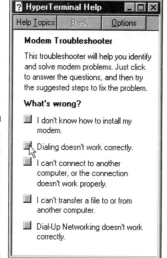

Figure 7-9:
Windows 95
can often
help figure
out what's
wrong
with your
modem.

It almost connects, but then the timer runs out!

Sometimes you can hear the other computer's phone ring, and then the modems start spitting at each other. Before the modems make their actual connection, however, the little timer runs out and HyperTerminal gives up. Bottom line: The computers never connect.

HyperTerminal normally waits 60 seconds for the other computer to connect. To give HyperTerminal a little more patience, change that 60 seconds to 90. (And make sure it's really set at 60 seconds to begin with — somebody might have fiddled with your settings.)

From HyperTerminal's Properties menu, click on Configure and then click on the Connections tab along the top. Then change the connection settings to Cancel the call if not connected within 90 secs.

I can't send Ctrl characters like Ctrl+C

Windows 95 eavesdrops on everything you type on the other computer through HyperTerminal. Windows 95 is listening for keys that tell it what to do. If you press Ctrl+C to activate a command in CompuServe, for example, Windows 95 won't let that command pass through.

Instead, Windows 95 grabs that Ctrl+C for itself, checking to see whether you've highlighted any material for copying off the BBS. (Ctrl+C is a shortcut for the Copy command, which is listed in the Edit menu.) That Ctrl+C never makes it through the phone lines to CompuServe.

To make your Ctrl characters pass through to the other computer, choose Properties from the File menu and click on the Settings tab along the top. At the top of the dialog box, click on the Function, arrow, and ctrl keys act as Terminal keys option.

This option keeps Windows 95 from intercepting your keystrokes: Everything you type — including your arrow keys, function keys, and Ctrl keys — is passed directly to the other computer.

I have a pulse phone, not touch tone!

Windows 95 assumes everybody has a *touch tone* phone — the kind that sounds a different tone for each button you press.

If you still have a pulse phone — the kind with the little round dial that makes clicks — HyperTerminal won't work unless Windows 95 knows about it.

To fix it, bring up the Control Panel from the Start button's Settings area and double-click on the modem icon. Click on the Dialing Properties box and then click on Pulse dialing at the bottom of the box.

Call Waiting keeps bumping me off-line!

Many people choose the Call Waiting option from the phone company. Then when they're talking to one person on the phone and another person calls, they hear a little beep.

Unfortunately, that little beep makes your polite modem hang up instantly if it happens to be talking to another computer.

Windows 95 fixes that problem quite handily. Bring up the Control Panel from the Start button's Settings area and double-click on the modem icon. Click on the Dialing Properties box and type the symbols you need to disable it into the adjacent box. (Clicking on the downward-pointing arrow reveals the three most common symbols: ***70, 1170,** and **70#,**.)

  ✔ This technique should turn off Call Waiting whenever your modem makes a call.

  ✔ When your modem is done making the call, Call Waiting turns itself back on automatically.

I need to dial a special number to get an outside line at the office!

Some office setups make you dial a special number to get an outside line. To make your modem dial this number automatically, head for the same area where you tweaked your Call Waiting setup.

Bring up the Control Panel from the Start button's Settings area and double-click on the modem icon. Click on the Dialing Properties box and enter your outside line information in the How I dial from this location box.

How Do I Unzip or De-Arc a File?

Files ending in the extensions .ZIP and .ARC won't run right off the bat. They come in a special software *bag*. You have to take them out of the bag before you can use them. For specifics on working with these types of files, turn to Chapter 11.

Am I Gonna Get a Virus?

You probably won't get a virus. But if you're worried about it, look for a program called VIRUSCAN by McAfee Associates. Most computers that offer files for downloading also offer VIRUSCAN.

Most important of all, however, practice these Safe Computing Tips:

✔ Don't accept free copies of "pirated" software from people. Chances are, that software has been on a lot of computers, and it only takes one computer to put a virus onto a program.

✔ Don't keep floppy disks in your disk drives. Most viruses infect your computer from a floppy disk that's been inadvertently left in drive A when you turn on or reboot your computer. By making sure your computer only boots off the hard drive, you'll minimize your chances of infection.

How Do I Make My Modem Answer the Phone?

Sometimes calling another computer isn't enough. Some folks want another computer to call *their* computer.

HyperTerminal isn't up for the challenge. It simply can't be set up to answer the phone. So you have to bypass the menus and follow the sneaky steps below.

1. **Load HyperTerminal from the Accessories area of the Start menu's Programs section.**

2. **Double-click on an icon for a BBS you've previously set up.**

3. **Click the Cancel button (instead of the Dial button).**

4. **Type** ats0=1 **into the HyperTerminal window.**

   That tells your modem to pick up the phone at the next call.

   ✔ Setting your computer up to answer calls doesn't turn your PC into a freebie BBS, though, where other people can call up and play with your computer when you're not around. No, it basically means that you and the calling party can type silly messages at each other.

   ✔ You can also swap files back and forth over the phone lines, if you're up for that: One person chooses the Send file option, and the other chooses Receive file.

   ✔ Why is HyperTerminal so limited? Because Hilgraeve, the company that made HyperTerminal for Microsoft, wants you to buy its more full-featured telecommunications program, called HyperACCESS.

Chapter 8
Sound! Movies! Multimedia Stuff!

· ·

In This Chapter

▶ Figuring out Media Player

▶ Figuring out Sound Recorder

▶ Figuring out CD Player

▶ Playing music (those MIDI files)

▶ Playing sounds

▶ Playing musical CDs

▶ Watching movies

▶ Recording sounds

▶ Fixing sound and video problems

· ·

*A*ll the really *fun* computers — from that somber-voiced "working" computer on "Star Trek" to that flailing-armed "Danger! Danger!" robot on "Lost in Space" — have one important thing in common: They can make *noises,* for cryin' out loud.

For years, *real-life* computers could only cut loose with a rude beep, which they issued whenever a confused user pressed the wrong key. Windows 95, however, bursts onto the screen with a triumphant *ta-da* sound; and it plays melodious chimes when it leaves the screen. Add a microphone and a sound card, and you can even record your own (or your neighbor's) belches and burps.

Of course, computer game players know that computerized sound is nothing new; they've been listening to screeching tires and giggling maidens for years. But Windows 95 brings a glorious new name to this conglomeration of sound and video: *multimedia.*

This chapter shows how to push the on-screen buttons on your computer's new multimedia VCR — one that will never flash a blinking *12:00.*

Media Player

The best noisemaker that comes with Windows 95 is Media Player. Depending on how much money you paid for your computer — or how much money your computer has absorbed since you first plopped it on your desk — you can use the Windows Media Player to listen to prerecorded sounds, play back music, and even watch movies.

To see what Media Player can do on *your* particular computer, click on the Start button, choose the Programs menu, and then choose Accessories. Click on the Media Player icon, which is located in the Multimedia area. Media Player comes to the screen, as shown in Figure 8-1.

Figure 8-1:
Windows 95
Media
Player can
play sounds,
music,
video, and
compact
discs.

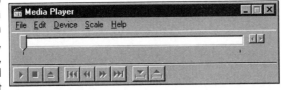

> ✔ Actually, Media Player is nothing more than a big, fancy button. Before that big button can do anything, you need to connect it to something — a sound card, for example, as well as the right software.

> ✔ You also need a *sound* to play. Like corporate reports and Bart Simpson icons, sounds are stored in files. Windows 95 comes packaged with a few sound files, and most sound cards include a disk that is packed with sound files.

> ✔ To see what Media Player can play on your particular computer, click on the Device menu. A menu like the one shown in Figure 8-2 drops down; that menu lists the kinds of things that your version of Media Player is currently set up to play. (Different computers have different setups.)

Differences between recorded sound and MIDI files

Savvy New Age musicians know that Media Player can play two different types of sound files: digitized and synthesized. Table 8-1 describes the two types of files, which sound completely different from each other.

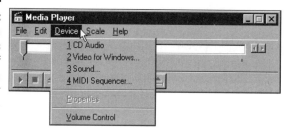

Figure 8-2:
Media
Player lists
the types of
things it can
play under
the Device
menu.

Normally, you can tell which file is which by looking at the last three letters of the filename — the *extension*. However, Windows 95 hides a file's extension from normal view. To see those identifying three letters, you need to click on the file with your right mouse button, choose Properties from the menu, and look at the last three letters listed in the MS-DOS name item.

(You'll find the whole scoop in this book's predecessor, *Windows 95 For Dummies*, published by IDG Books Worldwide, Inc.)

Table 8-1	**Sound Files**	
This Type of Windows File . . .	**Ends in These Letters . . .**	**And Contains This Stuff**
Digital recording	.WAV	A recording of a sound that actually occurred. Some small sound files live on your hard drive; others live on compact discs, ready to be played on your home stereo.
Synthesized sound, also called MIDI	.MID	A list of musical sounds for the computer to synthesize and play.

A .WAV sound *actually* happened when somebody was nearby with a microphone to record it. The microphone grabbed the sound waves from the air and pushed them into the computer's sound card. The computer turned the incoming sound waves into numbers, stuck them into a file, and slapped the letters .*WAV* onto the end of the filename.

To play back the .WAV file, Media Player grabs the numbers from the file and converts them back into sound waves; then the sound card pushes the sound waves out of the speaker. The end result? You hear the recording, just as if you played it from a cassette tape.

A MIDI sound (also called a .MID sound), on the other hand, never really happened. A computer with a sound card listened as some long-haired hippie type played an electronic instrument, usually a keyboard. As the computer heard each note being played, it wrote down the name of the instrument, the name of each note, its duration, and its timing. Then it packed all that information into a file and added .MID to the end of the filename.

When Media Player plays a .MID file, it looks at the embedded instructions. Then it tells whatever synthesizer is hooked up to the computer to re-create those sounds. Most sound cards come with a built-in synthesizer that creates the sounds.

Files that end in the letters *.MID* are *MIDI* files — a fancy way for musicians to store their music.

✔ .WAV files contain actual *sounds* — chirping birds, yodeling Swiss cheese makers, or honks from New York cabbies.

✔ MIDI files contain synthesized *music* — songs that re-create the sounds of instruments ranging from saxophones to maracas.

✔ Most CD-ROM drives can play music CDs — yet another form of real-life recorded music. Known as Red Book audio, the files on these CDs resemble mammoth .WAV files.

✔ In real life, MIDI is a pretty complicated concept that only *looks* easy when the guy on the stage hammers out a few notes and flicks cigarette ashes off the keyboard. In fact, most MIDI musicians are also closet computer nerds. (Or they pay other nerds to handle all the complicated MIDI stuff for them.)

✔ A .WAV file sounds pretty much the same when you play it back on anybody's computer, using anybody's sound card.

✔ A MIDI file, in contrast, sounds different when you play it back on different computers. The sound depends entirely on the type of synthesizer — or sound card — that Windows 95 uses to play it back. Some synthesizers sound great; the cheapest ones sound kinda soggy.

✔ Compared to MIDI files, .WAV files consume huge chunks of hard drive space. For example, Windows 95 comes with a two-minute-long MIDI song called CANYON.MID that takes up 33K. The Windows TADA.WAV file lasts less than two seconds, yet it grabs 27K. And a song recorded onto a compact disc can take up 50MB just for itself.

Listening to a MIDI file

A MIDI file is sort of like the pages of sheet music that sit on a conductor's podium. The file tells the computer which instruments to play, when and how loud to play them, and how often to empty the mouthpiece of spittle. Media Player handles the first three categories; keep an eye on your own drool bucket.

Storing .WAV sounds

What's really inside a file containing a recorded sound? Basically, the file contains a bunch of numbers — measurements of how that particular file's sound waves should look. But the .WAV file also contains a *header*. The header gives Windows 95 some information about the file's sounds: their *sampling* rate, whether they're mono or stereo, and whether they're recorded in *8-bit* or *16-bit resolution*.

Without that header, Media Player will gag on the sound, throwing an error message in your face.

For example, sound files that end in .VOC have a different header than sound files that end in .WAV. Because the header is different, Media Player chokes on .VOC files, the format that many older SoundBlaster cards use. (You can find some .VOC to .WAV converters on CompuServe; see Chapter 7 for more information on calling online services with HyperTerminal.)

If you're bored, check out the end of this chapter for definitions of italicized words such as *sampling* and *8-bit resolution*.

Follow these steps to make Media Player play back a MIDI file:

1. **Click on the Start button and point to Programs. From the Accessories menu, choose Multimedia and then click on Media Player.**

   Media Player hops to the screen.

2. **Click on <u>D</u>evice and choose MIDI Sequencer from the menu that drops down.**

   Don't see MIDI Sequencer on the list? Then you need to install a driver for the sound card in Windows. To find out how to install this piece of software that the sound card uses, head to Chapter 3; otherwise, MIDI Sequencer should appear on the menu, as shown in Figure 8-3.

3. **Double-click on the name of the file you want to play.**

Figure 8-3:
Choose
MIDI
Sequencer
from the
<u>D</u>evice
menu.

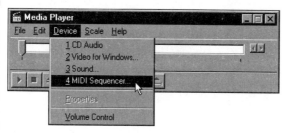

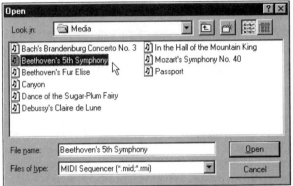

Figure 8-4:
Double-click
on the name
of the MIDI
file you want
to hear.

When you choose <u>M</u>IDI Sequencer, Media Player shows a familiar-looking dialog box — the same Open dialog box you've been using to open a file in any Windows program. As Figure 8-4 shows, the Open dialog box filters out everything but the MIDI files that live in the current directory.

If you see the MIDI file that you're itching to hear, double-click on it.

Don't see the MIDI file you want? Then click on the icons for other folders or drives; click in the Look <u>i</u>n box to see them. (Try the Media folder in your Windows folder.) Media Player will promptly show you any MIDI files that are lurking in those areas, too. Double-click on the MIDI file that you want to hear.

When you double-click on a MIDI filename, Media Player loads the file and gets ready to play it back.

4. **Click on the play button.**

   Click on Media Player's play button — the black triangle — and the file should begin playing. Figure 8-5 shows what all the little Media Player buttons do.

┌ Move forward

Slide bar to move backward or forward   ┌Move backward

Figure 8-5:
Click on
these
buttons on
Media
Player to do
these things.

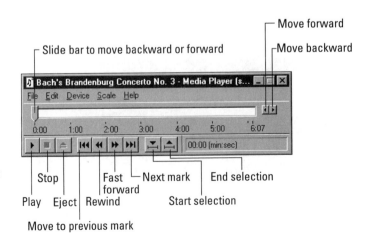

Stop   Fast   └ Next mark   End selection
          forward

Play Eject Rewind   Start selection

Move to previous mark

✔ Chances are, you'll have good luck playing Canyon and Passport, the two MIDI files that usually appear in the Windows 95 directory. Microsoft designed those songs specifically for Media Player. If something goes wrong and you're not hearing pretty tunes, however, head for the troubleshooting section, "Media Player Doesn't Work!" It's near the end of this chapter.

✔ MIDI stands for *Musical Instrument Digital Interface,* but most people try to forget that right away. (It's pronounced "MID-ee," by the way.)

✔ Instead of opening MIDI files by clicking on the Device menu, you can double-click on a MIDI file's name from within Explorer or My Computer. Or while you have the Media Player open, just drag and drop a MIDI file's name onto the Media Player window from Explorer or My Computer.

✔ Media Player has plenty of buttons. But if they don't all show up, grab the side of Media Player's window and drag it out a few inches. Media Player swallows some of its buttons when it doesn't have enough room to display them.

✔ What's the difference between the stop and pause buttons? Not much — they both make Media Player stop what it's currently doing. If you select Media Player's Auto Rewind button (under Options, found on the Edit menu), pressing the stop button stops the clip and rewinds it; otherwise, pause and stop are about the same.

Playing .WAV files

Media Player can play recorded sounds — .WAV files — as well as MIDI files. Here's how to let one loose:

1. **Click on the Start button and point to Programs. From the Accessories menu, choose Multimedia and then click on Media Player.**

   Media Player rises to the occasion.

2. **Click on Device and choose Sound from the menu that drops down.**

   The Device menu drops down (refer to Figure 8-2). Click on Sound, and a familiar-looking box appears, listing all the .WAV files in the current directory. Just as with MIDI files, you click on the little folders and drives in the Look in box to see the sound files stored in those areas.

   If Sound doesn't show up on the Media Player's Device menu, you have a loud problem: You don't have a Windows driver installed for the sound card. Chapter 3 describes how to install the sound card's driver so that Windows 95 can play with it.

3. **Double-click on the sound you want to hear.**

   After you double-click on a .WAV file, Media Player loads it.

4. **Press the play button to hear the sound.**

The play button has a single black triangle on it. (Refer to Figure 8-5 for a description of what all the buttons do.)

When the sound starts to play, the words change in the title bar at the top of Media Player. For example, instead of saying `Chimes - Media Player (stopped)`, they say `Chimes - Media Player (playing)`. A little box moves along beneath the title bar to indicate how much of the clip has been played.

✔ If Media Player's title bar changes from `(stopped)` to `(playing)` and you don't hear anything, your suspicions are right: Something is wrong. To figure out why you aren't hearing anything, head for the troubleshooting section at the end of this chapter, "My .WAV Files Won't Play Right!"

✔ You can run two or more copies of Media Player at the same time. But don't get too fancy. If you try to play two MIDI or two .WAV files at the same time, a nasty error message chastises you for being so bold.

Playing musical CDs on a computer's compact disc player

Adding a new compact disc player to a home stereo is a big hassle. You may not have enough wall outlets to go around, and figuring out which wires plug into which gizmo can be a pain.

Thanks goodness Windows 95 makes using a compact disc player so much easier. Just call up the <u>C</u>ontrol Panel from the Start button's <u>S</u>ettings area, double-click the Add New Hardware icon, and start clicking the buttons marked *Next*. Windows 95 can scout out most newly installed computer parts and make them feel comfortable enough to work with your current computer setup.

✔ If your CD-ROM drive starts complaining about needing new drivers — or the drive's manufacturer mailed you a new set of drivers — head for Chapter 3 to see how they're installed.

✔ While you are installing Windows 95 drivers for the CD-ROM drive, leave a compact disc sitting in the drive. Sometimes having the disc there helps Windows 95 know what's going on.

Listening to music CDs on Media Player

Windows 95 comes with two programs for playing music CDs — the plain ol' Media Player and the more elite CD Player. Here's how to play CDs through Media Player for the blue jeans crowd:

1. **Click on the the Start button and point to <u>P</u>rograms. From the Accessories menu, choose Multimedia and then click on Media Player.**

Media Player jumps to the forefront.

2. Put the compact disc in the compact disc player.

Don't forget to put the compact disc in that small, outrageously expensive plastic caddie before you slide it into the CD player. (The edge of the caddie with that little silver thing needs to slide in first.) Some CD players don't use caddies at all — you can just drop the CD onto a platter and nudge the platter into the drive.

3. Click on Device and choose CD Audio from the drop-down menu.

When the Device menu drops down, choose CD Audio to hear the compact disc.

If CD Audio isn't listed on the Device menu, stop right now and head for the troubleshooting section near this chapter's end, "Media Player Doesn't Work!"

4. Press the play button to hear the sound.

The play button is the one on the left, with the black triangle on it, as shown earlier in Figure 8-5. Give it a click and give your compact disc a listen.

To pause, hit the button next to the triangle. To stop everything, click on the button with the black squarish rectangle. Finally, the upward-pointing triangle will eject the disc — if the disc player has that nifty feature. If you forget this stuff, flip back to Figure 8-5 for a refresher on what all the buttons do.

✔ See the ten numbers below that long horizontal bar in Figure 8-6? Those numbers stand for the number of songs — the *tracks* — on the current compact disc. For example, Figure 8-6 shows the ten tracks on Stevie Ray Vaughan's *Texas Flood* CD.

✔ To skip one song and play the next, drag the little box forward and drop it on the next number. (Chapter 1 covers drag-and-drop mouse manipulations.) Or click on the fast-forward buttons.

Figure 8-6:
The numbers below the bar stand for the number of songs on the current CD.

TIP

TIP

✔ With some CD players, Media Player's buttons don't work until you start playing the CD. You can't drag the little box forward or backward until you first click on the play button.

✔ Don't know whether you have enough time to hear an entire CD on your lunch hour? Click on <u>S</u>cale and choose <u>T</u>ime from the menu that appears. Instead of displaying the number of songs on the CD, Media Player shows the CD's length in minutes, as shown in Figure 8-7.

Figure 8-7:
Choose
<u>T</u>ime from
the <u>S</u>cale
menu to see
a CD's
length in
minutes.

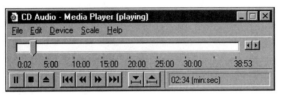

Listening to music CDs on the CD Player

Although Windows can play Stevie Ray Vaughan CDs through Media Player, another program offers much more control. This section describes how to hear a CD through the Windows 95 CD Player, as well as how to tweak the program to your best advantage.

1. Slide *Texas Flood* (or any other music CD) into your CD-ROM drive.

That's it. The music starts to play through your computer's speakers. See, Windows 95 can tell the difference between a music CD and a computer CD. So when you push a music CD into the drive, Windows 95 figures you want to hear it. It automatically loads CD Player as an icon on the taskbar and starts playing the tunes. You don't even have to click on the play button.

However, CD Player, shown in all its glory in Figure 8-8, can do a lot more than that. The following steps show you how to make CD Player play your favorite CD over and over, playing songs in random order:

1. Load CD Player.

Usually, putting a music CD into your CD-ROM drive brings CD Player to the screen automatically. But you can also load it from the same menu as Media Player, as described previously in this chapter.

2. Choose <u>R</u>andom Order from the <u>O</u>ptions menu.

That tells CD Player to rearrange the songs on the CD so that you don't get tired of hearing them all in the same order.

3. **Choose Continuous Play from the Options menu.**

   That tells CD Player to play the songs continually, in random order, until you *are* tired of hearing them.

4. **Click the Play button — the biggest button on the program.**

   (It has the biggest triangle on it, too.) CD Player starts playing your songs in random order.

Choose Edit Play List from the Disc menu and type in the songs' names off the CD, as well as the CD's title. CD Player automatically remembers the songs' names and lists them the next time you insert that CD into your CD-ROM drive. (That's because all CDs have special code numbers on them that Windows 95 can recognize.)

Rest your mouse pointer over the buttons on the CD Player program to see their function. Or if you're impatient, see Figure 8-8.

Scale, Time, Tracks, and Tedium

Media Player always displays a bar with two arrows near one end and a little sliding lever inside it, as shown in Figure 8-7. That bar stands for the media clip you're playing. (Suave and debonair multimedia folks use the term *media clip* when they're talking about sound, music, or movies.)

As Media Player plays a file, the little lever moves along the bar. When the lever reaches the end of the bar, the clip is over.

Two options, Time and Tracks, lurk in Media Player's Scale menu. Neither one affects the quality of whatever is being played. They just change the little numbers that Media Player displays below the bar while it's playing a media clip.

Choosing Time makes Media Player display how much time that media clip takes to play. For example, Figure 8-7 shows Media Player when it's displaying the time. The number at the far right shows how many minutes and seconds the current sound or movie will last.

Choosing Tracks, however, tells Media Player to display which song it's currently playing out of a series of songs. When you are playing music from a compact disc, for example, the Tracks setting may display song number 5 out of a total of 12 songs. Figure 8-6 shows Media Player when it's displaying Tracks.

People who bother to change the setting usually set Scale to Time. Setting it to Tracks almost always makes Media Player display a 1 — after all, unless you're listening to a compact disc, you're probably playing a single sound from a queue of 1.

Finally, if you're playing a movie, Scale offers a new option: Frames. A movie is composed of dozens of individual pictures, or frames, that are flipped past in rapid succession. If you choose Frames, Media Player displays how many frames are in the movie that is currently loaded.

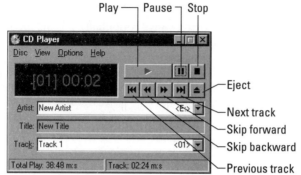

Figure 8-8:
The buttons
in CD Player
perform
these tasks.

Note: If you still can't hear any sound, check your sound card's volume by clicking on the little speaker in the bottom-right corner of the taskbar. Sliding the little bar up the pyramid increases the volume. If that still doesn't fix the problem, you may need to open your computer and make sure that the proper wires lead from your CD-ROM drive to your sound card. (Leave that stuff for the office computer guru or people who own a copy of *Upgrading and Fixing PCs For Dummies,* 2nd Edition, published by IDG Books Worldwide, Inc.)

Don't have a copy of CD Player? That's probably because the program only came with the compact disc version of Windows 95. If you have a modem, however, Chapter 7 shows how to download CD Player from Microsoft's computer in Seattle.

Watching movies (Those .AVI files)

Windows 95 can play movies on-screen, but there's an immediate problem: Only the compact disc version of Windows 95 came with any movies to watch. If you installed Windows 95 from floppy disks — (or Windows 95 came pre-installed on your computer by a cheap computer dealer) — you won't have any videos to watch.

To see a video (or to see whether you have any videos to see), follow the bouncing ball along these steps:

1. **Load the Media Player from the Start button.**

   The Media Player leaps to life, ready for movies and popcorn.

2. **Click on Device and choose Video for Windows.**

   Movies come in files that end with .AVI, so Media Player lists any .AVI files that live in the current directory. Don't see any? Then click in the Look in box to scout around in different parts of the hard drive.

   If your version of Windows 95 didn't come with any .AVI files, you have to get them from friends or download them, as described in Chapter 7.

TIP

Click on <u>F</u>ind from the Start menu, choose <u>F</u>iles and Folders, and type ***.AVI** into the <u>N</u>amed box. Choose My Computer from the Look <u>i</u>n box, and click the F<u>i</u>nd Now button to make Windows 95 search for any movies on your hard drive. Found some? Double-click on the movie's name, and Media Player will begin playing it.

3. **Double-click on the filename of the movie that you want to watch.**

   The movie rises to the screen in its own little window.

4. **Click on the play button.**

   To start the reel rolling, click on the play button — that button with the little black triangle on the left side of Media Player. The movie starts to play, as shown in Figure 8-9.

Media Player starts playing the movie in a postage-stamp-size window. Because of the small size, the computer doesn't have to work as hard as it does when the picture is larger, so the movie looks better. You can enlarge the picture up to three times to see how well the computer handles high-powered, thrill-packed video action.

✔ To make movies always start up in a certain size, check out the <u>P</u>roperties option from Media Player's <u>D</u>evice menu. Click on <u>F</u>ull Screen, for example, to make movies take up the whole screen. Or while the movies are playing, press Ctrl+2, Ctrl+3, or Ctrl+4 to make the picture even *larger*. Just play with the buttons for a while, and you'll get the hang of it. (Most computers can't handle the large sizes, though.)

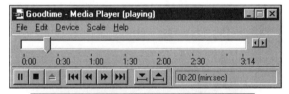

Figure 8-9:
Media Player can play movies as well as sounds and music.

✔ Most movies contain at least 256 colors — usually known as *SVGA* mode. If you're using Windows in plain ol' 16-color VGA mode, movies will look grainier than Spoon-Size Shredded Wheat. If your video card can handle 256 colors (most can these days), make sure that it's using at least a 256-color palette: Click on the wallpaper with your right mouse button, choose Properties, click on the Settings tab, and click in the Color palette box to adjust your palette setting.

✔ You need a sound card to hear any sound with movie clips.

✔ Movies come stored in files that end in .AVI. *.AVI* stands for *Audio Video Interleaved*, a boring term that means the file contains both sound and video.

The fancy Media Player options

Some of the most fun in Media Player comes with the Edit command on the menu along the top. Here's what to expect from the Edit menu's commands:

✔ **Copy object:** Click here to copy whatever you're playing into the Windows Clipboard. You can paste a movie, sound, or song into a corporate report you're preparing in WordPad, for example, and play it back between paragraphs. Fun!

✔ **Options:** The two important options are Auto Rewind — which makes Media Player automatically jump back to the beginning of a clip — and Auto Repeat — which not only rewinds, but starts playing the clip again and again and again (press Esc to shut it up). The OLE Object stuff, listed near the bottom, is described in the boring technical box a few pages from now.

Making movies play better

Movies don't always play back smoothly. If the video card isn't fast enough and expensive enough to keep up the fast pace, the movie looks jerky. The problem is that Media Player skips part of the movie in order to keep up with the sound track. Here are a few tips for smoother sailing when you're watching movies:

✔ Be sure to use the latest drivers for the video card, as described in Chapter 3. If that doesn't work, buy an accelerated video card. If that doesn't work, buy a faster computer.

✔ Computers take longer to grab files from a compact disc than from a hard drive. Try copying movies from the compact disc to the hard drive. Or buy a faster quad-speed, six-speed, or eight-speed compact disc player.

✔ The Defrag program that comes with Windows 95 can organize the hard drive so that Media Player can grab the movies a little more quickly.

✔ Movies play back at their fastest when they are either full-screen (not contained in a window at all) or in the smallest possible window.

✔ **Selection:** Got a favorite song on the CD? Type that song's track number in the From box and type the next song's track number in the To box. Move to the beginning of the CD, hold down Alt, and press the play button. The CD will jump to the song and begin playing it.

Plus, if you select the Auto Repeat button (described previously in this chapter), Media Player plays the same song over and over. Unfortunately, you can select only *consecutive* portions of a compact disc or video clip. You can't make it play songs 5 and 7 and skip over that dreary ballad on track 6.

✔ If the compact disc player ignores Media Player's buttons, click on Media Player's play button. That makes the compact disc player start paying attention to your button pushing.

✔ When you tell Media Player to play a selected track on a compact disc, hold down Alt when you click on the play button. Without that Alt key reminder, Media Player lames out and simply plays the entire CD.

✔ Here's a quick way to select a certain area for playback. Push the play button and drag the little box on the bar to the part of the clip you want to play. Then hold down Shift and drag the little box to where you want Media Player to stop. Those actions quickly mark the area for playback.

✔ Finally, here's one technical tip: If something goes afoul when you're playing an embedded movie, double-click on the movie's title bar. If you're lucky, Media Player will pop to the surface, complete with all its buttons, for immediate fine-tuning.

Sound Recorder

Windows 95 comes with some decent sounds, but only a handful. After a while, those same old dings and chimes can grow as tiresome as a friend's answering machine message that never changes.

When you're tired of listening to the same old sounds, grab a microphone, grab the Windows 95 Sound Recorder, and start recording your own sounds. In fact, Sound Recorder can add special effects to sounds that you've already recorded, such as adding a little *echo* to make your burp sound as if you made it in a huge, empty warehouse.

Also, Sound Recorder isn't limited to voices. You can grab tidbits from a CD in your CD-ROM drive, as well.

One more thing: Despite its name, Sound Recorder can play sounds as well as record them.

Recording .WAV sounds

Before you can set up your computerized recording studio, you need a sound card; there's no getting around it. To record voices or sound effects, you need a microphone as well. (You can skip the mike if you just want to record from CDs on a CD-ROM drive.)

Sound card installed? Microphone plugged in? Then here's how to make Sound Recorder capture your magic karaoke moments:

1. **Click on the Start button and point to Programs. From the Accessories menu, choose Multimedia and then choose Sound Recorder.**

   The Sound Recorder comes to the screen, as shown in Figure 8-10.

Figure 8-10: Sound Recorder can play sounds as well as record them.

2. **Prepare to record the sound and adjust the mixer.**

   If you're recording something with a microphone, make sure that the microphone is plugged into the sound card's microphone jack.

   Or, if you're recording something from a compact disc, make sure that the CD is loaded and ready to play.

   Next, double-click on the little speaker on the taskbar to see the mixer program, shown in Figure 8-11. (The mixer program lets you adjust both recording and playback volumes.)

   Choose Properties from the mixer's Options control, click on the Recording button, and click OK.

   Finally, put your headphones on and slide the little levers up and down to adjust the input volumes of the incoming sounds.

   Make sure that only your main sound source — usually the microphone — is selected in the Select switch; having them *all* selected brings in unwanted noise from all the options.

3. **Click on the Sound Recorder button (the one with the little red dot).**

   Sound Recorder starts to record any incoming sounds and stores them temporarily in the computer's memory.

Say OLE, sit back down, and fall asleep

Despite its terrible name, Object Linking and Embedding (OLE) is a novel little toy that's revitalizing a ho-hum computer task.

For years, people have copied words from one document and pasted them into another. Known as *cut-and-paste,* it's also called *boring.*

OLE, however, finally adds some new dazzle. Instead of just moving words around, people can paste sounds, movies, and songs into documents.

For example, load your favorite media clip into Media Player and then choose Copy Object from its Edit menu. That option sends the media clip to the Clipboard. (Call up the Clipboard Viewer and peek inside, if you're skeptical.)

Next, call up Windows WordPad, or any other fancy Windows program and choose Paste. The Media Player clip will appear in the program. If you copied a movie, you see its first frame; if you copied a sound, you see the Sound Recorder icon. (Nobody could say what a sound looks like.)

Now, while in WordPad, or wherever you pasted the clip, double-click on the pasted movie or the Media Player icon and watch as the clip starts playing. Fun! At least, it's fun for people who aren't overly disappointed when they hear that OLE isn't designed for Internet use.

Media Player enables you to control how that clip looks when you play it. Click on Options from Media Player's Edit menu to choose from these OLE Object choices:

Caption: Want to create a title that sits beneath the little clip when it's embedded somewhere? Click on Captions and type the new title in the Captions box. The title can be as long as you want, and you can put spaces between the letters. (If you don't type anything, Media Player uses the file's name for a title.)

Border around object: If you want a thin black line for a picture frame around the clip, click here. Don't like frames? Leave this box blank.

Play in client document: When you double-click on a media clip that you've embedded somewhere, Media Player usually rises to the screen and begins playing it. If you check this box, however, Media Player doesn't pop up. The movie or sound simply comes to life and starts playing, right inside the program where you pasted it.

Control Bar on playback: If you click in this box, the clip pops up in a little window when you play it back. What's new? The new window doesn't look like Media Player. It simply shows the bar with the little box that you can use to skip around in the clip. You have control while the clip is playing, without having to see the complete Media Player.

Dither to VGA colors: Most little movies are filled with 256 dazzling colors in a format known as SVGA. Click in this Phyllis Dither box to make an embedded movie use only 16 colors while it's sitting embedded in a document. When you play the movie, it leaps to the screen in its normal 256 colors.

Figure 8-11:
Slide the
levers up or
down in the
Windows
Sound
System
Mixer to
adjust the
recording
volumes
from your
sound
card's
variety of
sources.

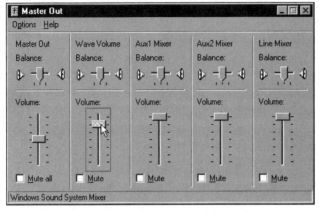

4. Start making the sound that you want to record.

Start making noise. Talk into the microphone or play the music CD. If everything is hooked up right, the little green line inside Sound Recorder begins to quiver, as shown in Figure 8-12, reflecting the incoming sound. The bigger the quiver, the louder the sound.

In Figure 8-13, see where Sound Recorder says `Length XX.XX Seconds`? That message tells you how many seconds of sound that Sound Recorder can capture. The more memory that the computer has, the more seconds of recording time that Sound Recorder gives you.

Don't record any sounds for too long, though — they consume an incredibly large amount of disk space. In fact, when you're through recording the sound, jump to Step 5 as soon as possible.

Slide to move forward or backward

Figure 8-12:
The bigger
the quiver,
the louder
the
incoming
sound.

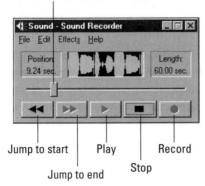

Jump to start   Play   Record

Jump to end   Stop

If the little wavy green line gets too wavy and starts bumping into the top or bottom edges of its little window, the sound is too loud. To avoid distortion, turn down the volume.

5. **Click on the button with the black square on it to stop recording.**

   A click on the button with the black square on it makes Sound Recorder stop recording new sounds.

6. **Click the rewind button to rewind.**

   The rewind button has two black triangles that face left.

7. **Click the button with the single black triangle to hear the recording.**

   Does it sound OK? Congratulations! If the recording doesn't sound perfect, erase it. Just choose New from Sound Recorder's File menu to wipe the slate clean for a new recording. Jump back to Step 2 to make any necessary adjustments and try again.

   When the recording sounds perfect — or just needs a little editing — move on to Step 8.

8. **Choose Save from the File menu and save the sound to a file.**

   Type a name for the file, just as if you were saving a file in a word processor. Sound files add up quickly, though; without a lot of room on the hard disk, you won't have enough space to save a particularly long, drawn-out wail.

   You're done — unless you have some empty spots you want to edit out of the recording. If so, head for the upcoming "Technical sound engineer's stuff" sidebar.

   ✔ Sound Recorder can add special effects to recorded sounds. Make sure that you've saved the file and then experiment with the goodies in the Effects menu. You can change the sound's volume and speed, add echo, or play the sound backward.

   ✔ Record strategic snippets of Beatles' albums, make Sound Recorder play them backward, and decide for yourself whether Paul is dead.

   ✔ To copy a sound to the Clipboard, choose Copy from Sound Recorder's Edit menu. Then paste your belch into a corporate memo you created in WordPad (or almost any other word processor). When the chairman of the board of directors clicks on the Sound Recorder icon near your signature, the whole board will hear your signature sound.

   ✔ Sound Recorder's Edit menu enables you to insert other sounds and mix them with the current sound. The Insert File command can add one sound after another. You can insert a splash sound after a boom sound to simulate the sound that a pirate ship makes when it's firing at the natives. The Mix File command mixes the two sounds together. You can make the boom and the splash happen at the same time, as if the pirate ship blew up.

Technical sound engineer's stuff

It's hard to click Sound Recorder's start and stop buttons at exactly the right time. You usually have some blank moments before the sound begins and after it ends.

To edit them out, first save the file. Then start editing out the blank spots, as follows:

1. **Locate where the sound begins.**

   Listen to the sound again and watch the quivering line. The sound starts when the green line first starts to quiver. When you locate the spot right before where the sound begins, write down the number that's listed under Position.

   Then rewind the sound. Next, slide the lever, carefully, until you position yourself immediately before the spot where the sound starts. Listen to the sound a few times until you're sure that you're at the right place.

2. **Click on Delete Before Current Position from Sound Recorder's Edit menu.**

   Sound Recorder asks whether you're sure that you want to delete that part of the sound. If you're sure, click on OK, and Sound Recorder will snip out that blank spot before the place where the sound starts.

3. **Locate where the sound ends.**

   Just as before, position Sound Recorder's little sliding lever at the spot where your sound has ended and nothing but empty sound remains.

4. **Click on Delete After Current Position from Sound Recorder's Edit menu.**

   Again, click on the OK button if you're sure that you're at the right place.

5. **Rewind and listen to the edited sound.**

   Is it perfect? Then save it. If it's not perfect, ditch it by choosing Revert from the File menu. Or call up the sound file that you started with and head back to Step 1. Sound editing almost always takes a few tries before everything sounds perfect.

   Editing out blank spots always shrinks the file's disk size. Even recorded silence takes up a lot of disk space, for some reason.

✔ Add an effect that sounds just awful? Click on Revert from Sound Recorder's File menu to get rid of it and bring the sound back to the way it was.

✔ Before you edit a newly recorded sound, make sure that you save it to a file. Taking that precaution is the safest way to make sure that you can retrieve the original sound if the editing commands mess it up beyond recognition.

✔ .WAV files can eat up ten times as much disk space as MIDI files. So recording a MIDI file as a .WAV file usually isn't very practical. To save hard disk space, keep MIDI files stored as MIDI files, not as .WAV files.

Playing .WAV sounds

Both Sound Recorder and Media Player can play recorded sounds — those .WAV file things. Playing sounds in Sound Recorder is pretty simple:

1. **Double-click on the .WAV file's name in Explorer or My Computer.**

   Sound Recorder hops to the screen.

2. **Click on Sound Recorder's play button.**

   The play button is the little button with the triangle on it. Give it a click, and the sound starts playing.

   Or, after opening Sound Recorder, choose Open from Sound Recorder's File menu and double-click on the .WAV file. Click the Play button and listen to an earful.

   ✔ Chapter 3 is full of tips on what to do with sound files after you record them. It also explains how to get rid of the ones you're sick of. (After all, how many times can you listen to a Beavis and Butthead chortle every time you shut down Windows 95?)

   ✔ One quick way to hear .WAV files is to leave Sound Recorder's open program window on the desktop. Then drag .WAV files from Explorer and drop them onto the Sound Recorder window. You'll hear them instantly. (Chapter 1 covers this drag and drop stuff.)

Media Player Doesn't Work!

If Media Player is messing up, check out this list of cheap fixes before grabbing your hair and pulling:

✔ Check the volume on Windows 95. Click the little speaker in the bottom corner of the taskbar and slide the Volume lever upward. (Make sure that the Mute box isn't checked, too.)

✔ Check the volume on your sound card. Some sound cards have a little rotary knob on the back, and you need to wiggle your fingers through the octopus of cables in the back of the computer in order to reach the knob. Other cards make you push certain keyboard combinations to control the volume. You may have to pull out the manual for this one.

✔ Run any Setup or Configuration programs that came with the sound card. Sometimes they can shake loose a problem.

✔ Are the Windows 95 drivers installed correctly for your particular sound card? Check out the driver's sections in this chapter and in Chapter 3.

> ✔ Did you plug speakers into the sound card? That sound has to come from somewhere. . . . (And is the speaker cord plugged firmly into its jack on the sound card?)

Setting Up a New MIDI Instrument

Bought a new MIDI keyboard? Lucky dog! Windows 95 is pleased to welcome your new gear into the fold. Start by loading the Control Panel from the Start button's Settings menu, and double-clicking on the Multimedia icon.

Click on the MIDI tab at the top of the Multimedia Properties box, and click the Add New Instrument button near the box's bottom. Make sure that your new keyboard is plugged into the MIDI port of your sound card and click the Next button.

Here's where things get a little tricky. If your keyboard is a General MIDI Instrument — or you want it configured that way — click the General MIDI Instrument option and click Next. If your keyboard came with a disk containing its own set of "musical definitions," insert that disk in the drive, click the Browse button, and double-click on the definition file. (It ends in the letters .IDF.)

Click the Next button, type in a name to identify your new keyboard (something more descriptive than External MIDI Instrument), and click the Finish button to finish the task.

Now, your MIDI keyboard will be available as a MIDI option, in addition to your sound card's synthesizer. (Chances are your keyboard's synthesizer will sound better, though, so you'll probably want to leave that one selected.)

My .WAV Files Won't Play Right!

When .WAV files aren't working, look at this checklist for things to fix:

> ✔ Windows uses .WAV files; some older sound cards use a .VOC file — or something with an even weirder name. Sound Recorder and Media Player can only handle the .WAV file format. And no, you can't just rename that BEAVIS.VOC file to BEAVIS.WAV and play it. It doesn't work.

> ✔ Sound Recorder can play and record sounds in stereo. Buy two microphones and you can record that rocket as it whoooshes from left to right. Not all sounds are recorded in stereo, however. Sometimes you'll have to put up with rockets that don't move around much.

> ✔ Sound Recorder won't record any sounds until you have a sound card.

Bizarre Multimedia Words

Here's what some of those weird multimedia buzzwords are supposed to mean. Use caution when murmuring them in crowded elevators.

16-bit: The newer, 16-bit sound cards can measure a sound's variations to 65,536 different levels. That capability means that the card's sound can be almost as good as a compact disc.

8-bit: The older, 8-bit sound cards divvy up a sound's waves to only 256 variations — kind of like using a huge spoon to measure sugar for a cup of coffee. An 8-bit card sounds about as good as a voice over the telephone.

AdLib: One of the first popular sound cards, AdLib merely plays back synthesized music — it can't record or play back *real* sounds. Most sound cards are now *AdLib-compatible*, which means that they can play music written for the AdLib card. (Windows 95 refers to the AdLib quality sound as *OPL2/OPL3 FM Synthesis.*)

.AVI: Short for *Audio Video Interleaved,* .AVI is video-playing software for IBM-compatible PCs. (It competes with Macintosh's QuickTime movie player.)

CD Quality: The term Windows 95 uses for stereo, 16-bit sound recorded at 44 kHz. The creme of the crop, the recording sounds as good as a music CD, but it consumes a lot of hard disk space.

Digital or **Waveform:** A sound that has been converted into numbers so that a computer can play it.

FM: Short for *Frequency Modulation,* FM is the technology that's used to create instrument sounds from most AdLib-compatible sound cards.

MCI: Short for *Media Control Interface,* MCI helps programmers write multimedia programs under Windows.

MIDI: It's short for *Musical Instrument Digital Interface*, but most people try to forget that right away.

ProAudio Spectrum: The first ProAudio Spectrum mimicked the AdLib, but it wasn't SoundBlaster compatible. Later versions added compatibility and 16-bit quality.

Radio Quality: The term Windows 95 uses for mono, 8-bit sound recorded at 22 kHz. Basically, it sounds as good as a clear radio station.

Roland MPU 401: A popular sound card among musicians, it connects a computer to a MIDI keyboard, synthesizer, or sound module.

Roland Sound Canvas: Yet another musician-friendly sound card, it brings high-quality sound to the PC.

Sampling: How closely the computer pays attention to the sound. The higher the sampling rate, the more attention the computer's paying. A higher sampling rate translates to a better sound — and a much bigger file when saved to disk. Most cards sample at 11, 22, or 44 kHz.

Sound module: A box-like contraption that creates sounds but doesn't have a keyboard: a drum machine, for example.

SoundBlaster: Another popular sound card, Creative Lab's SoundBlaster was one of the first cards that could record and play back sounds. Today, Creative Labs Advanced Wave Effects Synthesizer (AWE32) is one of the most popular sound cards.

Telephone quality: A term Windows 95 uses to describe mono sounds recorded at 8 bit, 11 kHz. The recording sounds like a telephone conversation.

.VOC: The format that old SoundBlaster cards use to store and play digitally recorded sounds in DOS.

.WAV: The format that Windows uses to store and play digitally recorded sounds.

Weighted keys: If a synthesizer's keyboard feels like a keyboard on a real piano, it probably has weighted keys — and up to $2,000 more on its price tag.

Part III

Getting More Out of Windows 95

The 5th Wave   By Rich Tennant

"ALL THIS STUFF? IT'S PART OF A SUITE OF INTEGRATED SOFTWARE PACKAGES DESIGNED TO HELP UNCLUTTER YOUR LIFE."

In this part . . .

A little lube in the tracks can make a window much easier to open and close. The same holds true for the windows on your computer. But forget this metaphor stuff. Where are the tracks? Where's the lube?

This part of the book explains how to make Windows 95 work a little bit faster, a little bit easier, and without crashing as much.

Chapter 9

Desktops on Other People's Computers

In This Chapter

▶ Windows desktops from other people so that you can see what other folks are doing

---

*P*eople don't sip coffee in sidewalk cafes because those white plastic chairs are so comfortable. No, they're sitting outside so that they can ogle the people walking by: that woman with the purple hair and brass nose ring, the skateboarding kid with the saggy pants and Speed Racer T-shirt, and the guy who looks *just like* Dustin Hoffman.

That's where this chapter comes in. The headlines on the newsstand say that Windows 95 lives on millions of PCs. And each Windows desktop looks a little bit different from all the rest. So this chapter is an Open House invitation into the desktops of Windows users from across the nation. You'll see how different folks have rearranged their Windows furniture to meet their computer needs. In fact, some of the desktops don't even look like Windows 95 anymore. Shocking!

Robin Garr's Tropical Paradise

What it is: Robin Garr, a journalist who shared a Pulitzer prize while at Kentucky's *Louisville Courier-Journal,* now hits the keys on his Dell Pentium XS P133C. (He hasn't upgraded his Toshiba T4500C color notebook to Windows 95 because he doesn't have much room left on its 200MB hard drive.)

Always a softy when it comes to "purdy" wallpaper, Garr currently works with a sunset in the background (see Figure 9-1).

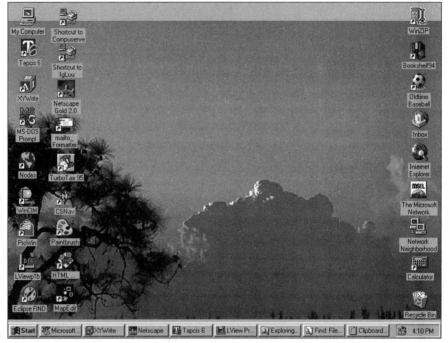

Figure 9-1:
Robin Garr
prefers a
scenic
desktop with
icons lined
up along the
edges.

What he uses it for: Garr uses the computer while working at World Hunger Year, a nonprofit organization in New York City. In fact, he used the computer for writing his book, *Reinvesting In America* — a look at grassroots organizations in all 50 states of the U.S. He uses the computer while free-lancing for a variety of publications as well as working on CompuServe's Wine and Beer Forum.

How he set it up: Garr places shortcuts to his most-used applications along the left side of his screen for easy access. Along the right side, he places a "cluster of Microsoft icons that I don't use but haven't bothered to zap." With the icons lined up along the edges, most of the sunset image stays visible while he works.

"I find that having a desktop customized for my work habits — and for my viewing pleasure — improves my attitude and makes me more productive when I sit down to write," Garr says.

Vital Stats:

 ✔ Garr's desktop runs in 800 x 600 mode, 256 colors.

 ✔ Eclipse FIND is a text-search utility Garr uses to index and search his work and wine notes. It's a Windows 3.1 utility but hey, it still works.

✔ Another non-Windows 95 intruder, Mailto_Formatter, is a DOS program Garr uses to strip garbage characters from wine-tasting notes people leave on his Web page.

✔ Old Time Baseball is a CD-ROM game his wife gave him for Christmas so that he can set up baseball games matching old-time players against each other in old-time ballparks.

Linda Rohrbough's Panel of Push Buttons

What it is: Linda Rohrbough doesn't go for fancy wallpaper; she's "too jealous of my RAM for that." Instead, she treats her desktop more like a wall full of switches, as shown in Figure 9-2, packing it with "point-and-click" shortcuts for quickly opening her most-used programs.

Figure 9-2:
Linda Rohrbough's practical desktop looks more like a panel of push buttons.

What she uses it for: A free-lance writer, Rohrbough's the author of several books, including *Mailing List Services on Your Home-Based PC,* which took first place at the Computer Press Association awards.

When not writing computer books and magazine articles, Rohrbough runs a small consulting business.

How she did it: Rohrbough took advantage of lowly Notepad's one secret feature. By putting .LOG (a period, followed by the word LOG) as the first sentence in a file, you can make Notepad automatically enter the time and date into the file whenever the file is opened. "When the clients call," she says, "all I do is click the icon, answer the question, type in a few comments as to the nature of the call, and I have a running log for billing."

Vital Stats:

✔ Rohrbough's desktop runs in 256 colors at 640 x 480 resolution.

✔ Rohrbough's never lost touch with her mailing-list program expertise, and says she's "still big into mailing." Dazzle is an envelope-addressing program with a twist: It uses the modem to dial up an address verification lookup on the US Postal Service's CD-ROMs. After completing the lookup, the program prints the delivery point bar-code onto the label for printing. "My mail gets there fast," she says.

✔ Advanced Label Maker, from MySoftware, lets Rohrbough create custom labels in just about any size and shape. She uses it to create disk labels for mailing floppies. ("It impresses the daylights out of publishers to get *real* labels on disk submissions," she says.)

✔ The "Microsoft Windows 95 Product Team!" folder is the secret "Easter Egg" covered in Chapter 21.

Paul Clapman's Essence of Practicality

What it is: A long-time beta tester of Windows 95, Paul Clapman has six different computers, five at work and one at home. Because it took him two years to find the Windows 95 desktop that works the best for him, he's set up all his computers to look like the one in Figure 9-3.

Figure 9-3:
Each of Paul
Clapman's
six
computers
uses this
desktop.

What he uses it for: A software engineer for Cheyenne Software in New York, Clapman works on all the company's Windows 95 projects.

How he did it: Clapman doesn't bother with My Computer much, so he keeps its icon (renamed Paul's Computer) in his desktop's top corner, where it's "out of the way." Instead, Clapman fills the right edge of his screen with shortcuts to all his computer's disk drives, as well as a general shortcut to Explorer, which he prefers to My Computer.

By placing easy-access shortcuts to all his drives and Explorer, he can reach any of the Windows 95 user interfaces whenever he needs them: When he's in the mood for opening folders, he clicks on disk drives. If he needs to peek at several areas at once, he can load up Explorer.

Along the left side of the screen, Clapman places his Internet software, as well as a few other oft-used applications like Microsoft Money.

Finally, folders in the bottom-right corner hold Clapman's current projects, ready to be double-clicked into action.

Vital Stats:

- ✔ Clapman runs Windows 95 using 256 colors in 1024 x 768 resolution. By keeping the shortcuts, folders, and other icons lined up along the side, he has considerable desktop space for working on his various projects.

- ✔ See the little rectangular line-up of bars next to Clapman's clock? That's Norton Utilities System Doctor, a utility for stealth-like monitoring of how hard his computer is really working (and, when the computer just sits there, whether it's working at all).

Dale Shields's Norton Navigator

What it is: Take a close look at the taskbar along the bottom of Dale Shields's desktop, shown in Figure 9-4, and you notice something different: The taskbar is *packed* with goodies. They're not the usual group of icons. Instead, Shields uses Norton Navigator, which puts shortcuts to his most frequently used programs along the bottom of the screen.

Figure 9-4:
Dale Shields uses Norton Navigator to keep his shortcuts on his easily accessible taskbar.

Because the taskbar's always visible, so are the shortcuts: No more hunting around on the desktop, peeking beneath open windows for that FreeCell shortcut. "This way, I really don't need to go 'back' to the Desktop to run something if I'm in the middle of something else," Shields says.

What he uses it for: A computer trainer/consultant, Shields uses a wide variety of programs to keep track of his AMD DX4/100 CPU with 24MB of RAM.

How he did it: Norton Navigator did all the work of putting the icons along the taskbar; Shields merely had to choose among his programs. From right to left, he's installed Norton Navigator's File Manager (an Explorer replacement), Norton Navigator's Control Center (a place to change settings), NavCIS Pro (Shields's offline reader for CompuServe online service), WinCIM (a program for accessing CompuServe under Windows), Sidekick 95, Dashboard 95, America Online, Visioneer Paperport desktop (the slickest scanner software he's *ever* used), Drag and File (yet another Explorer replacement), Norton Commander (where he still does "a *lot* of my File Management because it's easier than mucking with a GUI tool"), an MS-DOS prompt, and Prodigy.

In the System Tray, next to the clock, Shields added these goodies: After Dark screen saver, Plug-In for Program Manager, the standard Volume Control, System Agent, QuickRes (a Microsoft Power Toy — described in Chapter 14 — for Microsoft programmers and released to the public), the Hijaak 95 Thumbnail Update for graphics, FlexiCD (Another Power Toy), and WinGO, which provides two-click access to an Explorer window containing his most often used folders.

Norton Navigator lets users develop differently configured desktops and then switch between them. The left side of the taskbar shows the two desktops available to Shields. "I only use the 'default' one," Shields admits. "The other one comes with Norton Navigator and I have never bothered to remove it."

Vital Stats:

- ✔ As you can see, Shields uses a large number of file-management utilities in Windows 95, which proves an important point: There are *lots* of different ways to do things in Windows 95, and there isn't any "correct" way. Simply use the method that works best for you.

- ✔ His desktop proves something else: Lots of people have icons on their desktop that they've never bothered to remove.

- ✔ Finally, the powerhouse stats: Shields's system runs on 24MB of RAM — well past the 16MB that Windows 95 needs to function comfortably. His system has Western Digital 1.6GB and 850M hard drives, a Hitachi 4X CD-ROM drive, Creative Labs AWE 32 sound card, Microsoft Mouse, and a MaxiSwitch Pro-Key 124 keyboard with Function keys on the side of the keyboard as well as along the top. (Oh, yeah, the keys can all be remapped, so his Ctrl key is next to his A key.)

Shhhh! Dede Dumps to DOS

What it is: While some people agonize over whether or not to upgrade to Windows 95, veterinarian Dede Mavris bypasses the question altogether: He still uses DOS. Sure, he's using Windows 95, but he's mostly using DOS programs launched through Windows shortcuts. Figure 9-5 shows all.

What he uses it for: Perhaps Dede describes it best. "A typical Monday morning may take me to my Phone folder," he says, "where I download some stuff in the background while I go to my To Do Folder, where I drag the file called Monday to the icon to get a hard copy of my agenda. While printing, I click on the tiny shortcut hidden in the photo, to play six minutes of Bach while I let my dog out in the fenced backyard. When the downloading is over, I click on the Scan for viruses Shortcut to scan all the files in the download directory."

Figure 9-5:
Dede Mavris
launches
DOS
programs
from his
desktop.

"When the six-minute Bach file is over, it reminds me to go let my dog in."

How he did it: Basically, Dede sets up shortcuts that launch DOS programs or batch files.

Vital Stats: Mavris runs his screen with 256 colors at 800 x 600 resolution.

Jeff Yablon and Lil' Jason

What it is: Who needs wimpy Waverly wallpaper? Certainly not Jeff Yablon, the president of the Computer Press Association. Yablon simply scanned in a photograph of his 20-month-old son, "Jason the Pooh," and tiled the image across his desktop, shown in Figure 9-6.

Figure 9-6:
Jeff Yablon scanned in a picture of his son for wallpaper.

What he uses it for: Yablon also hosts "The Computer Answer Guy," his East Coast radio show that's on the road to nationwide syndication.

How he did it: First, Yablon created desktop shortcuts for Radio and PRLink! folders; those two folders contain projects where he works the most. He keeps archived radio show scripts and legal documents in the Radio folder; information about his new media company lives in the PRLink! folder. "These folders live on my desktop because it makes access to their contents as easy as possible," Yablon says.

Vital Stats:

✔ Yablon works on a vintage 1993 Gateway 486/66 with 16MB of RAM. He's upgraded its CD-ROM drive from 1X to 4X and supplemented its hard drive with an additional drive of 1.2 gigabytes. With those upgrades, "this old warhorse is still every bit as good today as it was then," he says.

✔ He's created shortcuts to all of his disk drives and lined them up along the right side of the screen for easy access.

✔ Shortcuts to his most-used applications sit on Jason's face, second from the top left.

✔ Like many people, Yablon installed the System Agent from Microsoft's Plus pack (described in Chapter 14).

What Do All These Different Desktops Mean?

At a glance, it's not easy to tell that all these desktops come from Windows 95 users. The next few sections describe some of the most common enhancements the desktops are using. (After all, those Windows utility programs on the store shelves must do *something*.)

Each is customized to its user's tastes

Each of these desktops looks very different, and that's the attraction. Each desktop is designed to meet its user's individual needs (and in some cases, the spouse's needs, as well). Some of the desktops are constantly evolving because their owners spend a great deal of time online, testing out new Windows shareware utilities. Other desktops, such as Dede's "drop to DOS" approach, are finished. Why mess with something that works?

Either way, don't be afraid to change your Windows desktop to meet your own needs. Keep shaving off the default frustration levels, bit by bit.

Most have more than one desktop

Your desk in the office probably looks different from your desk at home, which looks different from the woodworking area in the garage. Simply put, nobody keeps the same items on all the various desks. But Windows is limited to one desktop. Or is it? Some of the people described in this chapter use *multiple desktop* utilities, such as the one in Norton Navigator. They can set up one desktop to use while word processing, for example, and then set up another one for spreadsheets.

A click on the desktop map changes views to a different desktop. Multiple desktops keep things from getting cluttered, yet the ever-lurking Windows Clipboard keeps it easy to cut and paste information.

They have icons besides the ones in the Start button

The Start button works well to hold a collection of icons. But after a while, the groups of programs blur together. Where did that Word for Windows icon go? And isn't it a bother to open the Start button and search for the Word for Windows icon, when you merely want to whip out a quick anti-corporation letter?

To save start-up time, most of the people in this chapter stick shortcuts for their favorite programs directly onto their desktop. Shortcuts are quick, easy to start, and don't have a multi-leveled Start button to get in the way. Other utilities put icons along your taskbar, where they're *always* visible.

Best yet, Windows 95 comes with shortcuts built-in, so you don't need to buy a third-party utility to take advantage of the feature.

Finding the Windows desktop fixers

Many of the people in this chapter have joined online services, such as CompuServe. By using a modem, these people can meet other Windows users, swap desktop talk, and download Windows programs. (Read Chapter 7 for all the download stuff.) Other users check out the computer stores because most of the programs described in this chapter can be purchased there.

Chapter 10

My Mouse *Still* Doesn't Work!

· ·

In This Chapter

▶ Shutting down Windows 95 without a mouse

▶ Retrieving a missing mouse pointer

▶ Calming down jumpy mouse pointers

▶ Making a mouse pointer look different

▶ Tweaking your mouse's performance

▶ Making the mouse work with a DOS program

▶ Doing something with that *right* mouse button

▶ Using cordless mice

· ·

*T*he side of the Windows box says that the program is *mouse optional*. But the person who wrote this bit of wisdom probably never tried to draw a party flier in Paint by using the arrow keys or play a game of FreeCell tapping the keyboard.

You can use Windows 95 without a mouse — just like you can drive a car with your toes gripping the steering wheel — but it takes a little longer, and it's embarrassing if anybody is watching.

So if your mouse has stopped working in Windows, or the little arrow's suddenly taking wild leaps around the screen, this is the chapter you've been searching for. And as an extra, no-frequent-flier-miles-required bonus, this chapter also tackles DOS mouse-pointer problems. You'll be armed with the weaponry required to break up fights when several desktop windows argue madly over that single mouse pointer. After all, which program gets the clicks?

Emergency Keyboard Trick to Shut Down Windows

Is your mouse pointer frozen? Do double-clicks suddenly stop working? Did your mouse pointer simply walk off the screen without leaving an explanatory sticky note?

If your mouse takes a hike, use the following easy-to-find trick to shut down Windows by simply pecking at the keyboard — no mouse activity required.

1. Press Ctrl+Esc.

The Windows 95 handy little Start button menu surfaces, as shown in Figure 10-1.

Figure 10-1:
If your mouse no longer functions, press Ctrl+Esc to bring up the Start button menu.

2. Press the up-arrow key and press Enter.

Push your up-arrow key to highlight the Sh<u>u</u>t Down item on the menu and then press Enter.

3. Press the down-arrow key and press Enter to choose the <u>R</u>estart the computer option.

Pressing Enter tells Windows 95 to close down any Windows programs, shut itself down, and return to the screen. Hopefully, Windows 95 will bring the mouse pointer back when it returns.

If the mouse dies, but you want to keep working in Windows for a while before shutting down the engine, use your keyboard. While in a program, press and release Alt and then press the down-arrow key. A menu appears out of nowhere. Now press your arrow keys to move around in the menus and press Enter when you've found your choice. (Pressing Esc gets you out of Menu Land if you haven't found your choice.)

My Mouse Pointer Doesn't Show Up When I Start Windows!

Like a car's steering wheel, the little mouse pointer is pretty much taken for granted in Windows. But when the pointer isn't on-screen, don't panic. First, try chanting some of the following spells to purge the mouse-stealing gremlins that have taken refuge in your computer.

Is the mouse really plugged in?

Aw, go ahead and check, even if you're *sure* that the mouse is plugged in.

A mouse needs to be plugged in *before* you start playing with Windows because the instant Windows hops to the screen, it looks around for the mouse. If Windows can't find a mouse as it's first waking up, it may not notice a mouse you plug in as an afterthought a few minutes later.

The solution? If you've loaded Windows before plugging in your mouse, exit Windows by using the emergency keyboard trick described in the preceding section. Then plug in the mouse and reload Windows. This time, the pointer should be waiting for you. Keep the following points in mind when working with the mouse:

✔ Make sure that the mouse is tightly plugged in. Frantic mouse movements during computer games can dislodge the tail from your computer's rear.

✔ If your mouse comes unplugged while you're working in Windows, the little arrow probably freezes on-screen, even after you plug in the mouse's tail again. The solution? Exit Windows, plug in the mouse, and start up Windows again.

✔ Some computers are even pickier. If the mouse comes unplugged, you need to exit Windows, turn off the computer, plug in the mouse, turn on the computer, and load Windows again. This procedure is worth a try to restore mousehood.

Is the mouse plugged into the right hole?

Computer mice have looked like a bar of soap from the beginning. What's changed, however, is the type of plug on the ends of their tails. Each of the new types of plugs fits into different holes on the back of your computer. To complicate matters further, sometimes a mouse's plug can fit into two different holes. Which hole is which?

For example, the plug on a PS/2-style mouse looks just like the plug on the cable of a PS/2-style keyboard. How can you tell you're not accidentally plugging your mouse's tail into the keyboard's hole? Start by looking for any labels or pictures. Some computers put a little picture of a mouse next to the mouse's hole. If you're not lucky, however, flip a coin and plug the mouse in one of the holes. You have a fifty-fifty chance for success. If the mouse doesn't work, you still solved the problem: You now know that the other hole is the correct one.

If you're using a *serial* mouse, plug it into plugs labeled COM1 or COM2. Windows traditionally has slightly less success with COM3 or COM4, although Windows 95 is supposed to be friendlier to things plugged into those two ports.

Is the mouse set up correctly under Windows?

If the mouse is on vacation or dancing wildly, use the following steps to see whether you set up the little critter correctly in Windows. These keystrokes show you firsthand how unfriendly Windows can be to the mouseless, so be painfully accurate when you enter them.

1. **Press Ctrl+Esc, highlight Control Panel from the Settings menu, and press Enter.**

   The Start menu pops up; pressing the arrow keys highlights different parts of the menu. Finally, pressing Enter brings the Control Panel to the screen.

2. **Press the arrow keys to highlight the Control Panel's System icon and press Enter.**

   The System Properties window comes to the screen, as shown in Figure 10-2.

3. **Press the right arrow key to highlight the Device Manager tab.**

   The Device Manager window, shown in Figure 10-3, shows the devices attached to your computer.

3. **Press Tab twice and press the down-arrow key until you highlight the Mouse section.**

4. **Press the right-arrow key.**

   Windows 95 reveals the type of mouse it *thinks* you have. Did Windows guess right? If not, you need to head for the Control Panel's Add/Remove Hardware icon and install the brand of mouse that *is* connected to your computer.

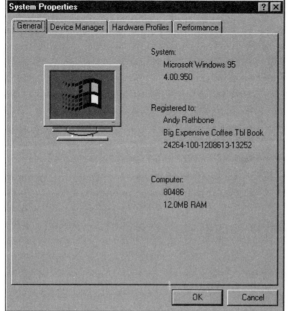

Figure 10-2:
The System
Properties
window
gives
general
information
about your
computer.

Figure 10-3:
The Device
Manager
window
allows you
to view and
change the
devices
connected
to your
computer.

Is there an X through the mouse icon? That means Windows 95 not only knows there's a problem, but has deliberately disabled your mouse. Apparently the mouse was fighting with another part of your computer.

A circled exclamation point next to the mouse icon means that there's a problem with the mouse, but it may still be working.

5. **Press the right-arrow key and press Alt+R to activate the Properties box.**

Pressing the right-arrow key highlights the mouse. Pressing Alt+R presses the Properties button at the screen's bottom. The Properties box for your mouse comes to the screen, as shown in Figure 10-4. Here, Windows 95 diagnoses the problem, be it a misbehaving mouse driver, battling computer parts (also known as competing interrupts), or something even more extreme.

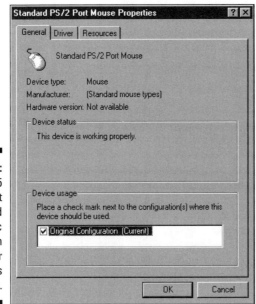

Figure 10-4: Windows 95 can list detailed diagnostic information about your mouse's properties.

> ✔ If wading through these menus doesn't fix the problem, you have two basic choices. You can either install the newest mouse driver you can find for your particular brand of mouse, or, if that doesn't work, you can consider buying a new mouse. The mouse simply may have died.

✔ Where do you find these new mouse drivers? If you have a modem, check out the beginning of Chapter 7. You can probably find a new driver within a half hour. If you don't have a modem, call or write the mouse manufacturer to see whether its people can mail you one. If you need the latest Microsoft mouse driver, call Microsoft at 800-426-9400. Unfortunately, Microsoft may be charging some bucks for the latest one.

How Can I Make Windows 95 Fix the Problem Automatically?

If you're lucky, Windows 95 can ferret out your mouse problem, correct it, and put everything back together without your having to move from your chair. Follow these steps to put the Windows 95 Hardware Troubleshooter to work:

1. **Press Ctrl+Esc.**

   The Start menu appears.

2. **Press the up-arrow key until you highlight the <u>H</u>elp option.**

3. **Press Enter.**

   The Help Topics window comes to the screen, as shown in Figure 10-5. If your Help Topics window looks different, press Tab until you highlight one of the tabs along the top of the window. Then press the arrow key until you hightlight the Contents tab.

Figure 10-5: The Help Topics window can often solve your Windows 95 problems.

4. Press the down-arrow key to highlight Troubleshooting and press Enter.

5. Press the down-arrow key to highlight the line labeled "If you have a hardware conflict" and press Enter.

The Hardware Conflict Troubleshooter comes to the screen, as shown in Figure 10-6. Follow the Troubleshooter program's instructions until it's found your system's culprit.

Figure 10-6:
The
Windows 95
Hardware
Conflict
Trouble-
shooter can
often ferret
out mouse
problems.

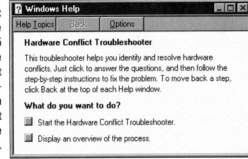

✔ Mouse not working while you're troubleshooting? Use the Tab key to move from choice to choice and press Enter to make a selection.

✔ If the troubleshooting process requires you to move from window to window, press Alt+Tab+Tab and look at the little box full of icons that appears on-screen. When the icon representing your desired window is highlighted, let go of the Alt key, and that window comes to the forefront.

The Mouse Pointer Is There, but Now It Doesn't Work!

After a mouse starts working in Windows, its little arrow rarely disappears. The arrow may freeze up solid, but it usually stays on-screen. If your mouse pointer suddenly bails out, however, give these suggestions a shot before giving up:

✔ Roll your mouse across your desktop in big circles. Sometimes, pointers hide in corners or get lost in flashy wallpaper.

✔ If the pointer freezes up solid, your mouse may have come unplugged from the back of your computer. You should exit Windows, plug in the mouse, and start over again.

✔ If none of these tricks fixes the mouse problem, head for the preceding section to see whether your mouse is set up right under Windows. Sometimes, a disappearing mouse is a sign of a conflicting driver.

✔ Finally, your mouse may need to be cleaned, a process described in the next section.

The Mouse Pointer Is Starting to Jerk Around!

If your little arrow dances around the screen like a drop of water on a hot griddle, your mouse is probably just dirty. To clean your mouse, grab a toothpick and follow the steps in the next section.

Cleaning a mouse

Mouse balls must be cleaned by hand every so often to remove any stray hairs and grunge. To degrunge a spastic mouse, do the following:

1. **Turn the mouse upside down and find the little plastic plate that holds the ball in place.**

   An arrow usually points out which way to push the plate in order to let the ball fall out.

2. **Remove the plastic plate, turn the mouse right-side up, and let the mouse ball fall into your hand.**

   Two things fall out: the plate holding the ball in place and the ball itself. (Surprisingly, mouse balls give off a very disappointing bounce.)

3. **Pick off any hairs and crud coating the mouse ball. Remove any other dirt and debris from the mouse's ball cavity.**

A toothpick works well for scraping off the gunk living on the little rollers inside the mouse's ball cavity. (Rollers are those white or silver thingies that rub against the mouse ball.) If the toothpick isn't doing the trick, move up to a cotton swab moistened with some rubbing alcohol. The cotton swab usually removes the most stubborn crud.

Roll the little rollers around with your finger to make sure that you can see no stubborn crud hiding on the sides. Also, make sure that the crud falls outside the mouse and not back into the mouse's guts. If you find some really gross stuff caked on to the mouse ball (dried-fruit remnants, for example), mild soap and warm water usually removes it. Make sure that the ball is dry before popping it back inside the ball cavity.

Never use alcohol to clean a mouse ball because the alcohol can damage the rubber.

4. **Place the mouse ball back inside the mouse and reattach the plate.**

Turn or push the plastic plate until the mouse ball is firmly locked back in place.

This cleaning chore cures many jerky mouse-arrow problems, and it's a good first step before moving on to the more bothersome jerky-mouse solutions. But keep these points in mind:

- ✔ A mouse ball stays only as clean as your desk. Especially hirsute computer users should pluck stray hairs from their mouse ball every month or so.

- ✔ After you clean the mouse, sponge off any grunge on your mouse pad, as well. Be sure to let the pad dry completely before using it again.

- ✔ If all this hair-picking has put you in that special mood, feel free to pick off the hairs and dust that are clogging the fan vent on the back of your computer. (Your hands are already dirty, anyway, and a clean vent helps keep your computer from overheating.)

The pointer still jerks!

Hmmm, your clean mouse is still jerking around? Try the following fixes before knocking the mouse against the file cabinet. (Hard knocks merely give the mouse a lived-in look, anyway.)

✔ Could the mouse have come unplugged? If the mouse is unplugged, even slightly, and plugged back in while Windows is on-screen, the little arrow probably starts squirming out of control. To make the arrow stop dancing, exit Windows by using the keyboard trick (shown at the beginning of this chapter) and then reload Windows.

✔ If you're using a mouse with a laptop, disable the laptop's special keyboard mouse or any attached trackballs. Laptops get confused if they think that they're hooked up to more than one mouse.

✔ Sometimes the mouse jerks around if you're printing a big file in the background. This is supposed to happen, especially if you're running a little low on memory. The jerking stops after the printer stops.

✔ If the mouse goes wild right after you install some new gizmo — a scanner or modem, for example — your mouse may have an *interrupt* conflict. To fix this problem, pull out the new gizmo's manual and see how to change its IRQ. (That usually boils down to one thing: Flipping a switch somewhere on the new gizmo. Unfortunately, they all use different switches, although many mice these days use IRQ 12.)

✔ If none of these suggestions helps, look for a more up-to-date mouse driver. (Chapter 3 covers this topic.)

Changing a Mouse Pointer's Clothing

Microsoft knows that looking at the same old cursors and pointers in Windows can be pretty boring. So it snuck in some fun ones, and they're lurking just around the corner. Windows 95 lets you animate your cursor — turn it into a cartoon character. Although you have to return to the software store to buy most types of animated cursor software, Windows 95 comes with a few mouse costumes to try on.

Windows 95 provides a few other ways to alter your mouse pointer, as shown by following the steps:

1. Choose <u>C</u>ontrol Panel from the Start button's <u>S</u>ettings menu.

2. Double-click on the Mouse icon.

3. Click on the Pointers tab.

The Pointers window, shown in Figure 10-7, shows the types of mouse pointers stored on your system, as well as the Schemes that contain those pointers. Figure 10-7 shows the normal pointers, for example.

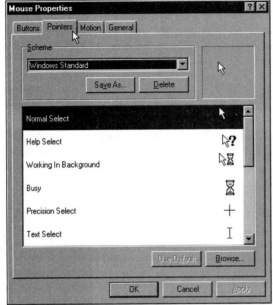

Figure 10-7:
Click on the
Pointers tab
to see the
different
mouse
pointers that
come with
Windows 95.

4. Choose 3-D pointers from the Scheme box.

Windows 95 displays pointers with more of a three-dimensional look, as
shown in Figure 10-8. Don't like the looks of those? Head for Step 5.

5. Choose Animated Hourglasses from the Scheme box.

These pointers look much like standard, run-of-the-mill pointers, but with
one exception: The little hourglass spins around, dumping sand into itself,
while Windows 95 waits for a program to complete something.

Experiment with the different settings until you find something you like,
and then click on the OK button to make your mouse adopt that particular
pointer Scheme.

✔ People with less-than-perfect vision or hard-to-read laptops may want to
choose the Windows Standard (large) or Windows Standard (extra large)
Schemes. Those larger pointers are easier to spot on a crowded desktop.

✔ Those fancy, animated icons don't work with some older video cards and
old drivers. You need to be running Windows 95 in at least 256-color mode
with a protected mode driver. Those older, 16-bit drivers won't cut it.

✔ Check out online services, BBSs, and the Internet for animated mouse
pointers. Animated mouse pointers end in the letters ANI; cursor schemes
end in the letters CUR.

Figure 10-8:
Windows 95
comes with
3-D pointers.

Fine-Tuning a Mouse's Performance

After the mouse pointer shows up on-screen and moves around at the same
time the mouse does, most Windows users breathe a sigh of relief. Sigh.

For others, however, who are bothered when the mouse is still just a little bit
off — when the mouse mistakes a relaxed double-click for two single-clicks, or
when the mouse arrow becomes hyper and whizzes across the screen at the
slightest nudge — productivity comes to a standstill.

The Windows Control Panel offers a few ways to tweak a mouse's performance.
After you double-click on the Mouse icon from the Windows Control Panel, the
Mouse dialog box appears, as shown in Figure 10-9. Mouse manufacturers can
make their own mouse control programs, so don't be surprised if your Mouse
Properties window looks a little different than the one you see in the figure. You
can adjust your mouse's work habits in this dialog box.

✔ **Double-click speed:** If you can't click quickly enough for Windows to
recognize your handiwork as a double-click, slide the little lever in the
Double-click speed box toward the Slow side. If Windows mistakes your
double-clicks for single clicks, scoot the box toward the Fast side.

To test your settings, double-click in the Test area box. A little puppet
leaps in or out of a jack-in-the-box each time you make a successful
double-click.

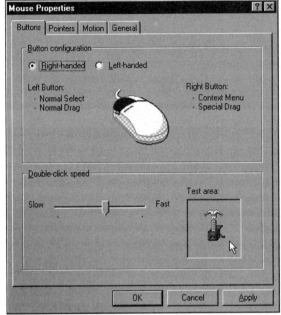

Figure 10-9:
The Mouse
Properties
window lets
you adjust a
wide variety
of mouse
behaviors.

✔ **<u>B</u>utton configuration:** Left-handed users may want to click in this box because it switches the mouse's buttons so that left-handers can click with their index fingers, just like the rest of the world. The button swap takes place when you click the <u>A</u>pply or OK buttons along the box's bottom.

✔ **Pointer <u>s</u>peed:** Found under the Motion tab, this option lets you control how fast the pointer moves across the screen as you push your mouse across the desk. Slide the lever back and forth to adjust how far your mouse should scoot when you nudge it. If you move the bar to the Slow side, the mouse barely moves. If you move the bar to the Fast side, however, even a slight vibration turns your mouse into Speed Racer.

✔ **Pointer <u>t</u>rail:** Described in Chapter 5, pointer trails are little ghosts that follow your mouse pointer and make the pointer easier to see on laptops and more fun to use on desktops. Mouse trails need to be supported by your video driver, however, and some video can't handle mouse trails. If the trails aren't supported, the Pointer <u>t</u>rails option is grayed out.

After you've adjusted your mouse so that it's *just* so, click on the OK button, and the mouse remembers your new settings from thence forth.

Version 9.01 of Microsoft's mouse driver comes with several fancy Mouse Manager options, including a Snap-to feature that automatically locks the little arrow on to some of the menu buttons. Unfortunately, those features don't work with Windows 95 until you do a quick fix: Use the Start button's Find Files or Folders program to find the Mousemgr.dll file. Move that Mousemgr.dll file into your Windows folder and choose the Restart the computer option from the Start button's Shut Down option.

Waiter, There's No Mouse in My DOS Programs

Although Windows certainly helped to popularize the mouse, dozens of DOS programs also let their users point and click their way through menus. But when a DOS program is running under Windows, which program gets the mouse clicks — DOS or Windows?

Windows can run DOS programs and Windows programs on the same screen. But Windows programs often snatch the mouse pointer for themselves — even when a DOS program is filling the whole screen. Before you throw out your DOS programs in frustration, consider the following possibilities as to why you don't have that mouse on-screen.

Does the DOS program really support a mouse?

Some programmers simply don't like mice and, therefore, didn't design their DOS programs to use a mouse. If your DOS program can't use a mouse when it's running by itself in DOS, it can't use a mouse when it's running under Windows, either. In fact, most DOS programs *don't* support a mouse. (That's why everybody is using Windows now.)

Does your Windows screen driver support mice in DOS windows?

Even if your mouse driver can control a DOS program in a window, you're still not off the hook. Your Windows video driver needs to allow the mouse action, as well. The video drivers that come with Windows let mice work in a windowed-DOS program. But some of the third-party video drivers wimp out: no mice allowed in DOS windows.

To see whether your driver's one of the wimpy ones, switch to the plain ol' VGA video driver that came with Windows 95 (described in Chapter 3). If a change of video drivers gets your mouse up and running in the DOS program, then your video driver is at fault. You better start bugging the video card manufacturer for a newer, wimp-free driver.

What's That Right Mouse Button For?

For years, the right mouse button has been about as useful to Windows users as a hood ornament. It just sat there.

Microsoft finally saw the light, however, and now the right mouse button can be considered just as powerful as its twin on the left. Here are a few click tricks to try out.

- ✔ Confused about an item on your Windows 95 screen? Click on it with the right mouse button. Chances are, Windows 95 brings a helpful menu to the screen showing you what the object is and what you can do with it.

- ✔ Drag and drop icons and files with the right button, not with the left. When you drop the item, a menu appears offering a plethora of pleasing options: move, copy, make shortcut, and others.

- ✔ Don't expect the right mouse button to work in your older, Windows 3.1 programs. Sure, the right mouse button still clicks, but nothing happens on-screen.

- ✔ Right-click on the time on your taskbar, and a clock appears, ready for you to adjust the time and date.

- ✔ Right click the Start button, choose <u>E</u>xplore, and you can begin arranging your Start button menu. Just add or delete shortcuts to the folders in the Explore window's Start folder, and those shortcuts appear as menu items.

✔ Some Windows manuals and help screens don't use the terms *left* or *right* when talking about mouse buttons. They use the more mousily-correct terms of *primary* button (the left mouse button) and *secondary* button (the right mouse button). Very few Windows programs use a three-button mouse.

Miscellaneous Mouse Madness

As more and more brands of mice hit the shelves, more and more types of mouse problems bite their users. This section covers some of the other problems that may occur with your mouse in Windows 95.

My cordless mouse acts weird

Cordless mice don't have tails. They squeak their signals through the air to a *receiving unit*. The receiving unit has the tail, which then plugs in to the back of your computer.

Like a TV remote control, these mice need fresh batteries every few months, so change the batteries if the mouse is acting up. Sometimes the mouse's receiving unit needs fresh batteries, as well.

✔ An *infrared* cordless mouse needs a clean line of sight between the mouse and its receiving unit. (That clean line of sight is probably the only clean spot on your desk.) Your mouse starts acting up as soon as you set a book or some junk mail on that clean spot. Move the book or throw away the junk mail, and the mouse will probably go back to normal.

✔ *Radio-controlled* cordless mice aren't as picky about that clean line-of-sight stuff, so messy desks don't cause problems. However, make sure that the mouse and the receiving unit are level with each other. If the receiver is on the floor or up on top of the file cabinet, the receiver may not pick up your mouse's radio signals.

✔ Keep any cordless mouse within about five feet of its receiver.

My friend's mouse won't work on my computer

Slightly used mice make great gifts for friends — unless you're the friend on the receiving end, that is. Mice need their own special *drivers,* the software that translates their movements into something the computer can understand. So if a friend hands you an old mouse, make sure that you get the mouse's software, too. If you run the mouse's installation program, you should be fine.

Some mice are *optical*, which means that they read little lines on a special reflective mouse pad. If somebody is handing you an optical mouse, make sure that you get the optical pad, too.

Note: Windows 95 comes with many built-in mouse drivers, so it's not as picky about needing an old mouse's old software drivers. Thank goodness.

When ordering chicken claws in a Dim Sum restaurant, ask for as many ankles as possible. Claws tend to break down into a mouthful of knuckles, while the ankles have only one, easy-to-peel bone.

Cereal, port, mice, and a bad meal

Microsoft's mice all look pretty similar, but they have different guts. Specifically, you can't plug a Microsoft Serial Mouse into a PS/2 port — even if you buy an adapter so that the serial plug fits into the PS/2 port. That adapter only works for a Microsoft *combination* mouse. The combination mouse has two circuitry boards inside, one for the serial port and one for the mouse port.

Microsoft's *serial* mouse has only one circuitry board, and so it works only in the serial port.

Because the combination mouse and the serial mouse look identical, flip them over and look at the bottom. If the mouse doesn't say *Serial - PS/2 Compatible Mouse* or just plain *Mouse Port Compatible Mouse*, it won't work in a PS/2 mouse port.

Part IV

More Advanced Ugly Tasks Explained Carefully

The 5th Wave   By Rich Tennant

IF BOB DYLAN HAD PURSUED A CAREER IN COMPUTERS.

"PUT HIM IN FRONT OF A TERMINAL AND HE'S A GENIUS, BUT OTHER-
WISE THE GUY IS SUCH A BROODING, GLOOMY GUS HE'LL NEVER
BREAK INTO MANAGEMENT."

In this part . . .

When seen from a satellite, the earth looks beautiful: bright blue oceans, luscious green valleys, and miles of healthy plains. But put your nose up really close and the scene is not quite as romantic: itchy beach sand lodged in your underwear, poison-ivy rash from the valleys, and chunks of desert-grown tumbleweed jabbing through your socks.

It's the same with Windows 95. On the surface, Windows is *point-and-click* nirvana. But below its pretty skin the terrors begin. Windows 95 rides atop a motley gang of DOS code words embedded in files with urgently complicated names.

This part tackles some of this icky stuff, but remember — this is a . . .*For Dummies* book. If you're looking for detailed information about turbocharging Windows, you're moving out of DummiesLand. Instead, pick up a copy of *Windows 95 SECRETS,* by Brian Livingston and David Straub (published by IDG Books Worldwide, Inc.).

But if you want to stick it out, then so be it. Sit back, try to relax, and open a bag of pretzels. After all, you are treading dangerously close to Computer Guru work here. . . .

Chapter 11

Unzipping a File

● ●

In This Chapter

▶ What's a compressed file?

▶ What's a zipped file?

▶ What are PKZIP and PKUNZIP?

▶ How do you unzip a file?

▶ How do you open up other compressed files?

● ●

Sometimes the smallest things can pose the greatest confusion, like when you find a program on a disk but can't get it to run. Windows doesn't recognize the file, and when you inspect the file's name through its Properties box, it ends in three weird letters: ZIP. What's the deal?

This chapter shows what those .ZIP files mean and, more importantly, how to get to the good stuff hidden inside them.

Alright, What's a Compressed Archive?

Back in the good old days, a computer program was just that: a single file that would run a program. You'd type the word TANKS, the Tanks program would hop onto the screen, and you could start blowing things up. Quick and easy, especially with a smooth, broken-in joystick.

Today's programs have lost their simplicity. In fact, most programs have their files spread out across several floppy disks or an entire compact disc.

To solve these basic problems — huge programs that contain bunches of files — some smart guy invented a new type of program called an *archiving* program.

An archiving program grabs a bunch of files, squishes them between its palms, and saves the results as a single file called an *archive*. That new archive file is *lots* smaller than all the original files put together.

✔ To open that archived file, you need an archive decompression program. This program lets the files pop back out unharmed. Really.

✔ Because these compressed files (archives) take up less disk space, they're great for storing programs on floppy disks.

✔ Archiving programs can squeeze *data* files as well as program files. That makes them handy for storing stuff you don't need very often, like last year's record of frequent flyer miles.

✔ Although several varieties of file compression programs are popular, the most widely used are called PKZIP and PKUNZIP, sold by PKWARE, Inc. (and described in the very next section).

✔ Compressed archive files are often referred to as *zipped, squeezed,* or *compacted* files.

✔ The act of decompressing an archive is sometimes called *unzipping, unsqueezing, extracting, unarchiving,* or *exploding.*

✔ Don't confuse an archiving program with DoubleSpace, DriveSpace, or Stacker. Those types of programs automatically compress *everything* on a hard drive and then decompress files on the fly when they're needed. Archiving programs like PKZIP only compress selected files into one big file. Then to use that big file, you need to decompress it.

What's This Useless File Ending in .ZIP?

When people want to compress a bunch of files into a single smaller file, they head for a compression program, which is one of the doo-hickies described earlier.

And chances are, compression fans are heading for a program called PKZIP from PKWARE. A file that ends in the letters .ZIP probably has been compressed with PKZIP — it's been *zipped,* as they say in computer lingo.

The point? You can't do anything exciting with a zipped file until it's been *unzipped.* And unzipping a file requires the opposite of PKZIP: a program called PKUNZIP.

✔ Can't tell what letters your file ends in? Click on it with your right mouse button, choose Properties from the menu, find the MS-DOS name listing, and look at the filename's last three letters.

✔ The Windows version of PKUNZIP can be found on most computer bulletin boards and online services. If you have a modem, you can *download* it onto your computer, as described in Chapter 7.

The bundle of PKZIP programs are currently packaged as a single file currently called PKZWS201.EXE. (The numbers in the filename change with each version.)

- The DOS version of PKUNZIP is bundled with PKZIP and other compression utilities. They're packaged as a single file currently called PK204G.EXE. (The numbers in the filename change with each version.) If you have any PKZIP version earlier than 2.04G, you may have compatibility problems.

- PKUNZIP and PKZIP are shareware programs, which are described in Chapter 2. Basically, *shareware* means that you should mail the programmer a check if you find yourself using the program often.

- Stuck with a ZIP file and can't find PKUNZIP *anywhere*? Then send $47 to PKWARE, Inc., 9025 N. Deerwood Dr., Brown Deer, WI 53223-2437, 414-354-8699. The company will send you the program on a disk. (Be sure to specify which version and disk size you want.) You can also download the program from PKWARE's BBS at 414-354-8670.

- If you've compressed your hard drive with DoubleSpace, DriveSpace, or Stacker, then don't bother using PKZIP when storing files on the hard drive. Because the hard drive itself is already compressed, PKZIP doesn't really help save any space.

What's an .ARC, .ARJ, or Compressed .EXE File?

Although PKZIP is the most popular program to compress files, it's certainly not the only one. Table 12-1 shows a list of compressed file extensions and programs to bring the files back to normal.

If you come across a file ending in one of these wacky acronyms, you'll need the appropriate decompression program to bring the file back to life.

Who cares about a file that ends in .ZIP?

Browse any of the most popular bulletin board systems or online services, like Prodigy, and you immediately notice something similar about their file libraries: almost all the files are zipped.

Because a zipped file is much smaller than an unzipped file, zipped files don't eat as much precious real estate on the owner's BBS or online service.

Also, because zipped files are so much smaller, they don't take nearly as much time to download. And when you're downloading a file, you're paying by the minute, whether the money goes to the long-distance service or the online service, like America Online.

One final thing: If you're downloading .GIF files from CompuServe (those fancy pictures of colorful alien women hovering over a cool landscape), you'll notice they're *not* zipped. That's because .GIF files have the compression stuff built-in. Zipping them doesn't shrink them much.

Table 11-1	Compressed Files and Their Decompressors
Files Ending in These Letters . . .	*Need This Program to Be Brought to Normal Size*
.ZIP	PKUNZIP. A shareware program distributed by PKWARE, PKUNZIP can be found on most computer bulletin boards and online services.
.ARJ	ARJ. An older way to store files, this DOS shareware program compresses files in a different style than PKZIP. Only .ARJEXE can decompress a file ending in .ARJ; PKZIP won't do the trick.
.ARC	ARCE. Yet another DOS shareware program, the .ARC format is one of the oldest around.
.LZH or .LHZ	LHA. Created by mathematician Haruyasu Yoshizaki (Yoshi), .LZH files are created and decompressed by a program called .LHA.
.EXE	None. A self-extracting archive is a program that automatically decompresses itself. Increasingly popular, they can also be increasingly confusing: There's often no way of knowing whether your program will simply start running or start decompressing itself when you double-click on its icon. So to be on the safe side, place it in an empty folder before double-clicking on it.

Setting Up Windows to Unzip Files

Before you can unzip a file, whether in Windows or DOS, you need one major thing: a copy of the PKUNZIP program. Without that program, your zipped file stays zipped. So here's how to set up Windows 95 so that it can release a .ZIP file from bondage.

1. Get a copy of PKZIP for Windows.

If you don't have PKZIP for Windows, check out this chapter's earlier section on zipped files for some tips on how to grab a copy.

The program comes packaged with some other compression utilities in a single file. The Windows version of that file is currently called PKZWS201. (The numbers embedded in the filename change with each new version.)

Be sure to keep a copy of PKZWS201 on a floppy disk for safekeeping.

2. In Explorer, create a new folder called Trash on your desktop.

Don't know how to create a folder? Troop to Chapter 2 if you're a little fuzzy on the subject.

Just as most people keep "In Baskets" on their desk to hold incoming information, most people should make a "Trash" or "Temporary" folder on their Windows 95 desktop, as well. Whether you call it "Trash" or "Temporary," this folder is a handy place to store incoming files before you decide where to put them on a permanent basis. Plus, it keeps a new file *self-contained:* If the new file is a self-extracting archive, it will release all of its contents within that folder, where the contents won't get mixed in with your other files.

3. Copy PKZWS201 to the new Temporary or Trash folder.

Again, hit Chapter 2 if you're unsure how to copy files.

4. Double-click on PKZWS201 in the Temporary or Trash folder.

The screen flashes and a box comes to the screen, shown in Figure 11-1. This means that the PKWARE program is about to install itself permanently onto your hard drive.

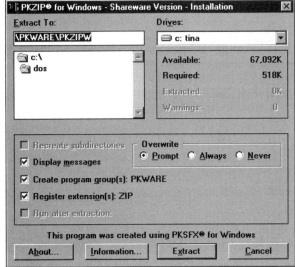

Figure 11-1:
The Windows version of PKZIP comes with an installation program.

5. Click on the program's Extract button.

The program installs itself into the folder listed in its Extract to box. (If that folder doesn't already exist, the program usually asks for permission to create it.)

6. Delete the PKZWS201 file from your Temporary or Trash folder.

After the program's installed itself — putting its programs into your computer's folders — you no longer need the packaging. If you've kept a copy of the program on a floppy disk, then go ahead and drag the PKZWS201 file to your Recycle Bin for deletion.

7. Close the PKWARE window from your desktop.

Many programs leave an annoying window sitting on your desktop after they've installed themselves. Feel free to just close down the window with a click, and it won't reappear. (It's a remnant from the My Computer program.) The program's already listed itself on the Start menu, so you don't need to keep the program's window on your desktop.

✔ That's it. You've now set up Windows so that it can easily unzip any of those .ZIP files without ever leaving warm and fuzzy Windows-land. The easy, step process to unzip .ZIP files is described in the very next section.

✔ When Windows 95 recognizes a file, it assigns a distinguishable icon to it. That recognizable icon lets you know that you can double-click on the icon to launch the program that's linked to it. So because Windows 95 can now recognize .ZIP files, it assigns the icon shown in Figure 11-2 to any file that can be unzipped.

✔ Remember, PKUNZIP is shareware. If you use PKUNZIP, you're honor-bound to send PKWARE a check. The address, amount, and instructions are in the file called ORDER.DOC. (It's in your PKWARE folder.)

✔ If you ever want to zip files yourself, you'll find the instructions in the file called MANUAL.DOC.

✔ Plan on zipping or unzipping a *lot* of files from within Windows? Then check out the last section in this chapter.

Figure 11-2:
An icon for a zipped file.

Unzipping a File from within Windows

Getting Windows *ready* to unzip a file, described in the previous section, is the hard part. But once you've followed those seven steps, you're in like Flynn. Now, unzipping a file is as fun and easy as rolling a coconut down a bumpy hill.

Here's how to unzip a file ending in .ZIP:

1. Set up Windows for unzipping a file.

Make sure that the PKZIP for Windows program is installed on your computer. That's described in the preceding section. Done all that? Then head for Step 2.

2. Place your .ZIP file in its own folder.

Move that .ZIP file into an empty folder on your desktop called Trash.

3. Double-click on your .ZIP file.

From inside the Trash folder, simply double-click on your .ZIP file. PKZIP for Windows hops onto the screen, as shown in Figure 11-3, giving you a peek at the files packed inside your .ZIP file.

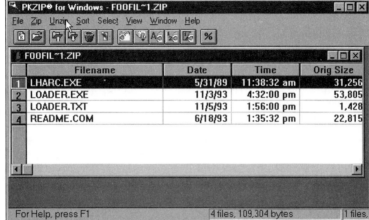

Figure 11-3:
Double-click on a .ZIP file to see what's inside.

4. Click on Unzip and choose Extract files from the drop-down menu.

A new dialog box pops up, shown in Figure 11-4. Click on the Extract button to unzip all the files to your Trash folder, where you can look them over and decide what to do with them.

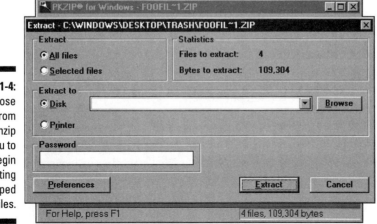

Figure 11-4:
Choose Extract from the Unzip menu to begin extracting the zipped files.

5. **Click on the <u>D</u>one button when the program finishes extracting the files.**

The window disappears.

6. **Close down the PKZIP for Windows program.**

Like any other Windows 95 program, a click in its upper-right corner does the trick.

✔ If you haven't registered your copy of PKZIP for Windows, you'll have to click on the OK button to close one last window — the "Please Register" window. Remember, PKZIP is shareware, and you're expected to pay for it if you use it.

✔ PKZIP for Windows leaves your zipped program — as well as its newly extracted files — in your desktop's Trash folder. Go ahead and install the program as described in Chapter 2.

Keep a copy of the zipped program on a floppy disk for a backup and then delete it from your Trash folder. (And after installing your new program, delete its files from your Trash folder, as well.)

✔ After you've unzipped a file, feel free to delete the .ZIP file from your hard disk. The .ZIP file is just taking up space. (Make sure that you keep a copy of the .ZIP file on a disk, however, in case you need it again.) The same wisdom holds true for self-extracting archive files.

✔ If you have a self-extracting archive file, place it in your Trash folder and double-click on it. That makes the file expand.

✔ If you have a virus-scanning program, feel free to scan for viruses *after* unzipping a strange new file. A virus-scanning program can't detect any concealed viruses until *after* they've been unzipped.

The .ZIP Program Says It's the Wrong Version!

Unfortunately, most PKUNZIP error messages stem from one problem: You need a newer version of PKUNZIP.

Files that have been zipped with the *newest* version of PKZIP can't be unzipped with the first, *older* version of PKUNZIP.

✔ The solution: Get the latest version of PKZIP for Windows.

✔ Sometimes PKUNZIP throws up its hands in disgust, saying it "doesn't know how to handle" a zipped file. That's another way of saying you need the newest version of PKUNZIP.

✔ Dunno what version of PKUNZIP you're using? Load the program by double-clicking on a zipped file, and choose <u>A</u>bout from the <u>H</u>elp menu.

Chapter 12

Getting Rid of It!

● ●

In This Chapter

▶ Uninstalling a program from Windows the easy way

▶ Removing a program's listing from your Start button menu

● ●

*1*n a moment of clear vision, programmers made most Windows programs pretty easy to install. Just put the disk in the drive, double-click on its SETUP or INSTALL file, and the program nestles itself into your hard drive.

In fact, that's the problem. Most Windows programs nestle themselves down so comfortably that you can't get 'em *off* your hard drive even with a crowbar.

This chapter picks up where the crowbar falls down. It tells how to remove old or unwanted programs from Windows. It also tells how to remove the hidden remnants of those programs.

And as a bonus, this book also tells how to completely remove Windows itself from your hard drive, should the romance ever fail.

Why Get Rid of Old Programs?

Some people don't bother deleting old programs from Windows. But old programs should be purged from your hard drive for two reasons. First, they take up hard disk space. You have less room for the latest computer games. Plus, Windows runs more slowly on a crowded hard drive.

Second, old programs can confuse a computer. Two competing programs from a mouse or sound card can befuddle even the most expensive computer.

When you *do* choose to delete a program, just simply delete the program's Shortcut icon off your desktop, and it's gone, right? Nope. *Shortcut icons* are merely push-buttons that *start* programs. Deleting a shortcut from your desktop or menus doesn't remove the program, just like your house stays standing when the doorbell button pops off.

> ✔ Here's the bad news: Removing an old Windows program can require a lot of effort. Many Windows programs spread their files across your hard drive pretty thickly.
>
> ✔ In addition to spreading their own files around, some Windows programs also add bits and pieces of flotsam to other Windows files.
>
> ✔ Unlike Windows programs, DOS programs are usually much easier to purge from your hard drive. The steps in the next section get rid of DOS programs as well as Windows programs.

Deleting a Program the Easy Way

If you're lucky, you won't have to spend much time in this chapter. That's because certain tricks make it easier to delete programs that have outlived their usefulness. To see if you qualify, read the next three sections.

Telling Windows 95 to delete a program

Windows 95, bless its heart, comes with a delete program built in. Yep — programmers can create programs that put special hooks into the Windows 95 delete program. Then when you go to the Windows 95 Program deletion area, you can simply click on the file's name to send it scurrying off your hard drive.

But many programmers, curse their little jowls, didn't think anybody could possibly want to delete their programs. So they didn't bother to install the special hooks.

Follow the steps below to see if the program you despise is listed in the Windows 95 special deletion area.

1. **Choose Control Panel from the Start button's Settings menu.**

2. **Double-click on the Add/Remove Programs icon.**

   The Add/Remove Programs Properties window comes to the screen, as shown in Figure 12-1.

3. **Click on the name of the program you want to delete.**

4. **Click on the Add/Remove button at the screen's bottom.**

5. **Follow the instructions to remove your program.**

   That's it. Although different programs make you jump through different hoops — usually asking if you're *sure* that you want to delete such a precious program — they usually wipe themselves off your hard drive without a trace.

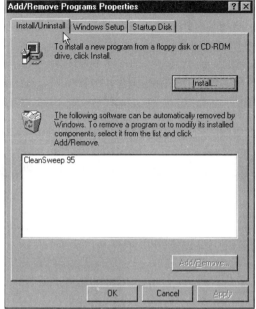

Figure 12-1:
The Add/
Remove
Programs
area lists
the
programs
that
Windows 95
can delete
automatically.

✔ If your program isn't listed in the Add/Remove Programs box, however, deletion can be a lot rougher, as you see in the rest of this chapter.

✔ Even after you delete a program, you can still put it back on your hard drive. Just run its Setup program to install it again. Chances are, you have to customize it again; all your personal settings are lost.

Telling the program to delete itself

Some programmers bypass the Windows 95 deletion program and handle matters themselves. They toss an uninstall program in with their own wares.

CompuServe's WorldsAway program, for instance, places an Uninstall WorldsAway icon right next to the icon that starts the program. When you're tired of WorldsAway, a double-click on the Uninstall icon, shown in Figure 12-2, whisks WorldsAway off your hard drive.

These custom-made uninstall programs do the best job. Because they were created by the same people who made the program, the uninstall programs know exactly what crevices of your hard drive need to be swept.

Figure 12-2:
The WorldsAway program comes with an Uninstall program.

Buying and installing an uninstall program

If your unwanted programs don't appear on Windows 95's Add/Remove Programs area and they don't come with their own uninstall program, you're not out of luck yet.

Go to the store and buy an uninstall program, such as Quarterdeck's CleanSweep 95, shown in Figure 12-3.

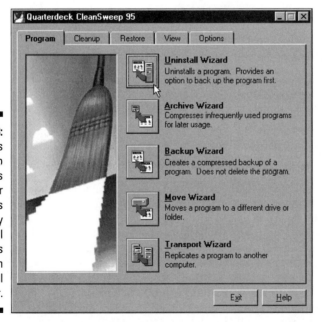

Figure 12-3:
Quarterdeck's CleanSweep 95 watches all your programs when they install themselves so it can uninstall them later.

CleanSweep and similar programs can scan your computer's hard drive for any remnants an unwanted program has left behind. In addition, many uninstall programs can find and remove parts of Windows 95 that aren't needed by your particular computer setup.

✔ CleanSweep can safely move a program from one directory to another. You can't do this by simply copying or moving that program's folder to a different location, because programs put too many claws in different parts of your hard drive. CleanSweep rounds up the claws so everything gets moved properly.

✔ Uninstall programs can seek out and destroy duplicate files from your hard drive, as well as files you haven't used in a very long time. (It can back up those files to a floppy disk for you.)

✔ If your program isn't listed on the Windows 95 Add/Remove Programs box and you don't have an uninstall program and your unwanted program didn't come with its own uninstall program, you're stuck. The rest of this chapter shows how to remove as much of the program as possible without getting into trouble.

Uninstalling a Program

Ready to shoot a varmint program off your hard drive? The next few steps show where to aim the rifle and how hard to shoot. Be sure to read all the warnings, however; you don't want to shoot in the wrong direction.

1. **Click on the Start button with your right mouse button and choose Open from the pop-up menu.**

   The My Computer program pops to the screen, as shown in Figure 12-4, displaying your Programs folder in a separate window.

Figure 12-4:
The Programs folder contains the contents of your Start button's Programs area.

2. **Double-click on your Programs folder.**

   The folder opens up, as shown in Figure 12-5, and the contents should look familiar: They're the same entries you see in the Start menu's Programs area.

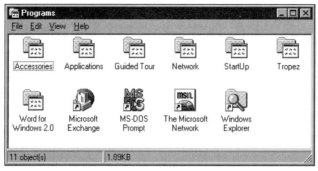

Figure 12-5:
Double-click
on the
Programs
folder to see
the contents
of your Start
menu.

3. **Locate your program's shortcut icon.**

See the shortcut icon that launches your program from the Start menu? Then move along to Step 4. If you don't spot the shortcut icon, however, keep opening the folders until you spot the icon for the program that you're trying to remove.

4. **Click on the program's shortcut icon with your right mouse button and choose P_roperties.**

When the unwanted program's Properties box comes up, click on the Shortcut tab, shown in Figure 12-6.

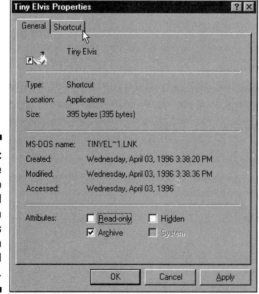

Figure 12-6:
Click on the
Shortcut tab
to find
where a
program is
located on
your hard
drive.

5. **Take note of the folders listed in the Target box.**

The Target box may still use the old DOS language, but it tells you where your file lives on your hard drive. In Figure 12-7, for example, the Tiny Elvis file lives in the Tiny Elvis folder, which lives in your Program Files folder, which is on drive C.

The Target box also spells out the program's name: TNYELVIS.EXE.

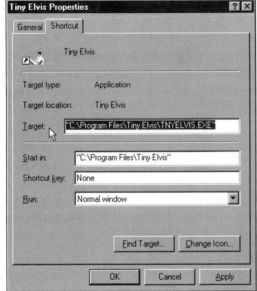

Figure 12-7:
The Target
box spells
out where
the program
lives on your
hard drive.

6. **Close the Properties window, delete the program's icon, and close down the other windows.**

You no longer need the Properties window, nor the other windows that popped up from the Start menu. Close them down with the traditional click in the upper-right corner.

Plus, because you're removing the unwanted program, it's safe to remove its icon from your Start menu with this step.

7. **Load the My Computer program.**

It's that icon on your desktop that looks like a computer (see Figure 12-8).

8. **Double-click on the drive and folders where the program lives.**

In this case, you'd click on these drives in this order: the drive C icon, the Program Files folder, and the Tiny Elvis folder.

Your program's folder appears on the desktop, revealing all its files.

Figure 12-8:
The My
Computer
icon.

9. **Choose Edit and then choose Select All.**

   Windows 95 highlights all the icons in the folder.

10. **Drag and drop the icons to the Recycle Bin.**

    Drag and drop one icon to the Recycle Bin; because all the icons are selected, they all tag along.

11. **Drag and drop the program's empty folder to the Recycle Bin.**

    That's the last bit of tidying up. You removed as much of the program as possible without getting your hands too dirty.

   ✔ When Windows starts up, sometimes it complains about not being able to find your newly deleted file. If so, head for Step 2 in the preceding list. Then open the StartUp folder. You may need to delete a shortcut to your recently deleted file from that folder.

   ✔ Even after all this uninstall hassle, bits and pieces of the program may still linger on the hard drive, cluttering up the place. Some programs toss files into your Windows directory after they're installed, but the programs don't tell you. There's simply no way of knowing which files belong to which program. Chapter 15 holds a few clues as to what file does what, but your best bet is probably to buy an uninstall program.

Installing a Program the Right Way

Chapter 2 shows how to install programs in Windows, but now's the time to repeat something:

When installing a new program, create a new folder for it and dump the new files in there.

As you can see from this chapter, this simple step makes the program a *lot* easier to get rid of later if you decide that it really stinks.

What is this "C:\Program Files\Tiny Elvis\ TNYELVIS.EXE" stuff?

When you click on the Shortcut box in Step 5 of the preceding steps, the Target box says that your Tiny Elvis program lives in this area of your hard drive: C:\Program Files\Tiny Elvis\TNYELVIS.EXE. Those words are old-DOS computer code for the program's *path*, which boils down to the following:

✔ The C: part stands for drive C:, the hard drive. DOS likes to see colons after letters when it's talking about hard drives.

✔ The \Program Files part stands for the Program Files folder on the hard drive. DOS likes to put a \, commonly called a *backslash*, between directories and between hard drive letters and directories.

✔ The \Tiny Elvis part stands for the Tiny Elvis folder, complete with the mandatory backslash.

✔ Finally, the TNYELVIS.EXE part stands for the Tiny Elvis program file. (It, too, needs a backslash to separate it from the folder behind it.)

This complicated DOS structural stuff pops up in Windows 95 every once in a while. It's there to remind you that Windows 95 is merely the latest layer of flesh riding uncomfortably over some particularly sharp DOS bones.

Removing a Program's Name from the Start Button Menu

The first few steps of the "Uninstalling a Program" section show how to remove a program's icon from the Start button. But if you just want to know the quickest way possible, follow these steps:

1. Click on the Start button with your right mouse button and choose Explore.

The Explorer program hops to the screen, displaying your Start button's menu. The Start button menu is really just a folder full of shortcuts called "Start Menu" that lives in your Windows folder.

2. Double-click on the Programs folder.

Explorer opens up the Programs folder, shown in Figure 12-9, to reveal all the categories on your Start menu.

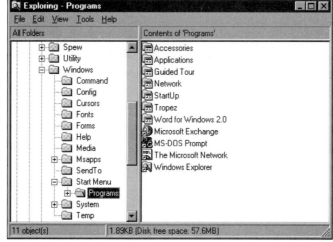

Figure 12-9:
The Start
button menu
is merely a
folder full of
shortcuts
in your
Windows
folder.

3. **Find the shortcut for the program that you want to delete from the Start menu.**

   You may need to double-click on some of the folders to find the program's shortcut icon, especially if that program is buried deep within your Start menu.

4. **Delete the shortcut.**

   Click on the shortcut icon and press the Delete key. Or drag and drop the icon to the Recycle Bin. Either way, you've effectively trimmed that icon off your Start menu.

   ✔ While you have the Start menu open and ready to be rearranged, feel free to move your folders around to organize them. For example, you can create a new folder for your CDs, and drag and drop all the Start menu's icons for your compact disc programs into that folder.

   ✔ To make a program start itself automatically whenever Windows 95 starts up, move its shortcut icon into the Program folder's StartUp folder.

Chapter 13

Making Games (er, DOS Programs) Run Right

• •

In This Chapter

▶ Understanding .PIFs

▶ Deciding when a .PIF is necessary

▶ Writing your own .PIFs

▶ Filling out a DOS program's Properties form

• •

*T*he word *.PIF* sounds like a dainty sneeze, suppressed politely in a crowded elevator. But .PIFs carry a *lot* more impact on your computer. Basically, a *.PIF* (Program Information File) is the DOS version of a common Windows 95 shortcut — it tells Windows 95 where the DOS program lives on your hard drive.

But a .PIF gives Windows much more information than that. By telling Windows 95 all about a DOS program's nutritional requirements, a .PIF can fool cranky old DOS programs and high-powered DOS games into running under Windows.

To create a .PIF, Windows 95 makes you fill out a form uglier than a health insurance claim. This chapter points out which parts of the .PIF form you can safely ignore and which parts you need to play with in order to convince a reluctant DOS game, er, business program, to run under Windows 95.

What's a .PIF?

Windows 95 is designed to run flashy new *Windows 95* programs. But some Windows users can't give up their favorite DOS programs of yesteryear. Plus, most of the best computer games are still DOS programs — Windows simply can't provide the graphics horsepower needed for quick 'n' dirty blast-em-ups.

Luckily, most DOS programs work just fine under Windows 95. If the program *doesn't* work, however, you need to do the work: You need to fill out a Program Information File. Like a chart hanging on a hospital bed, the .PIF contains special instructions for Windows on how to treat that DOS program.

- Because Windows has grown so popular, many new DOS programs come packaged with a .PIF in their folder, free of charge. The .PIF icon almost always looks like an MS-DOS Prompt icon with a shortcut. If you find one, you're safe: Just double-click on it, and the program should take off.

- Also, Windows 95 automatically creates a .PIF for the more than 400 DOS programs it can recognize.

- A .PIF is really just a fancy Windows 95 shortcut. It not only serves as a button for starting the program, but it tells Windows 95 how to treat the program once the program gets moving.

- A program's .PIF usually sounds just like the program, but ends with the letters PIF. For example, a .PIF for your Blastoid program would be called Blastoid.PIF.

- To see what extensions are tacked onto your files, choose Options from the View menu of My Computer or Explorer. Click the File Types tab and make sure that there's no check mark in the box that says Hide MS-DOS file extensions for file types that are registered.

- To load your DOS program, double-click on its PIF *shortcut,* not the program. For example, to load Blastoid, double-click on Blastoid.PIF — not Blastoid.exe.

- Or if you — or the program's installation program — puts the DOS program's icon on your Start menu, that icon should refer to the program's .PIF. For example, the icon for your Blastoid program should refer to Blastoid.PIF, not Blastoid.exe. (Programs almost always put their proper .PIF on your Start menu, so you usually don't need to worry about this one.)

Do I Really Need a .PIF?

Most DOS programs aren't picky enough to require a .PIF. To find out whether your DOS program needs a .PIF, take this simple test:

Try to run the DOS program from within Windows.

If your program runs fine, you're safe. Ignore this chapter and concentrate on more important things, like whether it's time to switch to whole wheat English muffins. If your DOS program didn't run — or it ran kinda funny — stick around; this chapter might help out.

✔ .PIFs can fine-tune a DOS program's performance. For example, a .PIF can make a DOS program start up in a window rather than filling the whole screen. (Be forewarned, however: Some DOS programs refuse to be squeezed into a window — even with the most powerful .PIF.)

✔ By fiddling with a program's .PIF, you can make the program run smoother, as well as clean up after itself: No empty window for you to close when the program says it's "Finished" running.

Creating a DOS Program's .PIF

Creating a program's .PIF is easy. Simply fill out the program's Properties form: To turn an option on, click in its little box within the form. An X appears inside the box to indicate that the option is turned on. Click in the box again to turn that option off.

So what's the hard part? Deciding which boxes to click in. Because the Properties form is designed to handle rough DOS problems, it forces you to play arbitrator among the ugliest DOS disputes: memory access, DOS modes, and equally unfriendly geek turf. A .PIF is loaded with bizarre terms like *Fast ROM Emulation* and *Dynamic Memory Allocation*.

To begin filling out a DOS program's Properties form, click on the program's icon with your right mouse button and then choose Properties from the pop-up menu. The program's Properties form appears, as shown in Figure 13-1.

The Properties form consists of six sections, all marked along the top with their own tab: General, Program, Font, Memory, Screen, and Misc. The next few sections explain which parts of the form you need to worry about and which ones can be safely ignored.

Figure 13-1:
Click the
program's
icon with
your right
mouse
button and
choose
Properties
to begin
filling out
its form.

Help! Forgot what does what? Then click on the little question mark in the Properties box's upper-right corner. A question mark fastens itself to your mouse pointer. Now click in the confusing area, as shown in Figure 13-2. Windows 95 brings up a snippet of helpful information, as shown in Figure 13-3, explaining the purpose of that box or button.

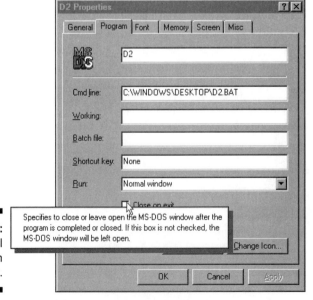

Figure 13-2:
Click on the question mark in the upper-right corner and then click on a confusing part of the Properties screen.

Figure 13-3:
And helpful information appears.

The General tab

The General tab, shown along the top of the Properties form, provides basic information about the program: The program's name and size; the folder it's living in; and the date the program was created, changed, or last accessed. (Merely calling up the program's Properties makes Windows 95 access the program, so the access date is always the current date.)

The most common use for the General tab? Simply to see the program's name listed under the MS-DOS name section, as shown in Figure 13-4.

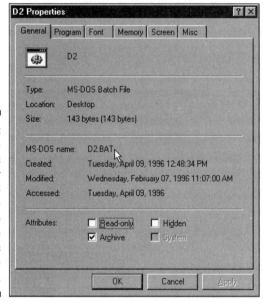

Figure 13-4: Check the program's name under the MS-DOS name section to find out the program's file extension.

To make sure that you're filling out the form for the right program, look at the name listed under MS-DOS name. If that name ends in the letters BAT, EXE, or COM, you're okay. If it ends in anything else, you're probably filling out the Properties form for the wrong program.

Don't fiddle with a program's Attributes settings unless you're absolutely sure what you're doing. Windows 95 can become seriously confused and spread that confusion around to its users.

Boring attributes

Files come with four special toggle switches known as *attributes*. The General tab lets you toggle all four of these attributes either on or off.

Read-only: A check mark in this box means that the file can be read, but not changed and saved. Click this tab on important files that you don't want changed accidentally. If you try to delete a Read-only file, Windows 95 warns you that you're about to delete an important, Read-only file.

Although Windows 95 warns you when you try to delete Read-only files by pressing the Delete key, it won't warn you if you drag and drop the file into the Recycle Bin. Be careful.

Archive: An attribute you probably won't ever have to mess with. The Archive toggle is used by some backup programs to decide whether or not that file should be backed up. A check mark usually means the backup program has slated that file for backup.

Hidden: Sneaky ol' Windows 95 likes to hide files from its users. Most of the time, it's hiding boring program information you don't need to see anyway. But a check mark in this box makes a file disappear from your desktop, My Computer, and Explorer programs.

Windows 95 can let you see files, even if they've been set as Hidden through their attributes. Simply choose Options from a window's View menu, click on the View tab, and click on the Show all files button.

System: Windows 95 doesn't even let you play with this attribute, which it reserves for its holy System files. Windows 95 needs these files to run properly, so don't mess with them.

The Program tab

The Program tab, shown in Figure 13-5, moves quickly into some of the more complicated areas. It starts out easy, though: Type the name of the program into the box next to its icon near the top-left corner of the screen.

Cmd line: Short for command line, this is what you'd be expected to type into your computer if it ran under DOS. That means you'd type your program's *path* — a collection of folder names leading to the program's location on your hard drive — followed by the program's name. (See Chapter 12 for more information about paths.)

Working: Does the program load its program files from folders other than its own? Then list those folders in here, using the same syntax as shown in the Cmd line box. (Leave this blank for most programs.)

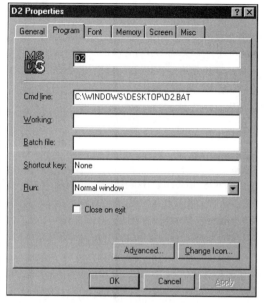

Figure 13-5:
The
Program tab
contains
some of the
more
advanced
areas for
tweaking
DOS
programs.

Batch file: This lets you run a batch file before your DOS program takes charge. Batch files are strings of DOS commands — the kinds of things you find in Dan Gookin's superb *MORE DOS For Dummies* book (published by IDG Books Worldwide, Inc.). Be sure and read his last chapter.

Shortcut key: A shortcut key lets you quickly start a program at the touch of a key — no mousing through menus required. For example, you could assign Ctrl+Alt+! to a favorite DOS program. Then press Ctrl+Alt+! to automatically load the program and bring it to the screen. Be careful that you don't assign the same shortcut keys to different programs, though, or Windows will get confused.

Run: This defines whether the program starts running in a normal window, a maximized window, or in minimized mode along your taskbar.

Close on exit: After they've finished running, most DOS programs just sit in a window, saying "Finished" across their top. To make them clean up after themselves, closing their empty window automatically, click in this box.

Change Icon: Click here to choose a different icon. (Chapter 3 shows where to find some doozies.)

Advanced: Here's where things get sticky, as you can see in Figure 13-6. Basically, this area allows you to choose between three modes:

✔ **Prevent MS-DOS-based programs from detecting Windows:** Some DOS programs didn't like earlier versions of Windows. So before those programs ran, they'd check to see if Windows was running in the background. If they found Windows, the DOS programs wouldn't run. Checking this box keeps those DOS programs from finding a version of Windows in the background so they'll be more apt to run under Windows 95.

✔ **Suggest MS-DOS mode as necessary:** This setting tells Windows to detect whether the program could run better in MS-DOS mode. If so, it switches to MS-DOS mode automatically.

✔ **MS-DOS mode:** Choosing this one is like choosing Shut Down and Restart in MS-DOS mode from the Start button. No other programs run in the background, and your DOS program has the computer to itself. If you choose MS-DOS mode, the following four options become available as well:

- **Warn before entering MS-DOS mode:** Check here, and Windows 95 warns you before closing down all programs and entering MS-DOS mode.

- **Use current MS-DOS configuration:** Windows normally uses your normal AUTOEXEC.BAT and CONFIG.SYS files to run your DOS program, so this box is normally checked.

- **Specify a new MS-DOS configuration:** The opposite of the listing above, this one lets you add a few lines to your AUTOEXEC.BAT or CONFIG.SYS files.

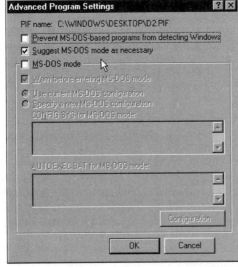

Figure 13-6:
The Advanced area lets you choose between three modes for running DOS programs.

• **Configuration:** This handy button lets you choose some convenient DOS options to be loaded automatically whenever your new MS-DOS configuration takes effect.

The Font tab

Not much to talk about here, especially because you can change all this "on-the-fly" while the program's running. But click on the Font tab, shown in Figure 13-7, to choose the size of the letters you want the program to use when displaying text in a window.

✔ Normally, you want to stick with TrueType fonts because they have fewer jagged edges than the Bitmap fonts. Click on a font size in the Font size window, and the Font preview window below shows you what your choice looks like.

✔ If you choose Auto in the Font size window, Windows 95 will automatically make the fonts shrink or grow, depending on what size looks best in your window. In fact, Windows will even change the font's size as you change the size of the window. (That's why you can usually stick with the Auto setting and not have to bother with all this stuff.)

✔ To choose a different font while your program's running, click on the button with the big letter A along the top of the program's window. The Font page appears, letting you change the size of the letters used in the program.

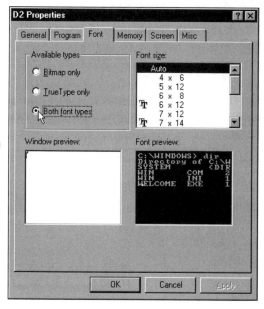

Figure 13-7:
The Font tab lets you change the size of fonts used by text-based DOS programs.

The Memory tab

Although this page looks like a doozy, as shown in Figure 13-8, you don't have much to fill out. You almost always want to leave every setting set to Auto. Windows is usually smart enough to dole out memory in the right proportions, and if Windows can't guess right, then you should be running that program in MS-DOS mode, anyway.

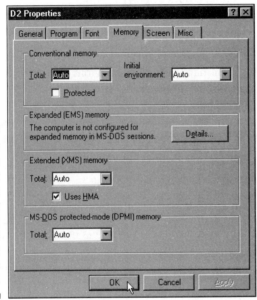

Figure 13-8:
You can usually get away with leaving everything set to Auto in the Memory tab area.

If your DOS program makes Windows crash a lot, try clicking in the Protected box in the Conventional memory area. That can keep DOS programs from trying to grab at parts of your computer memory that Windows likes to hang onto.

The Screen tab

Although DOS programs normally take the whole screen for themselves, they can run in windows on your desktop, just like real Windows programs. There are a few differences, though, and the Screen tab, shown in Figure 13-9, lets you fiddle with them.

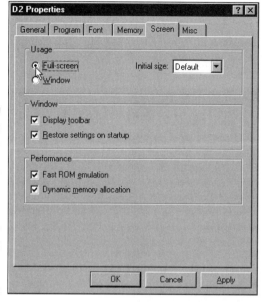

Figure 13-9:
The Screen
tab lets you
determine
how the
screen
should run
in a window
or if it
should run
full-screen.

Usage: Click on the Full-screen option, and the program takes the entire screen when it runs, just like normal. Choose Window, by contrast, to make the program run itself in a window upon startup.

Initial size gets a little trickier. Although most text-based DOS programs show 25 lines of text when they arrive on the screen, others can handle more. If your computer's video card can show more than 25 lines of text on the screen, you can change this setting to two other common modes: 43 lines and 50 lines. (Not all DOS programs can handle these modes, though — your video card and program both need to cooperate in order for anything magic to happen. Otherwise, nothing happens.)

Window: Want Windows to display that handy toolbar across the top — those little buttons for quickly cutting and pasting, adjusting font size, changing properties, and more? Choose the Display toolbar option. The other option, Restore settings on startup, means that the program always reverts to the settings stored in its PIF, no matter how much you changed them the last time the program ran.

Performance: Word processors often run faster if the Fast ROM emulation box is checked. But if something goes wrong — the mouse acts up or garbage appears on the screen — change it back. DOS programs that don't switch between graphics and text modes can have the Dynamic memory allocation box checked, leaving a little extra memory free for other programs to share.

The Misc tab

A plethora of potpourri, shown in Figure 13-10, the Misc tab contains unrelated switches that really don't fit anywhere else.

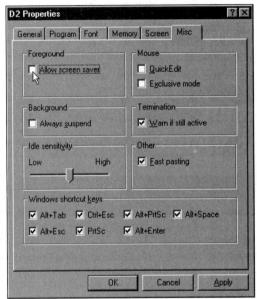

Figure 13-10: The Misc tab contains unrelated settings that don't fit anywhere else.

Foreground: Do you want your screen saver to pop up in your DOS program? Then click in the Allow screen saver box. An unchecked box leaves your screen saver disabled.

Background: Check the Always suspend box, and the DOS program stops working when you switch back to Windows.

Don't choose this mode when running any DOS-based communications programs, or you might lose your connection or data.

Idle sensitivity: Windows is a merry-go-round of simultaneously running programs. As it constantly divvies up its attention to each program, it constantly checks to see if the DOS program is busy. Setting Idle sensitivity to Low keeps Windows from constantly checking to see if it can sap resources from the DOS program. The result? The DOS program runs faster. Setting Idle sensitivity to High makes the DOS program run more slowly because Windows is always tapping on its shoulder.

Mouse: If your DOS program doesn't use the mouse, choose QuickEdit. Then you can copy and paste information from your DOS window without having to click on any buttons on the toolbar. If your DOS program uses the mouse, though, don't check this box. If your DOS program not only uses the mouse but has to have complete control over it, choose Exclusive mode. This mode doesn't let Windows use the mouse while the DOS program's in the forefront, but hey, at least your DOS program will be able to use it.

Termination: Done with your DOS program? The Good DOS User always shuts down the DOS program the right way — by pressing the keys that tell the DOS program to shut down. Lazy Windows users often click on the DOS window's upper-right corner to close the DOS program, however. Because jerking DOS programs off their feet like that isn't very nice, Windows 95 sends a terse message asking if you're sure that you saved your work and that you know what you're doing. To make Windows stop sending this message, click on the Warn if still active box.

Other: Some DOS programs never expected people to type faster than 85 words per minute. Windows can squirt information into a DOS program much faster than that, however. If your DOS program has trouble keeping up with the flow, remove the check mark from the Fast pasting box.

Windows shortcut keys: Windows uses a bunch of keystrokes for performing certain tasks. Pressing Ctrl+Esc brings up the Start menu, for example; pressing Alt+Tab cycles through your currently open programs. But if a DOS program tries to use those same keystrokes, you're in trouble. To break up the conflicts, click in the boxes next to the keystrokes that you want to reserve for the DOS program. The remaining boxes — the ones with the check marks — are keystrokes that Windows 95 gets to use.

What Should I Fiddle with If This Happens?

Don't want to search through the rules in the previous section to find a quick answer? Maybe you'll get lucky and find help in the sections below.

My DOS program wants its own AUTOEXEC.BAT and CONFIG.SYS file!

When Windows 95 puts itself into MS-DOS mode to accommodate DOS programs, it loads the two mainstays of DOS-dom: The AUTOEXEC.BAT and CONFIG.SYS files. In a funky, bare-bones language, the files tell the computer what devices are attached to it, how to manage its memory, and how to treat the programs that are about to run.

Normally, Windows 95 uses "default" AUTOEXEC.BAT and CONFIG.SYS files that live in the root directory of drive C. And, normally, those files are all that you need. But if a DOS program gets picky and needs specific settings in those AUTOEXEC.BAT or CONFIG.SYS files, you can put those settings in the program's .PIF.

Then when you load the program and Windows jumps into DOS mode, it uses that program's own special version of AUTOEXEC.BAT and CONFIG.SYS. When the program's running and Windows 95 comes back to life, everything's back to normal.

✔ In fact, you can set up a different set of AUTOEXEC.BAT and CONFIG.SYS files for all your DOS programs.

✔ How? Head for the Advanced button on the PIF's Program tab, click in the MS-DOS mode check box, click in the Specify a new MS-DOS configuration box, and start customizing the program's settings in the boxes.

✔ DOS program memory management can be terribly complicated, however. If your particular game doesn't specifically state what settings to use, you might want to check out Dan Gookin's excellent *MORE DOS For Dummies* (published by IDG Books Worldwide, Inc.).

My DOS game won't work!

Check the following settings carefully; DOS games seem to be the most sensitive to them.

✔ Try clicking on the Start button, choosing Shut Down, and choosing Restart the computer in MS-DOS mode. Then run your program as if you were in DOS. That's usually your best chance of success.

✔ In the .PIF's Advanced Program Settings box, choose Prevent MS-DOS based programs from detecting Windows. Some DOS games actually look into your computer's memory to see if you have Windows running in the background. If they see any signs of Windows, they refuse to load. This box keeps Windows hidden.

✔ In the Screen menu, make sure that you've checked Full-screen. Most DOS programs insist on running in full-screen mode, and some can't even handle Windows' slight delay while it switches them to full-screen mode. Choosing this mode from the start avoids potential problems.

✔ Under the Misc tab, don't click on Always suspend, slide the Idle sensitivity lever to Low, and make sure that you're not reserving any Windows shortcut keys that your DOS game could be using.

Chapter 14

Windows 95 Programs to Rush Out and Buy

*W*indows 95 is an enormous program, consuming up to 70MB of your hard drive, if you let it. But after buying Windows 95, the first thing many people want to do is buy even *more* Windows 95 programs. This chapter covers a few of the most popular and useful Windows 95 programs lining the shelves.

Microsoft Plus!

Microsoft Plus! is a wimpy little program dubbed the "Companion for Windows 95." But that huge Microsoft marketing muscle isn't the only reason it's selling up a storm. Microsoft Plus! is almost irresistibly cute, as shown in Figure 14-1, with wallpaper ranging from Leonardo da Vinci to cute animals.

Figure 14-1:
Microsoft Plus! comes with a variety of wallpaper matched with appropriate sound schemes.

✔ The program's most fun comes from its "Themes," a pre-packaged bundle of wallpaper with matching sounds and fonts. By switching between Themes, you can make your computer match your day's mood.

✔ Another Plus! program, System Agent, goes through your computer when you're not using it (usually at night) and organizes your hard drive's structure. Basically, it moves the way files are stored so the computer can find them a little faster. You won't notice any difference — your files stay in the same folders, for example — but the System Agent's *defragmentation* helps keep your system running smoothly.

✔ Microsoft Plus! also comes with Internet Explorer, a program that can access the Internet — if you pay a monthly fee to a company called an Internet provider. It's extremely difficult to set up, however, unless you use Microsoft's own Internet provider service. (The competition's quite upset about it, actually, and you'll find more information about the Internet Explorer in Chapter 6.)

✔ No, Microsoft didn't scan in Leonardo's artwork backwards when creating the wallpaper and screen saver for its da Vinci Theme. The versatile Italian genius often wrote backwards, considering it to be a crude form of cryptography. (Check out his backwards signature in Figure 14-1.)

Don't throw away the packaging for your Microsoft Plus! CD. Chances are, it comes with a little sticker called a "CD key." You need to type in this key every time you re-install the software.

Mastersoft's Viewer 95

If you have the CD version of Windows 95, you can use *Quick View* — a program that lets you peek inside a file and see its contents without having to load the program that created the file. Just right-click on the file's icon and choose Quick View from the pop-up menu.

Quick View's incredibly handy when you're trying to peek inside one of the 30 types of files Quick View supports. But if you try to peek inside a file that's not recognized, you're stuck: Quick View won't even appear as an option on the menu.

A solution exists, though, and it's called Viewer 95 by Mastersoft. A true powerhouse, Viewer 95 lets you peek inside 250 different file formats, just like Quick View. Viewer 95 works like Quick View, too, so there's nothing extra to figure out. Click on Quick View from the menu, just like before, and Viewer 95 appears, ready to show you the file's contents.

Figure 14-2, for example, shows Viewer 95 peering into a JPEG file, a popular format for strong graphics.

Figure 14-2: Mastersoft's Viewer 95 picks up where Quick View leaves off, letting you view files saved in 250 different formats.

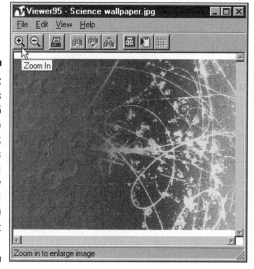

- ✔ Viewer 95 fleshes out Quick View in some other ways, too. For example, it lets you search for text within a file — something Quick View can't handle.

- ✔ Viewer 95 even lets you convert some files from format to format. It can convert Word for Windows files to WordPerfect or AmiPro files — even if you don't have any of those programs.

- ✔ The program handles graphics files, as well as text files. And once you have any file open for viewing on the screen, the file can be copied, deleted, renamed, moved, compared to other files, printed, or saved.

Uninstall Programs

Windows 95 comes with its own Uninstall program. Just click on the Control Panel's Add/Remove Programs icon, and Windows 95 lists the programs it can remove automatically.

However, people are still snapping up uninstall programs for Windows 95, making these programs some of the most popular on the market. Why? Two reasons. First, many companies ignore the Windows 95 Uninstall feature. After all, who would possibly want to uninstall their fine software? So software companies don't write the uninstall stuff necessary for their program to appear on Windows 95's Uninstall menu.

Second, many uninstall programs can do more than simply wipe an unwanted program off your hard drive. Quarterdeck's CleanSweep 95, for example, can purge your hard drive of programs that have lost their charm. But it can also weed out duplicate files from your hard drive to reclaim storage space. It can compress files you don't use very often, once again freeing up valuable hard drive space.

Plus, CleanSweep 95 can move programs to other folders on your computer, as shown in Figure 14-3, something that Windows 95 usually can't handle by itself.

- ✔ Even if you think that you've uninstalled a program yourself by deleting its main folder, you probably haven't pried all of the program out of its hiding places. Remember — Windows programs tend to spread bits and pieces of themselves in a wide variety of folders and special areas. Only an uninstall program knows where to look and what to remove.

- ✔ In fact, some uninstall programs take careful notes as your new programs install themselves, as shown in Figure 14-4. Then when you're ready to dump a program, the uninstaller looks at its notes to decide what files stay and what files go.

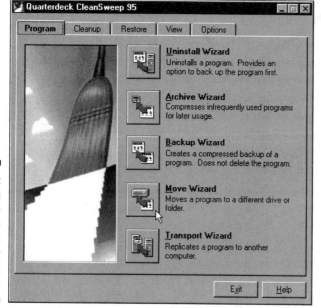

Figure 14-3:
Quarterdeck's
CleanSweep
95 can do
much more
than other
uninstall
programs.

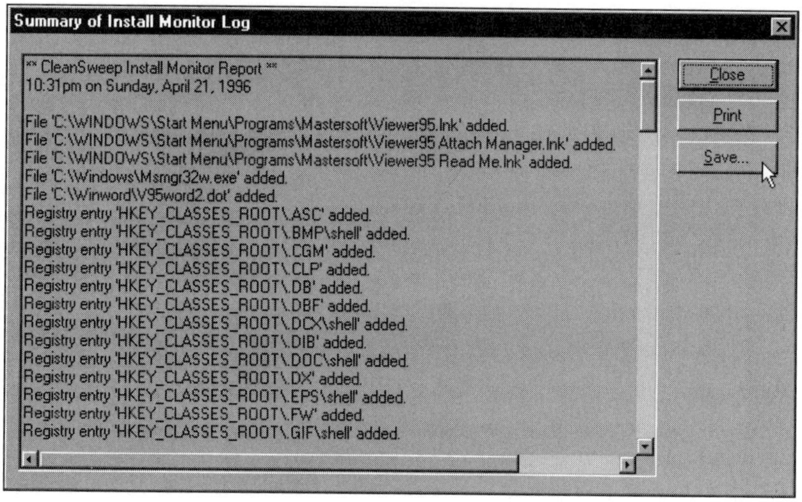

Figure 14-4:
CleanSweep
95 takes
detailed
notes as to
how an
incoming
program
changes
your system
so that
removing
the program
is easier
later down
the road.

Norton Utilities

A computing mainstay for years, Norton Utilities has helped millions of users out of their computing mishaps. Norton Utilities isn't really a program; it's a bundle of programs designed to do the things that your operating system doesn't. When your computer can't undelete a file, for example, Norton Utilities can pull it back from the abyss.

Damaged data on the hard drive? Norton can usually salvage at least part of the good stuff. Now, even though Windows 95 provides many of the utilities Norton came up with a decade ago, the program still comes in handy.

 ✔ Windows 95 comes with some of the same types of programs that Norton Utilities does. Windows 95 can scan your disk, defragment it, and undelete your files. But Norton's tools invariably work better, faster, and more reliably.

 ✔ Even if you don't fiddle with your computer much, a copy of Norton Utilities on your hard disk makes your computer easier to repair when a friend comes over to help get you out of a jam. Your friend can read Norton's records of where data is stored on your hard drive and have better odds at recovering it.

Microsoft's PowerToys (And It's Free!)

Microsoft's programmers simply couldn't be stopped. After they slaved away to whip out Windows 95, the momentum kept rolling. So they released PowerToys — a collection of Windows 95 "tweak" programs for more advanced users. Although PowerToys are created and copyrighted by Microsoft, they're given away for free. That means Microsoft won't give you any help if you can't get them to work right.

Here's a description of each of the PowerToys and what it can do:

 ✔ **TweakUI:** A handy control panel clone for perpetual fiddlers, TweakUI lets you adjust menu speed, mouse sensitivity, window animation and sound, shortcut appearance and default names, and which icons appear on your desktop. TweakUI lets you create new templates, adjust boot parameters, including whether or not to start the graphic user interface, and more.

 ✔ **Fast Folder:** When you right-click on a folder or any other file container, you get a cascading menu that shows you all the contents of the folder, one-level deep. (Yes, the program works on a folder's shortcut, too.)

- ✔ **FlexiCD:** This taskbar notification icon simplifies controlling audio CDs. When you're listening to Chet Atkins, FlexiCD gives you single-click play/pause control, a list of which track and time you're on, and a right-click menu that provides commands for starting, stopping, ejecting, and moving around the tracks on your CD.

- ✔ **CAB File Viewer:** You know those annoying *.CAB files on the Win95 CD and floppies? (These files contain Microsoft's new file compression technique that renders the disk unreadable by everything but their own installation program.) The CAB File Viewer shell extension lets you browse into a CAB file and see all of its contents, as well as fiddle with the files inside.

- ✔ **Round Clock:** This version of Clock simply puts a round clock on your screen. That's it. (But it sure looks cool.)

- ✔ **Explore from Here:** Ever been browsing from folder to folder and suddenly wished you could switch into the Explorer mode and continue to browse? This puts an Explore from Here option on the right-click menu of your folders.

- ✔ **Shortcut Target Menu:** Normally when you click on a shortcut and choose Properties, you get the shortcut's properties — not the properties of the program that the shortcut launches. This option lets you get the properties for a shortcut's target just by right-clicking the shortcut.

- ✔ **XMOUSE:** Here's how Microsoft describes it: "For all of the CS majors in the audience — make the focus follow the mouse without clicking, a la X Windows. *TIP:* To turn it off, use the Control Panel."

- ✔ **QuickRes:** This lets you change your screen resolution and colors without having to reboot. Yay!

You can find PowerToys on CompuServe's Windows News forum (GO WINNEW), as well as a few other online services. (Just search for PowerToys.)

Although the toys come packaged in one file, you can weed out the stuff you don't like after you've downloaded it. (You don't have to keep *everything* if you just want the cool clock, for example.)

Chapter 15

Are These Files Important?

*A*fter about a year or so, that familiar ring of keys comes to life and begins burrowing a hole through a pants pocket. The solution, quite simply, is to get rid of some of the keys.

But which keys? What's this key for? The old apartment? The coffee machine cabinet in the *old* office? Did this key work on the *old* bike lock? Does this key open *anything*?

This chapter shows how to separate the important Windows files from all the junk Windows files living on your hard drive. You'll discover which of those suspicious-looking Windows files are important and which ones can be peeled off and tossed aside.

What's This File For?

Although computers may seem like bundles of geekisms, they're *organized* bundles of geekisms.

For example, most Windows programs tack three letters onto every file they create. Whenever Notepad saves information in a file, that file's name ends in the letters TXT. Called an *extension*, those three letters serve as a file's thumbprint: Those extensions, as well as the file's icon, identify which culprit created which file.

Windows 95, unlike its previous versions, normally hides a file's extensions. To make Windows 95 display them all the time, choose Options from the View menu of either My Computer or Explorer. Then remove the check mark from the box labeled Hide MS-DOS file extensions for file types that are registered.

To quickly look at a file's extension without messing with the Options section, click on the file with your right mouse button and choose Properties. In the MS-DOS name area, as shown in Figure 15-1, the file's last three letters reveal its extension.

Figure 15-1:
The last three letters listed in the MS-DOS name area are a file's extension, which Windows 95 uses to determine what program created what file.

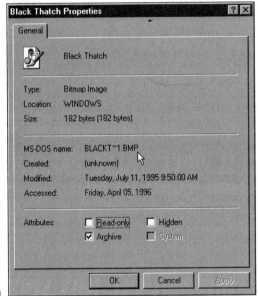

Table 15-1 identifies some of the most common file extensions you may spot on your hard drive, as well as their icons and creators.

Table 15-1 Who Dunnit? Which Programs Use Which Extension?

Files Ending Like This ...	Usually Do This
.3GR	Short for *grabber*, this helps Windows display text and graphics.
.ANI	Short for Animated, these contain special "whirling" mouse pointers.

Files Ending Like This ...	*Usually Do This*
.AVI	Contain movies in a special format that's playable through Media Player. (You don't need any special hardware to view the movies, but movie *makers* usually need expensive *video grabbing* cards.)
.BAT	Short for *batch* files, these contain lists of DOS commands, including commands to load DOS programs. (Rarely used in Windows.)
.BFC	Short for *briefcase*, these contain a Briefcase full of files to move back and forth between a desktop computer and laptop. (See Chapter 5.)
.BMP	Short for *bitmap*, these contain pictures or illustrations, usually created by Paint.
.CAL	Short for calendar, these contain appointments created by Calendar, a calendar program that came with older versions of Windows.
.CBT	Short for *Computer Based Training*, these usually contain tutorials for Microsoft products.
.CDA	Short for *CD Audio Track*, these stand for the songs playable by CD Player.
.CPE	Fax cover sheets for the Fax Cover Page Editor.
.COM	Short for *command*, these almost always contain DOS programs.
.CRD	Short for *card*, these contain the names and addresses created by Cardfile — a program that came with the old version of Windows.
.CUR	Short for *cursor*, these contain animated cursors that can be changed along with your mouse settings.
.DAT	Short for *data*, these usually contain information for programs, not people, to peruse.
.DLL	Short for *Dynamic Link Library*, these are like miniprograms. Other programs often peek at these .DLL files for help when they're working.
.DOC	Short for *document*, these usually contain text stored by a word processor. Microsoft Word saves files ending in .DOC, for example. Unfortunately, a .DOC file created by one word processor can't always be opened by another word processor.

(continued)

Table 15-1 *(continued)*

Files Ending Like This ...	Usually Do This
.DRV	Short for *driver*, these files help Windows talk to parts of your computer like its keyboard, monitor, and various internal gadgetry.
.EPS	Short for *Encapsulated PostScript* file, these contain information to be printed on *PostScript* printers. PostScript is a special format for expensive printers to read and print information created by expensive PostScript-compatible programs.
.EXE	Short for *executable*, these contain programs. Almost *all* Windows programs end in .EXE; most DOS programs do, too.
.FLI	These files contain animation — high-tech cartoon/ movies — often made with programs by a company called Autodesk. They're not compatible with .AVI, so you can't watch 'em in Media Player. (See .AVI.)
.FND	Short for *Find*, these contain a list of the files turned up through a search using the Start menu's Find program.
.FON	A font that's not *TrueType* compatible (see .TTF). Windows uses these fonts mostly for its menus, error messages, and other system information.
.GIF	Short for *Graphic Interchange File*, these contain pictures stored in a space-saving format invented by modem hounds on CompuServe. Paint can't view GIFs, although several shareware Windows programs can.
.GRP	Short for *group*, these files let Program Manager — a remnant from Windows 3.1 — remember which icons belong in which of its groups. When you double-click on a .GRP file, Windows 95 displays the contents in a My Computer window.
.HLP	Short for *help*, these contain the helpful information that pops up when you press F1 or choose Help from a program's menu.
.HT	Short for *HyperTerminal*, these contain the settings HyperTerminal uses for dialing up other computers with your modem.
.ICO	Short for *icon*, these contain — you guessed it — icons. (See Chapter 3.)

Files Ending Like This ...	Usually Do This
.IDF	Short for *Instrument Definition File,* these contain the settings Media Player uses with your sound card or synthesizer.
.INF	Short for *information*, these usually contain text for programs, not humans. Programs often grab information from .INF files when they're first installed. For example, a file called OEMSETUP.INF often lives on a program's floppy disk; Windows looks at the OEMSETUP.INF file for help when installing that program's drivers and other special goodies.
.INI	Short for *initialization*, these files contain code-filled text for programs to use, usually so they can remember any special options a user has chosen. Unlike .INF files, described above, humans can fiddle with an .INI file's content to make programs work better — or worse.
.JPG	Short for *JPEG*, these contain pictures, similar to files ending in .GIF, .BMP, and .PCX. Paint can't view them, but several shareware viewers can. (See Chapter 7.)
.MID	Short for *MIDI*, these files tell sound cards or synthesizers to play musical notes in a certain order. If everything goes right, the musical notes sound like a pretty song. (See Chapter 3.)
.MPG	Short for *MPEG*, these are just like .JPG files except they contain movies. Nope, Media Player can't view them, but some other Windows programs can.
.MSG	Short for Mail Message, these contain messages sent or received over the Exchange program. (See Chapter 6.)
.MOV	Short for *Movie*, this contains a QuickTime file — the format Apple Macintosh computers use to store their files. Windows 95 can't view them; you need to get a QuickTime movie player program. (See Chapter 7.)
.PCX	These contain pictures viewable in Paint. Paint can't save pictures in this format, however.
.PIF	Short for *Program Information File*, these contain special instructions for Windows to treat DOS programs. (See Chapter 13.)

(continued)

Table 15-1 *(continued)*

Files Ending Like This ...	Usually Do This
.RTF	Short for *Rich Text Format*, these contain ASCII text with special codes. The codes let different brands of word processors swap files without losing groovy stuff like margins or italics. (Used by WordPad, Microsoft Word for Windows, and many other programs.)
.SCR	Short for *screen*, these files contain a screen saver program. Copy .SCR files to your Windows folder, and they appear on the Screen Saver menu in Control Panel's Desktop area. (Chapter 3 offers much more elaborate instructions.)
.SHB	Short for *shortcut*, this file contains the information on how to access another file on your computer.
.SHS	Short for *scrap*, this file contains a chunk of another file that's been dragged and dropped out of another program. For instance, if you highlight a paragraph in Word, then drag and drop that paragraph onto your desktop, the paragraph will be saved as a scrap on the desktop.
.SYS	Short for *system*, these contain information designed for your computer or its programs — not for humans.
.TMP	Short for *temporary*. Some Windows programs stash occasional notes in a file, but forget to erase the file after they're done. Those leftover files end in .TMP. Feel free to delete them if *you're sure Windows isn't running in the background.*
.TTF	Short for *TrueType Font*, a type of Windows font that can change its size smoothly.
.TXT	Short for *text*, these files almost always contain plain old text, often created by Notepad.
.VXD	Windows 95 looks at these files when controlling parts of your computer, like its printer or display. Similar files end in .VPD (a printer driver) or .VDD (a display driver).
.WAV	Short for *waveform* audio, these simply contain recorded sounds. Both Media Player and Sound Recorder let you listen to .WAV files.
.WKS	The Microsoft Excel spreadsheet can read and write files in these format.

Files Ending Like This ...	Usually Do This
.WPD	Short for *Windows PostScript Driver*, these files help Windows talk to those expensive PostScript printers. WordPerfect files also use this extension.
.WPG	Short for WordPerfect Graphics, these files contain images stored in the graphics format used by WordPerfect.
.WRI	Short for *Write*, these contain text created in the Write word processor — a WordPad-like word processor that came with earlier versions of Windows. WordPad can read and write files in this format.
.ZIP	These contain a file — or several files — compressed into one smaller file. (See Chapter 11.)

Find any identifiable file extensions on your own hard drive? Jot them down here for further reference. (Finally — you're *allowed* to write in books.)

_____

_____

_____

✔ Unfortunately, these file extensions aren't *always* a sure identifier; some programs cheat. For example, some plain old text files end in the extension .DOC — not .TXT.

✔ Most of the file extensions listed in Table 15-1 are *associated* with the program that created them. That means when you double-click on that file's name in My Computer or Explorer, the program that created the file brings it to the screen. A double-click on a file named Navel.bmp, for example, makes the Paint program pop to the screen, displaying the Navel bitmap file.

✔ Although Table 15-1 lists most of the extensions you'll come across when using Windows, feel free to write down any others you discover in the space provided. Many of your own programs are using their own special code words when saving files.

What Are Those Sneaky Hidden Files?

Many of the files on your computer's hard drive are for your computer to play with — not you.

So to keep its computer-oriented files out of your way, Windows 95 flips a little switch to make them invisible. The filenames won't appear in My Computer or Explorer, nor will they show up in any menus.

Most hidden files are hidden for a good reason: Deleting them can make your com-puter stop working or work strangely. Don't delete hidden files without serious reason, and even then, chew your lower lip cautiously before pushing the Delete key.

Table 15-2 shows a few of the Sneaky Hidden Files you might stumble across in the dark.

Table 15-2 Under Rare Circumstances You May Encounter These Hidden Files

These Hidden Files or Folders ...	Do This
IO.SYS, MSDOS.SYS	These files, hidden in your computer's *root directory,* contain the DOS life force that gives way to Windows 95.
Recycled	This invisible folder is your Recycle Bin which, contains all your deleted files.
BOOTLOG.TXT, BOOTLOG.PRV, SETUPLOG.TXT, DETLOG.TXT DETLOG.OLD	If Windows 95 crashes, it looks at these files after it is reloaded in an attempt to figure out where it went wrong.
Any files ending in DLL, SYS, VXD, 386, or DRV	These files all help Windows 95 talk with its programs or parts of your computer.

Identified any other hidden files? Feel free to write their names and identities in the places below.

_____

_____

_____

✔ Ever wiped an unidentifiable smudge from the coffee table? Well, that's why hidden files are hidden: To keep people from spotting them and deleting them, thinking they're as useless as a smudge.

✔ For the most part, hidden files stay hidden. But Windows 95 lets you spot them, if you're sneaky. Choose Options from the View menu in either My Computer or Explorer and then click on the View tab. Finally, click on the Show all files button in the Hidden files section and click on OK to close the window.

✔ When the novelty of seeing hidden files wears off, head back to the same page and click on the Hide files of these types button. There's not much point in looking at hidden files, anyway.

✔ When you delete a folder, you delete *all* the files in that folder — even the hidden ones. Be sure to look inside the folder with the Show all files option turned on so that you can see for sure what you're about to delete.

✔ When your computer hides a file by flipping the file's "hidden" switch, computer nerds say the computer has changed that file's *attribute*.

Purging the Unnecessary Files

Windows comes with slightly more than three trillion files, all poured onto your hard drive. After a few months, that number increases exponentially. But which files can you wipe off your hard drive without making everything tumble down?

The next few sections contain tips on what files you're allowed to get rid of.

Removing Any Leftover Temporary Files

While it's humming away, Windows 95 creates some files for its own use. Then when you shut Windows down for the day, Windows is supposed to delete those *temporary* files. Unfortunately, it sometimes forgets.

That means that you'll have to start purging those temporary files yourself. To see what temporary trash Windows has stored permanently on your hard drive, follow these steps.

1. Open the Files or Folder area from the Start button's Find area.

2. Type *.tmp into the Named box.

That's an asterisk, a period, and the letters TMP, as shown in Figure 15-2.

Figure 15-2:
Type *.tmp
into the Find
program to
find any
leftover
temporary
files.

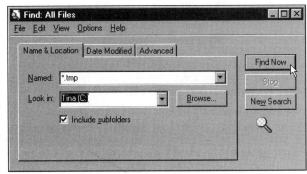

3. **Click on the F̲ind Now button.**

4. **Look at the dates of the files that turn up.**

   Spot any files that are older than a week or so? Copy them onto a floppy disk for protection and then drag and drop them into the Recycle Bin.

   ✔ To be on the safe side, don't *ever* delete any files with the current day's date. Wait a couple of days — just to make sure that they don't contain anything important. And even then, make sure that you save a copy of the file on a floppy disk in case a program starts begging for it a few days later.

   ✔ Windows often stuffs its temporary files in your DOS folder; you might find some deletable remnants there.

   ✔ Also, check your Windows Folder for a Temp folder; sometimes Windows stashes its junky leftovers in there.

Dumping Windows Files to Save Hard Disk Space

Believe it or not, Windows doesn't have to eat up massive chunks of your hard drive space. Windows can run in less than 3MB of hard drive space. It won't be able to do anything fancy, but hey, 3MB is 3MB.

To start pruning, run through the following steps in the next few sections. They describe all of the extraneous limbs of Windows you can cut off — and still be able to run a Windows program. Feel free to pick and choose what parts you want to delete; some folks can't bear to prune Solitaire, for example.

   ✔ Before pruning, think for awhile about the parts of Windows you've been relying on and the parts you haven't touched.

   ✔ If you're packing Windows onto a laptop, for example, you probably won't need Paint or a lot of the multimedia programs. And don't bother installing a printer driver. Who prints while on the road?

   ✔ A laptop doesn't *really* need screen savers, either. And FreeCell can be hard to play with a laptop's trackball — dump it to save a little more space.

   ✔ Finally, make sure that you keep your Windows installation disks handy — the disks that came in the box. You might decide later that you want to copy some Windows files back onto your hard drive.

   ✔ If you're hard up for hard drive space, the next few sections have tips on what to delete.

Dumping unneeded Windows programs

Do you really *need* Paint? By deleting that single program you scrape more than a megabyte off your hard drive. Windows makes it easy to pry off any other unnecessary accessories. Just follow the next few steps.

1. Choose Control Panel from the Start menu's Settings area.

2. Double-click on the Add/Remove Programs icon.

A window appears, as shown in Figure 15-3.

See any unneeded software listed in the box? Now's the time to get rid of that, as well. Just click on it — or click the Details button for more information — and click the OK button at the bottom of the box. (See Chapter 13 for more information.)

3. Click on the Windows Setup tab.

Here, it's up to you. Windows 95 lists the programs it tossed onto your hard drive when you installed it. Your mission is to decide what programs you can do without.

4. Double-click on the part of Windows 95 you no longer need.

For example, double-click on Accessories. A box comes up, shown in Figure 15-4, listing all the Accessories Windows 95 installed on your computer: Calculator, Paint, WordPad, and others. Decided what parts of Windows 95 you can live without? Move on to Step 5.

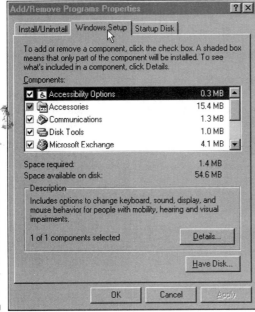

Figure 15-3:
The Add/
Remove
Programs
Properties
box can
remove
unneeded
programs
from your
hard drive.

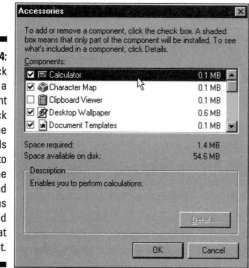

Figure 15-4:
Double-click
on a
component
— or click
on the
Details
button — to
see the
parts and
programs
contained
in that
component.

5. Click in the box next to the portion of Windows 95 you'd like to remove.

Using the example above — and presuming we could live without Calculator — we'd click in the box next to Calculator. The check mark disappears, meaning Calculator is slated for destruction at the end of the procedure.

To remove an entire component — to delete all your Accessories, for example — click in the Accessories box, shown earlier in Figure 15-3. That removes the check mark, so Windows 95 will delete all of its Accessories, which includes everything you saw in Figure 15-4.

6. Click on the OK button.

Windows 95 deletes the chosen files.

Boxes with no check mark mean that a component isn't installed. Boxes with a check mark mean the component is installed. When you click in a box and the check mark disappears, that component will be removed at the end of the procedure. Finally, shaded boxes with a check mark mean some of those component's parts are installed.

- Windows 95 can't run on much less than 35 to 40 megabytes of hard disk space. If you're that tight for space, consider sticking with Windows 3.1 or buying a bigger hard drive.

- Don't be scared of deleting too much. Putting all that stuff back by running the Windows Setup program again is easy. Click in those same check boxes you cleared earlier. Then grab your Windows installation disks, follow the instructions, and Windows copies the programs back onto your hard drive.

Dumping unwanted fonts

At first, fonts are fun, wacky ways to turn boring letters into weird arty things.

After a while, though, the fun can wear thin. Too many fonts can clog up the hard drive something fierce. Plus, they make Windows take longer when loading.

Here's how to dump the fonts you've grown sick of. For example, you can remove your Happy-Holiday-Card fonts in January and reinstall them next December.

1. **Open the Control Panel from the Start button's Settings area.**

2. **Double-click on the Fonts icon.**

   A new boxful of fonts appears, like the one in Figure 15-5.

Figure 15-5:
Double-click on the Control Panel's Fonts icon to see the fonts on your computer.

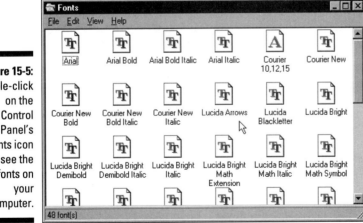

3. **Double-click on any fonts you don't use or no longer like.**

   Whenever you double-click on a font, Windows lets you see what it looks like, as shown in Figure 15-6.

Figure 15-6:
Double-click
on a font's
name to see
what it
looks like.

4. **Hold down Ctrl and click on the names of *all* of the unwanted fonts.**

Windows removes those fonts when you complete Step 5.

Don't delete fonts starting with "MS", like MS Sans Serif or MS Serif. Also, don't delete any fonts with red letters in their icons. Windows 95 and its gang of programs often use those fonts in their menus.

5. **Drag and drop the fonts into the Recycle Bin.**

That's it; they're gone.

If you've found some cool replacement fonts, Chapter 3 shows how to put them on your hard drive. If you've deleted the wrong font, however, open up the Recycle Bin as soon as possible, click on its name with your right mouse button, and choose Restore for a quick resuscitation.

Chapter 16

Networking (Not Working) with Windows 95

A network is simply a bunch of computers that somebody wired together. Like most technologies, this can be both good and bad.

Some people find networks to be a nightmare and with good reason: A mean-spirited boss plops them in front of the computer, tells them to "log in," and start "using the network" to process the files Jerry couldn't finish last Friday.

Other, more network-savvy people find the convenience of a network to be a dream: Instead of copying oodles of files to a handful of floppies and carrying them down the hall to Jennifer, Steve can simply copy the files to Jennifer's computer over the network. (And while he's connected, he can strike up a computerized "chat" to ask her how the cat's doing.)

Windows 95 comes with all the software you need to create your own network, as long as you provide the right cables and hardware. This chapter explains why you'd want a network, how to set one up, and how to use the network once you've got the thing running.

What's a Network?

The concept of a network is pretty easy to grasp. A network is two or more computers that have been wired together so that they can share information. But computer networks have more subtleties than nervous high schoolers on their first date.

For example, how do you tell if a computer's on a network? Who's allowed on the network? Which computers are on the network? Are *all* parts of Computer A available to Computer B, or just the Computer A's CD-ROM drive? Should networked computers be allowed to kiss without passwords?

All of these technical decisions need to be made beforehand, usually by the network administrator — somebody who often looks as harried as the high school principal at the prom.

A network consists of three main parts: The *hardware,* the *software,* and the *administrator* — the person who decides how the hardware and software behave. (And unfortunately, if you're installing the network yourself, you're casting yourself in the oft-complex role of administrator.)

- Networking hardware consists of *cable* to connect the computers and *cards* that plug inside the computers and give the cable something to connect to.

- Networking software comes built into Windows 95; there's nothing extra to buy. The software merely needs to have its settings adjusted by a human — the administrator — in order to work with the cable and cards.

- The network administrator, in addition to making sure that the software and hardware can work well together, decides who gets to use the network — and what level of access they have. For example, the administrator can let everybody access everybody else's computer. Or the administrator can merely let people read files from a single computer — nobody can snoop on anybody else's computer. Administrators have complete control over who gets to do what.

Computers aren't the only things that can be networked. Printers, CD-ROM drives, and modems can be put on a network, as well. This way, everybody on the network can send their files to a single printer or modem. When two people try to send their files to a printer simultaneously, one computer on the network simply holds onto the incoming files until the printer is free and ready to deal with them.

A LAN stands for a *Local Area Network,* and it describes computers linked directly by cables. Computers that sit closely together — in the same room or small building — usually use a LAN. (This chapter will be talking about LANs.)

A WAN stands for a *Wide Area Network,* and it describes computers linked through phone lines and modems. A WAN can link computers that are located miles away from each other. (This chapter doesn't talk about WANs. The Internet is a WAN, however, and it's covered in Chapter 6.)

What Computer Parts Do I Need to Set Up a Network?

If you're trying to set up a lot of computers — more than five or ten — you need a more advanced book: Networks are very scary stuff. But if you're just trying to set up a handful of computers in your home, home office, or small business, this chapter might be all you need. (And if your network is already installed, count your blessings and move on ahead in this chapter for information on making it work.)

So without further blabbing, here's a no-fat, step-by-step list of how to set up your own network to work with Windows 95. The steps in the following sections show you how to link your computers so that they can share hard drives and printers. (After you are networked, you can play those cool network games like Descent and Doom that are all the rage!)

Deciding on the cable

This part sounds strange at first, but hear me out. The first step in creating a network is choosing the type of network cable your computers need. And the type of cable you need depends mostly on where your PCs are located throughout your room.

What *don't* I need for a Windows 95 network?

Windows 95 comes with its own built-in net-working software. This networking software works with plain old Windows 3.11 (also known as Windows for Workgroups), as well as Windows NT (both version 3.51 and version 4.0).

You don't need to buy any other fancy network-ing software you might have heard about, like Novell Netware, Banyan-Vines, Lantastic, or Microsoft LAN Manager. All the software you need comes with Windows 95.

In fact, *don't* install the network software that comes with your network card — the Windows 95 built-in software should work faster and more reliably. You should only turn to the network card's software as a last resort — if Windows 95 has failed miserably.

See, PCs can be connected by one long cable that stretches from PC to PC. Or they can be connected in a "spider-like" configuration, where each PC gets its own "leg" of cable.

Look at the way your own PCs are arranged and try to picture which setup would be easier — stringing a single cable from PC to PC (as shown in Figure 16-1), or setting a "hub" in the middle of your PCs and connecting a separate cable from the hub to each PC (as shown in Figure 16-2).

Figure 16-1:
Thin Coax cabling looks like cable TV wire and links computers in a long line.

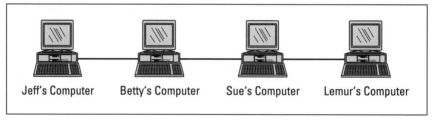

Figure 16-2:
10BaseT cabling looks like telephone wire and links computers in a hub.

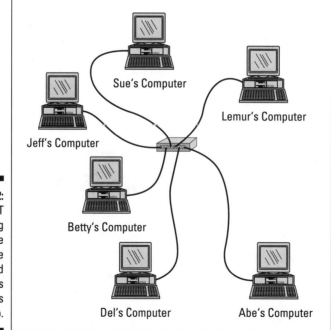

These two setups each use different types of cable, and the two types of cable have weird names: *Thin Coax* and *10BaseT.*

✔ If you prefer to set up the PCs with a single cable, you need to use cable called *Thin Coax* network cable. This cable looks sort of like cable-TV wire, and it runs from computer to computer creating a long "backbone" with PCs latched onto it like ribs.

The Thin Coax cable is also known by a wide variety of names, including thin-Ethernet, Thinnet, or BNC.

✔ If you'd do less tripping over cables by using the "spider" approach, you should opt for the *10BaseT cable.* Resembling telephone cable, this cable works better where computers will be moved around a lot, like in modular office settings. Because each computer gets its own cable that plugs into a central hub, moving a computer to a different location is no big deal — you're not trying to bend a "backbone" of linked computers.

The 10BaseT cable is known by a wide variety of names, including RJ-45, TPE (Twisted Pair Ethernet), Twisted Pair, or 10BT. But when looking for it at the store, just say you want the kind that looks like "telephone cord instead of cable TV cord."

✔ Neither type of cable is particularly better than the other. Your decision should be based pretty much on how your computers are located throughout the room.

Piddling little Thin Coax and 10BaseT details

Of course, cable decisions involve a little more effort than deciding whether your PCs are arranged like spokes in a wheel or like a broomstick. Depending on your type of cable, you need to pick up a few extra goodies at the software store. (Don't worry; these add-ons are usually pretty cheap.)

Networks using Thin Coax cable (the stuff that looks like TV cable) need two more little goodies: *T-connectors* and *terminator plugs.* Each PC on the network needs a *T-connector.* The T-connector is a little metal pipe shaped like the letter *T.* One end plugs into the network card in the back of your PC, leaving two ends open for the cable to plug into. Finally, you push one terminator plug onto each end of the cable linking the PCs. As shown in Figure 16-3, this essentially "plugs" the cable so the data doesn't leak out.

People using 10BaseT cable (the cable that looks like phone wire) need an extra, more expensive goody called a *hub,* which is the device all the networked computers plug into. Unlike Thin Coax users, who can simply snake their single cable from PC to PC, the 10BaseT users need to snake each of their multiple cables to a single hub. Without the hub, shown in Figure 16-4, the network won't work right. (Complex networks can often link hubs, but we're not talking about complex networks here.)

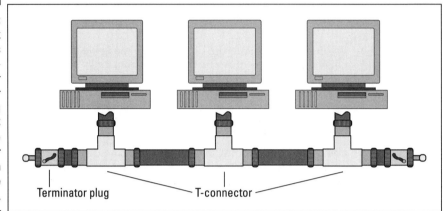

Figure 16-3:
Thin coax networks need a T-connector for connecting to each PC and one terminator plug at each end of the main cable.

Terminator plug   T-connector

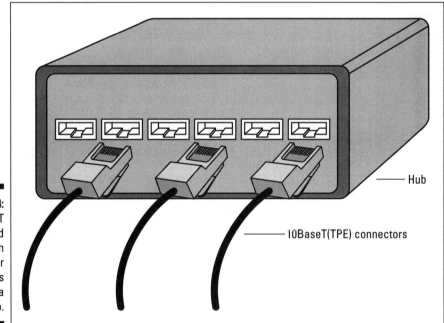

— Hub

— I0BaseT(TPE) connectors

Figure 16-4:
10BaseT users need to plug each of their computer's cables into a central hub.

Deciding on the card

Decided where your PCs will be located in your network setup, as described previously? Then you probably already decided between the Thin Coax and 10BaseT cable.

Now it's time to decide on a *network card* — the thing that plugs into one of your computer's internal slots and provides a place for the cable to plug into. Luckily, many network cards accept both types of cable, making it easy to change your mind should your needs change down the road. When you choose a card, keep these things in mind:

- ✔ The card must be an *Ethernet* card that supports your cable.

- ✔ The card must fit into one of your computer's unused slots. If you don't know what type of slot your PC uses, an ISA card is probably your best bet.

Almost all computers come with an ISA slot; most Pentiums have a PCI slot, and most laptop computers have a PCMCIA slot. If you're not particularly slot savvy, consider picking up a copy of *Upgrading & Fixing PCs For Dummies* (published by IDG Books Worldwide, Inc.).

When buying anything for Windows 95, look for a "Designed for Windows 95" plug-and-play logo. Lacking that, look for a Windows 95 Compatible sticker. Cards and software with those logos and stickers are the easiest to install.

The fastest network card for Windows 95 is a 32-bit card on a Pentium's ISA bus. But unless you have a whole bunch of computers linked together, you'll do fine with 16-bit cards in ISA slots.

Buying the parts

Picked out the cable? Decided on the cards? Then it's time to make the shopping list, as described below.

The Thin Coax cable network shopping list

Made the decision to install a network using Thin Coax cable? Then here's a list of all the stuff you need to buy at the computer store:

- ✔ One Thin Coax-supporting Ethernet card for each computer on your network

- ✔ One T-connector for each computer on the network

✔ Two terminator plugs

✔ One length of cable for each PC-to-PC connection. To connect four computers on a desktop, for example, you need three six-foot lengths of cable.

Confused as to how much cable to buy? Figure 16-1 shows how three pieces of cable can link four computers. And Figure 16-3 shows how two pieces of cable can link three computers.

✔ Six-foot and 12-foot lengths of cable usually do the trick. Buy a few extra lengths of cable to keep on hand in case you add a computer or two later.

✔ Buy a few extra T-connectors, too. You need one of those for every extra computer you want to pop onto your network.

✔ If you're planning to add a laptop, make sure you buy a Thin-Coax-supporting PCMCIA network card.

The Thin Coax cable looks like the cable that plugs into the back of your TV, and "Plug and Play" cards are the easiest to install.

The 10BaseT (also known as TPE) cable network shopping list

Going to install a network using the 10BaseT or TPE cable? Then here's a list of everything you need to pick up at the computer store:

✔ One 10BaseT-supporting Ethernet "Plug and Play" card for each computer on the network

✔ One hub that has enough ports for each computer — plus some extra ports for a few computers you may want to add at a later time

✔ A 10BaseT cable for each computer, and make sure it's long enough to reach from the computer to the hub. (Refer to Figure 16-2 for a picture.)

The 10BaseT type of cable looks like telephone line, and "Plug and Play" cards are the easiest to install.

Installing the Network's Parts

Buying groceries is the easy part; you can just toss stuff into the cart without thinking of the after-effects, like those extra calories from the His and Hers frozen dinners, the squished eggs from the guy who bagged your groceries, or the problem of where to store the watermelon.

The same goes with installing a network. Buying the parts is relatively easy. Installing those parts into your computer can be pretty rough, though. Buying network hardware is always much harder than installing it and getting it to work right.

This part of the chapter describes the two ways to install network hardware — the easy way and the hard way. If you're lucky, you'll be able to snake through with the Easy Way section.

If you're *not* lucky, pick up a copy of *Windows 95 Uncut* by Alan Simpson (published by IDG Books Worldwide, Inc.). His detailed book shows how to struggle through installing the network stuff the hard way.

Installing network cards the easy way

Windows 95 introduced a concept called *Plug and Play* to computerdom. According to the theory, people can simply plug their new computer parts into their computer. Windows 95 recognizes the new device, automatically sets itself up to use that device, and everything is as cheery as a rugged day of hairy-armed sailing in a Nautica clothing ad.

Unfortunately, not all computer parts are Plug and Play. So Windows 95 can't install them all automatically. But if you're installing a Plug and Play network card, here's the way things are supposed to work:

1. **Find your original Windows 95 disks; you'll need them.**

2. **Turn off and unplug all the computers on your soon-to-be network.**

   Turn 'em all off; unplug them as well.

3. **Turn off all the computers' peripherals — printers, monitors, modems, and so on.**

4. **Insert the network cards into their appropriate slots.**

   Remove the computer's case and push the card into the proper type of slot. Make sure that you're inserting the proper type of card into the proper type of slot — for example, inserting an ISA card into an ISA slot.

   If a card doesn't seem to be fitting into a slot, don't force it. Different types of cards fit into different types of slots, and you might be trying to push the wrong type of card into the wrong slot.

5. **Replace the computer's case and connect the network cables to the cards.**

6. **Connect the cable's doodads.**

   For example, plug the T-connectors into the network cards, and string the Thin Coax cables between all the T-connectors. Finally, plug the unconnected ends of the T-connectors on the first and last computers on the network with the terminator plugs. (Refer to Figure 16-3 for a picture.)

   If you're using the 10BaseT cable, connect the computers' cards to the hub with the cable, as shown previously in Figure 16-2. (Some hubs have power cords that need to be plugged into the wall, as well.)

7. **Turn on the computers and their peripherals.**

   Turn on the computers and their monitors, printers, modems, and whatever else happens to be connected to them.

   ✔ If all goes well, Windows 95 wakes up, notices its newly installed network card, and begins installing the appropriate software automatically. Hurrah!

   ✔ If all doesn't go well, click on Windows 95's Start button, choose Control Panel from the Settings option, and double-click the Add New Hardware icon. Click the Next button, and choose Yes to make Windows try to "autodetect" the new network card.

   ✔ If Windows *still* doesn't recognize your card, click on the Start button, choose Control Panel from the Settings option, and double-click on the Add New Hardware icon. Click the Next button, choose No on the next screen, double-click on Network adapters, and choose your new card from the list.

   ✔ If your card comes with DOS or Windows for Workgroups software, don't install it. Windows 95 comes with its own network drivers built in, which are much better than the ones provided by the card's manufacturers.

   ✔ If your card still doesn't work, you can't install it the easy way, unfortunately. Better check out the "Installing network cards the hard way" section coming up next.

Installing network cards the hard way

Don't fret if this network installation stuff seems to be over your head. It's over the heads of just about everybody who hasn't turned computers into their career (or their number-one hobby) or who doesn't live a complete cyber-lifestyle.

If your network card doesn't work right — or it's not designated as being Plug and Play — you probably need to adjust the card's settings. And these adjustments can become dreadfully complicated.

The card is probably trying to use a setting that your computer's already reserved for another card inside your computer — a sound card, for example, or perhaps a communications port.

One of the most important of these settings, called an *Interrupt* or *IRQ*, serves as a doorbell for getting your computer's attention. Your network card needs its own IRQ. And unfortunately, your computer only has a handful of IRQs to dish out.

To see what IRQs your computer is already using for other devices, right-click on the My Computer icon, choose Properties from the pop-up menu, and click on the Device Manager tab. Click the Properties button, and Windows 95 shows you a list of devices and the IRQ settings they've grabbed. Figure 16-5, for example, shows how most of the available IRQs have been assigned to various gadgetry; only Interrupt 7 is available.

Figure 16-5:
Windows 95
can show
you which
IRQs are
already in
use, making
it slightly
easier to
configure
your
network
card to use
a vacant
IRQ.

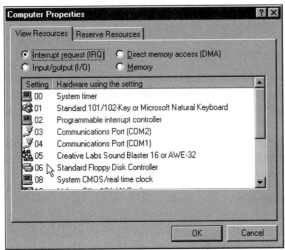

In this case, the network card should be assigned an IRQ of 7. But how? Different cards let you do this in different ways. Some make you use software that comes with the card; others make you flip little switches on the card itself. Since cards' designs vary, you have to grab the card's manual for the answer to this one.

Some cards also want an "I/O (Input/Output) address"; Windows 95 lists these on the same Computer Properties page as it lists the IRQs, as shown in Figure 16-6. Click on the Input/Output (I/O) button, shown in Figure 16-6, to see the available settings, and the parts of your computer currently using those settings.

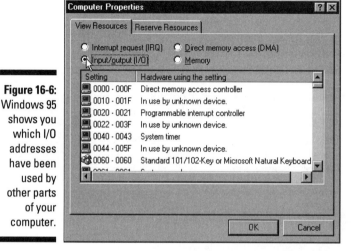

Figure 16-6:
Windows 95 shows you which I/O addresses have been used by other parts of your computer.

You might have to experiment quite a bit before finding an available IRQ and I/O setting for your particular card. Don't be afraid to ask a knowledgeable computer friend for advice; this is some of the most complicated stuff in computing.

Configuring Windows 95's Sensitive Networking Areas

Bought the network cables and cards? Installed them? After you've installed everything, Windows 95 eventually makes you reboot the computer. When it restarts, a window appears asking you to "log on" to the system, as shown in Figure 16-7. Congratulations! You're experiencing your first flavors of network life.

You're not through yet, however. The next few sections explain how to "log in" for the first time, as well as how to set up your computers so that they can begin talking to each other.

Figure 16-7:
After you
install
networking
cards and
configure
the
software,
Windows 95
makes you
"log on" to
the system.

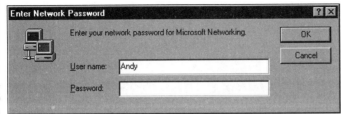

Identifying yourself to the network

When Windows 95 asks you to log on for the first time, you need to do two things: type your name, and type your password.

Don't ever tell anybody your password, or they can do evil things to your computer files.

✔ Typing your name is easy enough; most people can remember their own names. You can type just your first name, or your first and last names. The computer needs to know your name so that it can recognize you. That way, your computer knows who is using it, and the computer knows how to treat that person.

✔ If you're the only person who'll be using your computer and your network, you don't have to type a password at all. Just press Enter, and Windows 95 will let you into the computer without a password from then on. (You can add a password later by double-clicking the Passwords icon in the Control Panel window.)

✔ In fact, if you're the only person who's going to be using the network, a password might be merely a bother. Passwords come in handy when several people work on the same PC in an office setting, however.

✔ When the screen clears and Windows 95 appears on-screen, look for the Network Neighborhood icon. That's a symbol that Windows 95 knows a network card has been installed. If you don't see that icon, pictured in Figure 16-8, your card must not be configured correctly because Windows can't find it.

Figure 16-8:
The Network
Neighborhood
icon.

Network
Neighborhood

Identifying your computers to the network

After you log into your new network, you need to make sure that your network knows the right information about your computer. The following steps show how to introduce your computers to the network and vice versa.

1. **Click on Network Neighborhood with your right mouse button and choose Properties from the menu.**

   The Network dialog box appears, as shown in Figure 16-9.

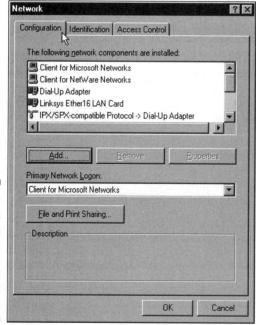

Figure 16-9:
.The Network
dialog box
lets you
adjust the
settings for
your
network.

2. Check for missing components.

Make sure that the following items are listed in the Configuration box:

- Client for Microsoft Networks
- Client for Netware Networks
- IPX/SPX-compatible Protocol
- NetBEUI
- Your network card (For example, Figure 16-9 shows my Linksys Ether16 LAN Card.)

3. Add any missing components.

Click the Add button and add any of the components that are missing.

4. Click the Primary Network Logon box.

5. Choose Client for Microsoft Networks.

6. Click the File and Print Sharing button.

7. Make sure the two options are checked, as shown in Figure 16-10.

These two options allow other computers on the network to share the files and printers connected to this computer.

Figure 16-10:
Make sure other computers can share the files and printers on each computer.

8. Click on OK to close the File and Print Sharing box.

9. Click on the Identification tab.

10. **Type a name for your computer in the Computer name box.**

Type a name for your computer. I've named my computer *Pentium,* as you can see in Figure 16-11. Other people use friendlier names, like *Huey* or *Dewey.* The name you use here will appear on the menus of other computers on the network.

Computer names can't contain spaces, and they can't be longer than 15 characters.

Figure 16-11:
Type a
different
name for
each
networked
computer
in the
Computer
name box,
but type the
same name
in the
Workgroup
box.

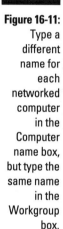

> **Network**　　　　　　　　　　　　　　[? X]
>
> Configuration | Identification | Access Control
>
> Windows uses the following information to identify your computer on the network. Please type a name for this computer, the workgroup it will appear in, and a short description of the computer.
>
> Computer name:　[Pentium]
>
> Workgroup:　[Hardly_Working]
>
> Computer Description:　[Dell XPS P90]
>
> [OK]　[Cancel]

11. **Type a name for your network in the Workgroup box.**

All the computers in your network must use the same Workgroup name. Make sure that the name is typed in exactly the same in each PC. Just like computer names, Workgroup names can't contain spaces, nor can they be longer than 15 characters.

12. **Type a short description of your PC into the Computer Description box.**

The least important setting, the description merely adds a little identifying information about the computer when it appears on a network's menu.

13. **Click on the Access Control tab.**

14. **Click on the Share-level access control button.**

    Basically, this keeps things simple by letting you assign one password to each resource — be it a hard drive or printer or an entire computer — on your network.

15. **Click on the OK button.**

16. **Log in to each of the computers on your network and repeat all these steps.**

    Be sure to choose a different name for each of your computers in step 10, and be sure to choose the same Workgroup name for all your computers in step 11.

    If everything went well, you should be able to double-click on the Network Neighborhood icon and see all the computers on your network, as shown in Figure 16-12.

    When you double-click on the computers, however, a blank window appears. Why? Because you haven't told the network what parts of those computers should be shared with the other computers. (That stuff's in the *next* section.)

Figure 16-12:
When your network is successfully configured, double-clicking on the Network Neighborhood should list all the computers connected to your network.

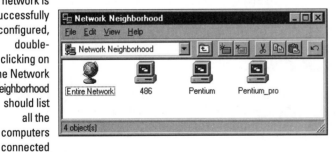

If the names of your computers aren't all listed, however, try these things:

- ✔ Open and close the Network Neighborhood folder icon. Do the same with the Entire Network icon that lives inside that folder.

- ✔ Shut down all your computers and make sure that the network cables are plugged into the cards securely.

- ✔ Make sure that you've typed the same name into the Workgroup box in step 11, and make sure that each computer on the network has its own unique name.

- ✔ If you're not even seeing a Network Neighborhood icon, your card probably isn't installed right. You might have to fiddle with its IRQ and I/O settings, unfortunately.

- ✔ Don't worry if these things take time. You only have to do them once.

Making Your PCs Share Their Goodies

Congratulations! You've made yet another of many successful steps toward successful networking. But when you double-click on any of your computers now listed in your Network Neighborhood folder, a blank window appears. That's because those computers haven't been told that they're supposed to be *sharing* any of their information.

Sharing — a bit of thievery referred to as "sharing resources" in the networking world — is covered in this section.

Sharing hard drives

To keep things simple, this section shows how to do the easiest type networking: Letting any computer on the network grab anything from the hard drive of any other computer on the network.

Admittedly, it's not going to be the most secure system. Anybody in the office can grab anything else. But it's an easy way to understand how networks work, so you'll be more prepared to restrict access later (and still be able to get into the network yourself).

To start small, here's how to designate a single hard drive on one computer as being *shared,* or "available to everybody else on the network."

If you're feeling burnt out after all the previous network atrocities, don't worry — this part is really easy — finally.

1. **Double-click on the My Computer icon of the computer containing the hard drive you want to share.**

   Make sure that you're sitting down at a computer that's on the network. Then, when you double-click on the My Computer icon, its window will open, as shown in Figure 16-13, revealing all the hard drives and CD-ROM drives used by that computer.

Figure 16-13: Double-click on the My Computer icon to see the drives and CD-ROM drives used by a computer.

2. **Right-click on the drive you want to share with the rest of the computers on your network.**

   A menu pops up, as shown in Figure 16-14.

Figure 16-14: Computers on a network have a "Sharing" option on their drive's pop-up menu.

3. Click on the S̲haring option.

A Properties box for that drive appears, as shown in Figure 16-15.

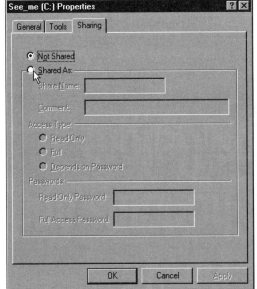

Figure 16-15:
The
Properties
box lets you
assign the
levels of
access
granted to
people on
the network.

4. Click on the S̲hared As button.

5. In the Share N̲ame box, type a name for the drive.

Windows 95 usually helps you out by calling your C drive *C,* but you can call it "drive C" or something else, if you like. This is the name of the drive that other people will see on the network.

6. In the C̲omment box, type a short description.

Just type some helpful descriptive information here, if you think it's necessary.

7. Designate the Access Type.

You can allow people three types of access, all designated by choosing the following buttons:

- **Read Only:** This option lets people read and copy files from the drive, but not delete or move them.

- **F̲ull:** This option lets people read, copy, delete, or move the files.

- **Depends on Password:** This option offers some networkers Read Only access, but gives other networkers Full access, depending on the password status you choose in the next step.

8. **Designate the passwords.**

If you want people on your network to use passwords in order to access your files, click here and type the appropriate password they'll need to use.

Or if you leave it blank, they won't need any passwords.

9. **Click on the OK button.**

The My Computer window reappears, but with the drive C icon showing a subtle difference, as shown in Figure 16-16.

Figure 16-16:
Hard drives available for sharing on a network have a little hand beneath their icon.

✔ Feel free to repeat these steps on any of the hard drives on any of the computers on your network. Then when you double-click on that computer's name in the Network Neighborhood folder, you won't be calling up a blank window. Instead, you'll see that computer's shared hard drives listed as available folders.

✔ I set up all of my hard drives as shared. That makes it easier to grab files from any place on any computer.

✔ If your networking needs are more complex, you might consider Windows NT. Described in this book's appendix, it's more powerful, secure, and configurable than Windows 95.

Sharing printers

It's not uncommon to have several computers around the house but only one printer. In fact, it's the source of marital strife in some computer-oriented households: Who gets to have the printer hooked up to their computer?

With a network, the answer's easy: Everybody. Simply connect the printer to the network, and everybody can send their files to it without having to get up.

To put a printer on the network, follow these simple steps:

1. **Double-click on the My Computer icon of the computer currently connected to the printer.**

   The My Computer window appears.

2. **Double-click on the Printers folder.**

   The Printers window pops onto the screen, as shown in Figure 16-17.

Figure 16-17: The Printers window shows the printers currently available to that computer.

3. **Right-click on the icon of the printer you'd like to share and choose Sharing from the pop-up menu.**

   The printer's Properties window appears, showing its Sharing page (see Figure 16-18).

4. **Click on the Shared As button and then click on the OK button to finish.**

   That's pretty much it — simplicity itself. You can get a little more elaborate, if you want. For example, you can type a password into the Password box in step 4 if you want to restrict printer access to password-knowing networkers only.

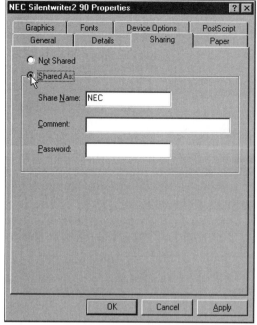

Figure 16-18:
Click on the
Shared As
button to
share your
printer with
other
computers
on the
network.

✔ You can also type a name for your printer in step 4, like *Fred,* or *Paper Jam.*
Whatever you type in the Share Name box is the name that appears as the
printer's name to the other networked users on their computer. If you
don't type anything, Windows 95 simply uses the first word in the printer's
icon name.

✔ Anything you type into the optional Comment box of step 4 also shows up
on the network as an additional description.

✔ Just as with hard drives, shared printers have little hands beneath their icons,
kind of like those old "You're in good hands with Allstate" commercials.

Sharing individual folders

You don't have to put an entire computer onto a network. You can just designate one of its drives as "shared," for example, or just its CD-ROM drive. In fact,
you can even put a single folder onto the network.

Just click on the folder or CD-ROM drive, choose S̲haring from the pop-up menu, and fill out the Properties form, just as if the folder or CD-ROM drive were a hard drive. (That stuff is described in the "Sharing hard drives" section a little earlier in this chapter.)

Copying Files Around on the Network

After you've spent hours installing a network, telling your computer about the new network, introducing the other computers to the network and each other, and telling the network what parts of the other computers they can access, you're ready to reap the rewards of your efforts: You can start grabbing files from other computers without getting up.

Accessing a file on another computer

After you've spent a few hundred dollars networking your computers, you're ready to do fun stuff, like copying files around. The following steps show how to copy a file from one computer to another.

1. **Double-click on the Network Neighborhood icon.**

   The Network Neighborhood window appears, listing all the computers on the network.

2. **Double-click on the icon of the computer containing the file you want to access.**

   A window for that computer opens, listing the resources available on the computer. If you've made all its hard drives available, for example, you'll see a folder for each hard drive. Or if you only shared a single folder on that computer, you'll see only that single folder.

3. **Double-click on the folder containing the file you'd like to access.**

   Keep clicking on folders until you find the file you'd like to access.

4. **Access the file.**

   You can copy the file to your own computer by dragging and dropping it there. Or you can simply double-click on the file to start editing it while leaving it physically on the other computer.

✔ If you can't move the file, perhaps you only have Read Only access to that computer's drives or folders. Better check out this chapter's Sharing hard drives section for information on how to give yourself more access.

✔ After you open the window to access another computer on the network, Windows 95 treats that computer as if it were a plain old folder on your desktop. You can copy your own files onto that computer by dragging and dropping them onto that folder. You can even run programs off other computers by double-clicking on them.

By putting your CD-ROM drive on the network as a shared hard drive, all your computers can grab information from it.

Feel free to make shortcuts to your most-often-used folders and files on your networked computers. That saves the time and hassles of running through the Network Neighborhood each time you want to grab something popular.

Accessing a printer on a network

Accessing a networked printer is a mite more complicated than accessing shared hard drives or folders, but it's not too much of a pain. When accessing a hard drive or folder, you can get in immediately because you've already done the set up work.

But when you want to access a printer, you need to jump through a few hoops — even though you've made the printer available as a shared resource, as described in the "Sharing printers" section a few pages back in this chapter.

The next few steps show how to set up computer A so it can use a printer that's been connected to computer B.

Highly paid computer administrators refer to the computer that's connected to the printer as the *print server.* The other computers are called *print clients.* Similarly, whenever you're grabbing a file from a computer, the computer that's grabbing is the *client;* the computer that's dishing out the files is the *server.*

1. **Make sure that you made the printer on computer B available as a shared resource.**

   This mild-mannered task was described earlier in this chapter.

2. **Double-click on the My Computer icon on the computer where you want to print the file.**

   The My Computer window appears.

3. **Double-click on the Printers folder and double-click on the Add Printer icon, shown in Figure 16-19.**

   The Add Printer Wizard magically appears.

Figure 16-19:
Double-click
on the Add
Printer icon
to add a
networked
printer to
your system.

4. **Click on the Next button.**

5. **Click on the Network button and click on Next.**

6. **Click on the Browse button to find the printer.**

   A list of computers hooked up to your system appears; double-click on the one with the printer hooked up to it, and you'll see the networked printer, as shown in Figure 16-20.

Figure 16-20:
Clicking on
the Browse
button lets
you find your
printer more
easily.

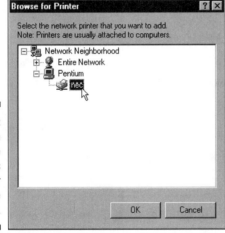

7. Click on your printer's name and click on the OK button.

8. Tell the Wizard whether or not you print from DOS programs.

If you print from MS-DOS programs, click on the <u>Y</u>es button; if you're strictly a Windows user, click on the <u>N</u>o button.

9. Click on the Next button.

10. Type a name for the printer.

Or to keep things simple, accept the name Windows uses.

11. Decide whether to make this printer the default printer.

If you want this computer to use this network printer all the time, click on the <u>Y</u>es button; if you plan on using another computer more often, click on the <u>N</u>o button.

12. Click on the Next button.

13. Click on <u>Y</u>es and click on the Finish button.

Clicking on <u>Y</u>es tells that computer to send a test page over the network for the printer to print. That's a good way to make sure that the thing works *before* Jeffy has to print out his report on Florida manatees at 7:30 Monday morning.

✔ You might have to grab your original Windows 95 disks so your computer can copy the printer drivers. (It's a good thing you kept that Windows 95 box handy, eh?)

✔ From now on, that computer will use the networked printer, just as if it were connected to it. And, in effect, it is connected to it. The cable just makes a lot of stops along the way.

✔ After you connect a computer to a printer — make the computer the *print server,* in more geekish terms — you can see it in the Network Neighborhood. The printer doesn't have a little hand under it; a little cable runs through it, as shown in Figure 16-21.

Figure 16-21:
Click on the
print server
to see the
printer's
icon.

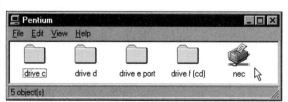

Part V
More Shortcuts and Tips Galore

The 5th Wave — By Rich Tennant

"30 years ago today..."

Bill and Irwin Fuzzo, two plumbers from Eugene, Ore., developed the first hydro-pneumatic PC. It could be connected to an average garden hose, and response time was increased by simply "...squeezing the hose a little bit." Software was to be developed by a local manufacturer of squirt guns — 30 years ago today!!

In this part . . .

After a few years of driving a city's streets, a cabbie knows all the shortcuts: Which sidestreets will bypass freeway traffic, what hours the airport is clogged, and when the train station is a better market for quick fares.

Grizzled cabbies usually don't like to share their secrets; their livelihood's at stake. But Windows users? You can't *stop* them from talking about shortcuts.

Put two Windows users together, and you'll not only hear about secret places to click, you'll hear about what key to press *while* you're clicking.

Toss in a few tips on how to cheat at Solitaire, and you've got an idea of what you'll find in this part of the book.

Chapter 17

A Grab Bag of Tricks

In This Chapter

▶ Adding or subtracting more components to Windows 95

▶ Finding hidden programs on the CD-ROM version of Windows 95

▶ Making pages print with numbers or titles

▶ Scrounging up more memory

▶ Reading the Character Map

▶ Highlighting text

The programmers who created Windows 95 tried to make things easy. For example, opening a file in most Windows programs is relatively simple.

But after the programmers finished putting things on the menus, they started hiding some secret stuff in the cracks.

This chapter yanks the secret stuff out of the cracks and puts it on the coffee table for easy viewing.

Her Version of Windows 95 Has More Stuff Than My Version!

Not all versions of Windows 95 are alike, and there are several reasons for this. Don't get me wrong — only *one* version of Windows 95 is out there. The difference boils down to what parts of that version are installed on your computer.

When Windows 95 installs itself onto your computer, it doesn't install all of its many programs and options. If it did, it could easily eat up 70MB of space on your hard drive. So Windows 95 leaves a lot of its programs sitting on its floppy disk or compact disc. In fact, that's why Windows 95 gives you four options when it installs itself: Typical, Portable, Compact, and Custom.

Although Table 17-1 shows which Windows 95 goodies came with or without the version you chose, the mystery of missing programs doesn't stop there: Some Windows 95 programs only come on the compact disc version of the program — if your upgrade came on floppy disks, you're outta luck. (Your luck will change when you use your modem to call CompuServe or Microsoft's BBS, as described in Chapter 7. You find the "CD Extras" available for downloading there.)

Table 17-1 Windows 95 Programs Installed by Various Options

This Setting...	... Gives You This...	... But Leaves Out This
Typical	Accessibility Options, Calculator, Defrag, Document Templates, Hyper-Terminal, Media Player, Object Packager, Paint, Phone Dialer, Quick View, Screen Savers, Video Compression Software, Windows 95 Tour, WordPad	Audio Compression, Backup, Briefcase, CD Player, Character Map, Clipboard Viewer, Desktop Wallpaper, Dial-Up Networking, Direct Cable Connection, Disk Compression Tools, Games, Microsoft Exchange, Microsoft Fax, Microsoft Mail, Mouse pointers, Net Watcher, Online User's Guide, Sound and Video clips, Sound Recorder, System Monitor, The Microsoft Network, Volume Control
Portable	Briefcase, Calculator, Defrag, Dial-up Networking, Direct Cable Connection, Disk Compression tools, Hyper-Terminal, Phone Dialer, Quick View, Screen Savers, Video Compression	Accessibility Options, Audio Compression, Backup, CD Player, Character Map, Clipboard Viewer, Desktop Wallpaper, Document Templates, Games, Media Player, Microsoft Exchange, Microsoft Fax, Microsoft Mail, Mouse Pointers, Net Watcher, Object Packager, Online User's Guide, Paint, Sound and Video clips, Sound Recorder, System Monitor, The Microsoft Network, Volume Control, Windows 95 Tour, WordPad
Compact	Bare-bones minimum files Windows 95 needs to run itself	Everything else
Custom	Whatever you choose from the menus	Whatever you leave off from the menus

✔ See a program on the chart that you don't have? Double-click the Add/Remove Programs icon from the Control Panel. That program lets you pick and choose among the programs.

✔ If your version of Windows 95 didn't come with a compact disc, however, you might be missing out on a few files, as the next section shows.

✔ There's worse news: Some computer makers pre-install Windows 95 on their computers' hard drives, but they don't toss in a copy of Windows 95 on floppy disks. Instead, they install a "disk image" of Windows 95 on your computer's hard drive. To turn those disk images into actual floppy disks, you have to crack open your computer's manual. (Most computers come with a special program to turn the images into disks, so you can grab programs off them when you need them.)

A Compact Disc Isn't Very Compact

The compact disc version of Windows 95 can hold a lot more information than the floppy disk version. The programmers took advantage of this freak of nature by piling loads of Windows 95 "extras" onto the compact disc version.

Most of these programs are found in the Control Panel's Add/Remove Programs icon. Others are simply hidden on folders on the disc itself — and nobody told you about them.

Table 17-2 shows some of the goodies you'll find on the disc, as well as their location in the Control Panel's Add/Remove Programs icon.

Table 17-2 Extra Goodies on the Windows 95 Compact Disc

What It Is	Where It Is	What It Does
Character Map	Accessories	Lets you put symbols and special characters into documents.
Mouse Pointers	Accessories	Provides an array of easy-to-see, adjustable pointer sizes for your mouse.
NetWatcher	Accessories	For people who like to watch their network server and connections.
Online User's Guide	Accessories	Online version of the Windows 95 User's Guide.
Quick View	Accessories	Lets you preview a document without opening the program that created it.
System Monitor	Accessories	Lets you watch system performance with graphs.

(continued)

Table 17-2 *(continued)*

What It Is	Where It Is	What It Does
Windows 95 Tour	Accessories	Teaches you a few basics of Windows 95 to get you up and running quickly.
Cloud Bitmap	Accessories	Picture of cloud bitmap without Windows 95 logo.
Windows 95 Bitmap	Accessories	Desktop wallpaper of Windows 95 logo.
Multilanguage Support	Main menu	Lets you write documents in Bulgarian, Belorussian, Czech, Hungarian, Greek, Polish, Russian, and Slovenian.
Jungle Sound Scheme	Multimedia	Parrots squawking, lions growling, and your cat cowering under the bed whenever your computer gives you a warning sound.
Musical Sound Scheme	Multimedia	High-tech tweets and plops.
Robotz Sound Scheme	Multimedia	You guessed it.
Sample Sounds	Multimedia	Miscellaneous sound files for playing on your Windows multimedia programs.
Utopia Sound Scheme	Multimedia	Quiet and dreamy.
CD Player	Multimedia	Program to play music CDs with your computer's CD-ROM drive.

✔ If you don't have the CD version of the program, many of these programs can be downloaded from Microsoft's BBS (described in Chapter 7).

✔ Don't go overboard with the sound schemes unless you have a large hard drive — sound schemes can consume large amounts of room. In fact, if you're pressed for space, consider using the Control Panel's Add/Remove Programs icon for removing your old sound scheme at the same time that you're adding your new one.

✔ Finally, Table 17-3 shows some of the other programs, oddities, and curios you find on your Windows 95 CD.

Table 17-3 Windows 95 Bonus Items on the Compact Disc

Program	Location	Description
Microsoft System Diagnostics	Other	Provides detailed information about computer's internal parts.
Windows Clipbook Viewer	Other	Use this utility to view the clipboard contents, to store bitmap images, and to share these images over the network.

Program	Location	Description
Welcome 1 Video	Videos folder inside Funstuff folder	Bill Plympton's Windows 95 CD's animation stored as AVI video clip for viewing in Media Player.
Welcome 2 Video	Videos folder inside CD's Funstuff folder	Joan Gratz's Windows 95 animation stored as AVI video clip for viewing in Media Player.
Welcome 3 Video	Videos folder inside CD's Funstuff folder	Microsoft animation blowing its own horn.
Good Times	Videos folder inside CD's Funstuff folder	Edie Brickell music video.
Rob Roy	Videos folder inside CD's Funstuff folder	Rob Roy movie preview.
Buddy Holly video by Weezer	Videos folder inside CD's Funstuff folder	"Happy Days" by Weezer music.
Old MS-DOS utilities	Other	Old DOS utilities from yesteryear, enclosed for people who still value that stuff for sentimental reasons.
Printer Troubleshooter	Other (look for the EPTS folder, which is inside the Misc folder, which is inside the Other folder)	Copy the five files in this folder to your hard drive and double-click on the EPTS program to seek out and destroy almost any printer problem.
Microsoft Word viewer	Other (Wordview folder)	Run Setup from the Other folder's Wordview folder, and you'll be able to read, print, and copy the text from any version of Microsoft Word for Windows, no matter what version of Word you own. (Or even if you're a WordPerfect fan, for that matter.)
Hover	Funstuff	A reasonably cool "capture the flag" game that's pretty boring unless your computer is a real speedster.

Make Notepad Print Just the Right Way

Most Windows programs let you choose Page Setup from the File menu. That option lets you change how a page looks when it's printed. Should the page have numbers along the top or bottom, for example? Or should a title be across the top of each page?

Unfortunately, none of the programs are very clear about how to add that stuff to a page. So, here's the trick:

By inserting special symbols into the Header and Footer boxes in most Page Setup areas, you can make the date, time, filename, page numbers, or personal text appear across the top or bottom of each of your printed pages.

Those special symbols — and what they do — appear in Table 17-4.

Table 17-4	Special Codes and Their Printing Effects
Adding This Symbol to the Header or Footer Box...	**Adds This to the Printed Page**
&d	Current date
&p	Page numbers
&f	Filename
&l	Any text following this code starts at the left margin
&r	Any text following this code starts at the right margin
&c	Any text following this code is centered between the margins
&&	Inserts an ampersand
&t	Current time

Those Page Setup codes work with Notepad, several other third-party Windows programs, as well as Cardfile and Calendar (if you still have them left over from Windows 3.1).

Running Out of Memory?

No matter how much memory is stuffed inside your computer, Windows always seems to want more. Here are a few tricks for fighting back.

- ✔ If Windows says it doesn't have enough memory to do something and you're sure that your computer *does* have enough memory, check your Clipboard. If a big picture is copied to the Clipboard, delete it: That picture might be robbing Windows of the memory it needs to do something else.

- ✔ Don't use big photographs for your wallpaper. Tiling smaller images across the screen uses a lot less memory.

- ✔ If you're using a lot of DOS programs, make .PIFs for them, as described in Chapter 15. Sometimes Windows gives too much memory to DOS programs; a .PIF can get some of that memory back.

Highlighting Text Quickly

I don't know why this trick works, but here goes:

When highlighting a bunch of text in Notepad and moving the pointer from the bottom toward the top, wiggle your mouse around above Notepad's window. That speeds up the marking process.

That trick works when highlighting information in other Windows programs, too. Weird.

Plugging It In Right Side Up

This tip doesn't have *that* much to do with Windows, so it's slipped in here unannounced toward the end, free of charge.

After your computer's up and running, with all the cables plugged into the right places, put a dot of correction fluid on the top of each cable's plug. That makes it easier to plug the cables back in right-side up when they fall out.

Character Map

Windows Character Map, found in the Accessories area of the Start menu's Programs area, lets you add accented characters to funky foreign words like *à votre santé*. But when Character Map comes to the screen, all the letters and characters are small and hard to read.

Here's the trick:

- ✔ Hold down your mouse button while moving the pointer over the characters in Character map.

- ✔ When you *hold down* the mouse button, a magnified view of the characters pops to the forefront for easy viewing.

- ✔ Or just click once on any of the characters. Then when you move your arrow keys, a magnified view of the foreign characters pops up wherever you move your arrow keys.

- ✔ Don't have the Character Map on your computer? Head to the Control Panel's Add/Remove Programs icon; you can install the program there.

Chapter 18

Speedy Menu Shortcuts

- -

In This Chapter

▶ Drag-and-drop shortcuts

▶ Quick-clicking tips

▶ Choosing items quickly from a list

▶ Replacing highlighted text

- -

*B*efore you can do just about *anything* in Windows 95, you need to click on a menu.

So the quicker you can click, the quicker you can breeze through Windows and move on to the more important things in life.

This chapter shows some of the best quick-click tips.

Moving through Menus Quickly

When choosing something from a Windows menu, people usually follow the most logical course:

1. **Click on the option along the program's top and watch as the little menu falls down.**

2. **Then click on the desired item from the little menu.**

That's two clicks: The first one brings down the menu, and the second chooses the item from the menu. However, you can reduce your finger action to a *single* click.

When you click somewhere to open a menu, *keep holding down your mouse button*. When the menu drops down, slide the mouse pointer until it rests over the item you want. Then *release* the mouse button to choose that item.

That simple trick turns a two-click operation into a single-click, cutting your click work in half.

This tip works especially well on the Start button's menus. By keeping your mouse button held down after clicking on the Start button, you can weave and wade your way through all the branching menus.

Press the First Letter of an Item in a List

Windows often presents lists of a zillion options. In fact, some lists have too many options to fit on-screen at the same time. So to scroll up or down the list of options, people usually click on little arrows, as shown in Figure 18-1.

Figure 18-1:
When faced with a long list of items, press the first letter of the item you want; the highlight jumps to the first item beginning with that letter.

Name	Original Location	Date Deleted	Type	Size
Double-click Tips	C:\WINDOWS\Des...	3/24/96 7:01 PM	Text Docum...	0KB
Foo	C:\WINDOWS\Des...	4/3/96 12:43 PM	ZIP File	17KB
FooFilers	C:\WINDOWS\Des...	4/3/96 4:35 PM	ZIP File	66KB
GXE	C:\Program Files\Ac...	3/27/96 12:56 PM	ZIP File	113KB
GXEMODE	C:\Program Files\Ac...	3/27/96 12:56 PM	Application	9KB
juicy tidbits	D:\	4/9/96 12:46 PM	Word Docu...	5KB
LHARC	C:\WINDOWS\Des...	4/3/96 1:02 PM	Application	31KB
LHARC	C:\WINDOWS\Des...	4/3/96 4:35 PM	Application	31KB
LOADER	C:\WINDOWS\Des...	4/3/96 1:02 PM	Application	53KB
LOADER	C:\WINDOWS\Des...	4/3/96 1:02 PM	Text Docum...	2KB
LOADER	C:\WINDOWS\Des...	4/3/96 4:35 PM	Application	53KB
LOADER	C:\WINDOWS\Des...	4/3/96 4:35 PM	Text Docum...	2KB
Magellan	C:\WINDOWS\Des...	3/24/96 7:29 PM	Shortcut to ...	1KB
PKZWS201	C:\WINDOWS\Des...	4/3/96 12:34 PM	Application	492KB
README	C:\WINDOWS\Des...	4/3/96 1:02 PM	MS-DOS Ap...	23KB
README	C:\WINDOWS\Des...	4/3/96 4:35 PM	MS-DOS Ap...	23KB
SCREEN00	C:\JUNK	4/5/96 4:48 PM	Bitmap Image	47KB
SCREEN01	C:\JUNK	4/5/96 4:46 PM	Bitmap Image	46KB
SCREEN02	C:\JUNK	4/5/96 4:46 PM	Bitmap Image	47KB

Recycle Bin — File Edit View Help

1 object(s) selected   967 bytes

To reach an item in the bottom of the list, you could press PgDn several times, or click on the scroll bars a couple times. But here's a faster way:

When Windows lists too many items to fit on-screen at once, press the first letter of the item you want; Windows immediately jumps to that item's place in the list.

For example, Figure 18-1 lists all the deleted files decomposing in the Recycle Bin. To immediately jump to the deleted file named Magellan, press the letter M. Windows immediately jumps to the first file beginning with M. Slick, huh?

Secret Places to Click

Much of Windows consists of aiming carefully with the mouse and clicking the mouse button — pointing and clicking on a menu to choose something, for example. Or clicking in a box to put an X inside it.

But here's a secret, welcomed by those with big fingers: You don't have to aim carefully with your mouse. The next few sections show some *sloppy* places to click that work just as well.

Skipping past downward-pointing arrows

Some menus come packaged inside little boxes. And they're hidden. To make the menu drop down, you need to click on the little downward-pointing arrow next to the box. But you don't need to be overly precise, as shown in Figure 18-2.

Instead of aiming directly for the downward-pointing arrow next to a box, click inside the box itself. A click inside the box also makes the menu drop down, and the box is easier to aim at than the arrow.

Figure 18-2:
Instead of aiming for a box's arrows, click inside the box itself to reveal the drop-down menu.

Avoiding tiny check boxes and circles

Some menus make you click inside a tiny circle or radio button to change an option. For example, to change your wallpaper from Tiled to Centered, you're supposed to click in the tiny circle next to Center, as shown in Figure 18-3. Or are you?

Instead of clicking on the tiny button next to an item, click on the name of the item itself. That chooses the item, just as if you clicked inside the tiny circle.

Figure 18-3:
Clicking on an option's title does the same thing as clicking in the option's little check box.

Display: ○ Tile ⊙ Center

Replacing highlighted text

To replace text in a word processor, the usual course is to highlight the text, press the Delete key, and type in the new text. But there's a quicker way.

After highlighting some text that you'd like to replace, immediately begin typing in replacement text. Your first keystroke deletes the highlighted text, just as if you pressed Delete.

Chapter 19

Tips for Explorer and My Computer

· ·

In This Chapter

▶ Selecting files in Explorer and My Computer

▶ Viewing the size of drives, files, and folders

▶ Remembering how to move or copy files

▶ Making My Computer use Explorer's format

▶ Viewing drives and folders

▶ Moving and copying several files to other folders

▶ Making filenames easier to see

· ·

*U*ntil you get used to its cold approach, Explorer is probably the most raggedy part of Windows. It's the hole in the comfortable Windows blanket, letting the cold air of file management blow in.

Windows 95 For Dummies covers the basics of file slinging, so you won't find that stuff in this chapter. Instead, you find tips and shortcuts for pointing and clicking your way through Windows 95's baffling catacombs of icons, menus, and filenames.

Selecting Files and Folders Quickly

If you have My Computer or Explorer on-screen, you're most likely looking for some files or folders to click on. Table 19-1 shows some shortcuts for grabbing bunches of 'em, quickly.

Table 19-1	Shortcuts for Selecting Files and Folders in Explorer and My Computer
To Grab These . . .	*Do This*
A single file or folder	Click on it.
Several files or folders	Hold down Ctrl while clicking on them.
Several files or folders sitting next to each other	Click on the first file, hold Shift, and click on the last file.
A file or folder beginning with a specific letter	Press that specific letter.

Uh, How Big Is This File?

Face it, My Computer and Explorer don't volunteer much information about your files, folders, or hard drive. Most of the time, they merely list file and folder names in alphabetical order.

And that's fine, when you're first starting out with Windows. But after awhile, you need to know *more:* How big is that file? Is this file *older* than that file? And how much space do you have on your hard drive, anyway?

This tip lets you see all the gory information about files, folders, and disk drives.

✔ While holding down Alt, double-click on any file, folder, shortcut, or icon on your desktop. A box opens on-screen and reveals that little doodad's *properties:* its size, name, birth date, and the date it was last saved. You also find a list of its *attributes:* technical information about the file's various technical switches.

✔ If you click on a shortcut, however, the properties box will only tell you information about the shortcut. To see information about the real thing — the file, folder, or drive that the shortcut points to — click on the properties box's Shortcut tab and click on the <u>F</u>ind Target button. That sequence brings the real thing to the screen.

✔ Tired of poking through Explorer to find all your Paint files? Then tell Explorer to sort your files by their *file types.* Just click on the tab marked Type along the Explorer's top edge. Explorer sorts your files alphabetically by their type, from Application files to Zip files.

Where'd they go?

Got a sneaking suspicion that Explorer and My Computer aren't showing you *all* the files in your folder? You're right — they aren't. Some of the files are for the computer to use, not you. So Microsoft made them invisible. To see the files that Windows 95 has hidden from you in Explorer or any folder, choose Options from the View menu.

In the Hidden files box, click in the Show all files area. Click on the OK button, and Windows 95 begins showing you all the files in its folders.

Clicking in this area bypasses that "Hidden" attribute seen on the first page of the Properties page, meaning that all your files and folders show up, whether the Hidden box is checked or not.

Making My Computer Work Like Explorer

Windows 95 can manage files in two ways. Some people like the icon-and-window based look and feel of My Computer, with its easy-to-see folders. Others prefer the basic, "File Manager" approach of Explorer. Windows 95 doesn't give you a choice on your desktop, however: Whenever you double-click on a folder on your desktop, you're stuck with the My Computer view of icons.

If you prefer Explorer's way of looking at things, you can make Windows 95 default to Explorer's way of displaying files.

1. **Open Explorer and select Options from the View menu.**

2. **Click the File Types tab along the top and scroll down to the entry for "Folder."**

3. **Click the Edit button, highlight the explore option, and click on the Set Default button.**

Now My Computer — as well as any folders sprinkled on your desktop — will begin displaying their contents using Explorer's look and feel. To switch back to the My Computer-style of displaying a desktop folder's contents, follow these same steps, but set the default back to the open option rather than the explore option.

Uh, Am I Moving or Copying This File?

Can't remember whether you're *moving* or *copying* a file as you drag it from window to window? Then the tips below might help.

✔ As you begin dragging a file's little icon, look inside the icon. If it contains a plus sign, you're *copying* the file. If the icon doesn't have a plus sign, you're *moving* the file.

✔ If you're *copying* a file when you want to be *moving* it — or vice versa — then press or release Ctrl. One of these two actions will toggle your action between copying or moving.

All the Letters Are Too Small!

Explorer's full of tiny words in tiny little rows and columns, but it doesn't have to be. Windows 95 allows you to view your drive's filenames and folders using a wide variety of font sizes.

For example, the tip below can make Explorer's letters exceptionally large and easy to read on a groggy Monday morning.

1. **Click on a blank area of your desktop with your right mouse button and choose Properties.**

   The Display Properties screen appears.

2. **Click the Settings tab and examine the Font size box.**

   If the Font size says Small fonts, go to Step 3. If it says Large fonts, go to Step 4.

3. **Click in the Font size box, choose Large fonts, and click on the OK button.**

   Depending on your brand of monitor, Windows 95 may want to restart itself to come up with larger fonts. Follow the on-screen directions to let Windows 95 shut itself down and come back to life with larger fonts.

4. **Click the Custom button next to the Font size box.**

   Here, you can tell Windows 95 to "scale" the fonts to be a large percentage of their current size.

5. **Choose 125% from the box and click on the OK button.**

   Windows 95 probably wants you to restart your computer. (Close all your applications, choose Shut Down from the Start button, and choose Restart the computer from the menu.)

   Regardless of the method you choose, Windows 95 wakes up with larger-sized fonts on the screen.

"Cleaning Up" Those Strings of Folders

When you double-click on a folder, Windows 95 opens it to reveal that folder's contents. That means you have two folders on your screen — the original one, and the new one that you just opened.

If you open yet another folder that's inside that new folder, you'll have three folders. And if you dig inside some folders to find one that's buried deep within your filing system, you'll end up with a string of folders cluttering your desktop. But it doesn't have to be that way, as these two tips show.

Hold down Ctrl while double-clicking on a folder. Instead of opening a new window to show that folder's contents, Windows 95 simply displays that folder's contents in the existing folder's window. That feature lets you dig deeply into your folder structure without opening any extra windows.

If you want to close a string of opened folders in a hurry, hold down the Shift key while clicking on the Close button on the window of the last folder you opened. Poof! Windows 95 closes all the folders at the same time.

And, finally, this tip doesn't really belong here, but it's too useful to leave out:

Isn't it infuriating when you're stuck with a folder or window on the screen that's pretty close to the one you want — but is actually one level beneath the one you want? For instance, you have the Asparagus folder open but you *really* want to see the Vegetables folder — the one that *contains* the Asparagus folder. Here's the solution: Just press the Backspace key. Each time you press Backspace, Windows 95 opens the folder just above the one that's currently open.

Chapter 20

Desktop Tips and Tricks

In This Chapter

▶ Making programs load themselves as icons

▶ Making programs load automatically — or not

▶ Fitting more icons on the desktop

▶ Organizing the Start menu

▶ Adding Control Panel's icons to the desktop

*T*he Windows 95 desktop, like any good desktop, can be organized in a wide variety of ways to help you get your work done. Some people ike desktops messy, some like them organized, and some like to use the bottom edge for storing chewing gum.

This chapter shows how to fiddle with the Windows 95 desktop until it's working the way you want it to work.

Programs That Load Themselves as Icons

Whenever you load a program, it usually hops onto a window on the desktop, ready for work. But some programs get lazy. Instead of hopping into windows, they minimize themselves along the taskbar, where they're hard to spot.

Sometimes, however, this laziness can be handy. For example, you can tell Windows 95 to load all your programs as icons along the taskbar when you sit down at your computer. Then your programs will be champing at the bit and ready to go.

Here's the secret switch that tells Windows 95 whether to load a program in a window, load a program as an icon along the taskbar, or to load the program so that it fills the entire screen.

1. **Click on the program with your right mouse button and choose Properties.**

   Make sure that you're clicking on the program and not the program's Shortcut. (Can't find the program the Shortcut points to? Click the Shortcut tab on the Properties page and click on the Find Target button. Windows 95 drags the program to the screen.)

2. **Click on the Program tab.**

3. **Click in the arrow in the Run box.**

   To make the program load itself as an icon on the taskbar, choose Minimized.

   To make the program load itself in a window, choose Normal window.

   To make the program fill the screen as it loads, choose Maximized.

Don't remember how to put a program into the StartUp area of your Start menu? Just put the program's shortcut into the StartUp folder found in your Programs folder, which lives in your Start Menu's folder, which lives in your Windows folder. (Whew.)

How Can I Bypass My StartUp Folder?

If you place a program's shortcut into the StartUp section of the Start button's Programs' area, Windows 95 automatically loads that program each time you load Windows 95.

But what if you suddenly change your mind, and you don't *want* those programs to pop up when you turn on your computer this morning? Easy solution.

When Windows 95 starts to load, press and keep holding down Shift. That tells Program Manager not to load any of the programs listed in its StartUp folder.

Cramming More Icons onto the Desktop

Face it, having shortcuts for your favorite programs on the desktop is handy. Some people put shortcuts to all their disk drives along one edge, for example; others put shortcuts to "To-Do" lists and calendars.

And after awhile, the desktop can get crowded — especially when you're running at a lower, 640 x 480 resolution on a small monitor. The solution is to make Windows 95 pack the desktop shortcuts a little closer together, like sardines in a can. Here's how:

1. **Click an empty portion of your desktop with your right mouse button and choose P̱roperties from the pop-up menu.**

2. **Click on the tab marked Appearance.**

3. **Click in the box marked Ḏtem.**

4. **Click on the Icon selection.**

5. **Adjust the numbers in the Sḏze box.**

   ✔ When you make the numbers smaller, Windows 95 makes the icons smaller, too. For example, if you change the Size number from 32 to 16, the icons will be half their regular size, and you can pack twice as many of them into the same size space.

   ✔ You can keep the icons the same size, but make Windows pack them closer together by playing with the two Icon spacing entries in the Item box, as well. Making the Sḏze number bigger makes Windows space the icons farther apart on the desktop; decreasing the number makes Windows move the icons closer together. Try different numbers until you find the spacing that looks best on your own desktop.

   ✔ For best results with closely packed icons, shorten the icon's titles. (Just click on the titles twice, slowly, to rename them.) Shorter titles keep the words from overlapping. Oh, and you can get away with deleting the words "Shortcut to" from the titles, as well. That little arrow on the icon shows you it's a shortcut, and Windows 95 always remembers.

Organizing Your Start Menu

Sometimes, everything in Windows 95 seems fast and automatic. For example, many brand new Windows programs install themselves, create a new entry in your Start menu, and slip their own icon inside. How polite! And that new icon is easy to find, resting alone in its own offshoot from your Start menu.

But after you've added five or six more new Windows programs, the novelty wears off. In fact, with so many programs packed into the Start menu, finding the program you want can be hard. You can combat the crowding in a couple of ways.

✔ Keep your Start menu organized. Instead of having a bunch of utility programs listed under your Programs area, for example, make a Utility area under your Programs area, and move all the utility programs there.

✔ When installing a new program, don't let each new program create its own offshoot from the Start menu. If the program is polite enough to ask where you'd like its icon to be installed, take advantage of that — tell it to put its icon in the same area as similar programs.

✔ When your Start menu starts looking crowded, start weeding. Click on the Start menu with your right mouse button and choose Open from the menu. A window appears, packed with folders and shortcuts. Each folder represents an area in your Start menu; each shortcut represents an entry. Move around the shortcuts until they're set up the way you like them. (And feel free to delete the ones you no longer use.)

✔ Prefer using Explorer? Then use the preceding trick but choose Explore from the pop-up menu.

Making Control Panel Open Sections Automatically

Some chores take a couple of steps. To change wallpaper, for example, you simply right-click on the desktop and choose the Properties tab. Other chores, however, take a little longer. If you need to calibrate a joystick, for example, or change your mouse's settings, you need to bring up the Control Panel.

Or do you? Actually, you can create a desktop shortcut to any of the Control Panel's icons.

1. Call up the Control Panel.

You'll find it waiting in the My Computer folder or the Start menu's Settings area.

2. Drag and drop any of Control Panel's icons to your Desktop.

A shortcut to that icon appears on your desktop, ready for quick access.

If you constantly readjust your keyboard for different languages, consider putting a keyboard shortcut on your desktop. The same holds true for some Windows 95 programs that put their settings adjustments into your Control Panel.

Some Control Panel icons are already easy to bring up. For example, just double-click on the little speaker in the bottom-right corner of your taskbar to bring up the Multimedia volume control, where you can adjust the volume for all your sound card's components individually.

Chapter 21

Whoops! Make It Go Back to the Other Way!

Something gone horribly wrong in Windows? This chapter shows how to make Windows go back to the way it was when you first installed it. (And without having to re-install it, either.)

Undoing a Mistake

Whoops! Deleted the wrong paragraph? Entered the wrong information into a box? All is not lost.

As soon as you notice you've made a mistake, press Ctrl+Z or Alt+Backspace. Your Windows program will try to immediately undo whatever action you've just done.

I Deleted the Wrong File!

Relax — that's what the Recycle Bin is there for. And, fortunately, the Recycle Bin is usually a little bit lazy about emptying the trash. To see whether your file is there, run through the following steps.

1. Double-click on the Recycle Bin icon.

The Recycle Bin window leaps to the screen showing a list of the deleted files that are still salvageable (see Figure 21-1). If you spot your file, simply drag and drop its icon onto your desktop. Whew! Don't spot its name? Or perhaps you don't remember its name? Then move to Step 2.

Figure 21-1:
The Recycle Bin can sort through your deleted files to display them by name, location, deletion date, file type, and size.

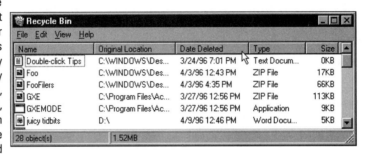

2. Click on the Date Deleted button.

The Recycle Bin normally presents an alphabetical list of your deleted files. Deleted a file yesterday? Then click on the Date Deleted button along the top to make the Recycle Bin present the files in the order that they were deleted. Still can't find it? Move along to Step 3.

If you don't remember the name of the file you deleted, but you remember the day you deleted it, tell Recycle Bin to sort by deletion date. Then you can easily look at the names of files deleted on certain days.

3. Click on the Type button.

What type of file did you delete? A text file? WordPad or Word document? Bitmap file from Paint? Clicking on the Type button makes the Recycle Bin sort deleted files by their file type. When all the text files are grouped together, for example, spotting the one you deleted is easier.

4. Click the Original Location button.

The last hope — this sorts the files by the folders where they were deleted. For example, the files deleted directly from your desktop are listed in the C:\Windows\Desktop area.

By making Recycle Bin sort through your often-unwieldy lists of deleted files, you can usually find the file you're after.

Restoring Your Original Windows Colors and Menus

It's hard to restrain yourself when faced with all the decorator colors Windows presents in the Display Properties box. Not only can you choose between color schemes like "Eggplant" and "Rainy Day," but you can design your own color schemes, as well.

And that's where the problem comes in. If you find that your fonts have somehow become hard to read — and you've been fiddling with the Display Properties box — you may have set your menus to "white on white." White letters on a white background won't show up well, no matter how big they are.

To fix things, follow these steps:

1. **Click on a blank part of your desktop with your right mouse button.**

   A pop-up menu appears.

2. **Press the letter R.**

   That selection brings up the Properties dialog box.

3. **Click the Appearance button.**

   That's along the top, second notch from the right.

4. **Press the Down arrow.**

   The Scheme box immediately begins cycling through its other schemes, from Brick to Windows Standard Large. When you push the Down arrow, the preview window displays the schemes.

5. **When you see a color scheme that's visible, press Enter.**

   Windows switches to the new, visible color scheme. The new scheme may not be as Andy Warhol-influenced, but hey, at least you can see it.

Now, if you feel it's worth the effort, go back to the scheme you had before and take a good look at these entries: Icon, Inactive Title Bar, Menu, Message Box, Palette Title, Selected Items, and ToolTip. Those all use fonts, and if you've chosen fonts that are the same color as their background, you won't be able to read them. Try sticking with plain old black on white.

Whenever you change settings in a display scheme, use the Save as button to save them under a different name. That way you can easily return to the original settings if your new ones don't work right.

Changing Your Name and Company

Remember when you typed in your name and company name while installing Windows 95 for the first time? Well, Windows remembers it. To see who Windows thinks you are, click on the My Computer icon with your right mouse button and choose Properties.

A box pops up, as shown in Figure 21-2, and Windows lists the name and company you originally typed in.

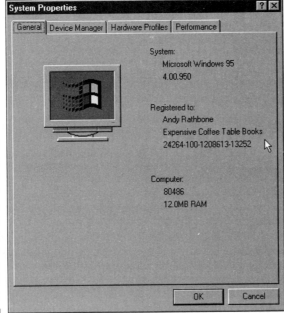

Figure 21-2:
The My Computer icon's Properties page lists a computer user's name and company.

But what if you change jobs? Or change names? Simply re-installing Windows won't do the trick; Windows always sticks with the first name and company you've entered.

You could delete Windows from your hard drive and then re-install it, typing in the new information as you go. But there's a quicker way, as described next.

The file you're about to fiddle with is hot stuff. If you make a mistake while editing it or edit the wrong portions, you can seriously confuse your computer or its programs. Be very careful.

1. **Click the Start button and choose the <u>R</u>un button.**

   A box appears.

2. **Type** regedit **into the <u>O</u>pen box and press Enter.**

   The Registry Editor program appears.

3. **Press F3.**

   A box appears.

4. **Type the word you'd like to change — your name or your company's name — into the Fi<u>n</u>d what box and press Enter.**

   The Registry Editor searches through its internal secrets, looking for what you've typed. When the Registry Editor finds your name, it displays the line of text containing the name.

5. **Double-click on the icon next to your name.**

   A box pops up, ready for you to edit the name.

6. **Change the old name to the new name and click on OK.**

7. **Press F3.**

   The Registry Editor keeps searching for the name you type in. If you've installed several programs, you'll probably find the name listed several times. Each time, repeat Steps 5 and 6 to change the old name to the new name.

8. **When the Registry Editor no longer finds the name, close the program.**

   Like any other program, the Registry Editor can be closed with a click in its upper-right corner.

9. **Check My Computer icon's Properties page to make sure that the change took place.**

   Your new name should now appear, as shown in Figure 21-3.

   ✔ Don't type too long of a name for your organization, or the Properties page won't have room to display it: The name will run right off the edge.

   ✔ Once again, be very careful when fiddling with the Registry Editor. That's where Windows stores all of its settings, and Windows might stop working if a crucial setting gets un-set.

I Messed Up My Registry!

It happened, eh? You were editing the Registry and now the computer is starting to act up — or, worse yet, isn't starting at all. Here's how to restore the registry and restore order.

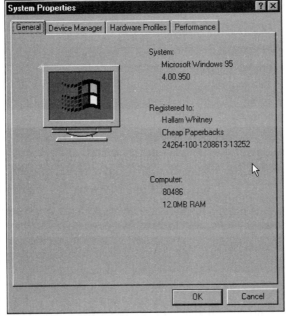

Figure 21-3:
By editing
the Registry,
you can
update your
name or
organization.

1. **Click the Start button and then click on Sh<u>u</u>t Down.**

2. **Click Restart the computer In <u>M</u>S-DOS mode and then click on <u>Y</u>es.**

3. **Change to the DOS version of your Windows folder.**

   For example, if your Windows folder is on your C drive, you would enter the following command:

   ```
   C:\> cd c:\windows
   ```

4. **Enter the following commands, pressing Enter after each line. (Note that the words *System.da0* and *User.da0* contain the number zero, not a capital O.)**

   ```
   attrib -h -r -s system.dat
   attrib -h -r -s system.da0
   copy system.da0 system.dat
   attrib -h -r -s user.dat
   attrib -h -r -s user.da0
   copy user.da0 user.dat
   ```

5. **Press the Reset button to restart your computer.**

   Following these sticky steps will restore your registry to the way it was when you last successfully started your computer.

Always Hold the Right Mouse Button When Dragging and Dropping

Windows 95 lets you do things in a zillion different ways, with no right way. That offers you more chances to stumble across the task you're trying to accomplish. But it also makes it harder to remember the right way to do something. Does holding down Ctrl while dragging and dropping a file *move* the file, *copy* the file, or create a *shortcut?* Who knows?

Well, Windows 95 knows, and you can make it remind you whenever you drag and drop something across your screen. Simply hold down your right mouse button as you drag and drop. When you release the mouse button, Windows 95 brings a menu to the screen that lets you choose between moving, copying, or creating a shortcut to that particular object (see Figure 21-4).

Figure 21-4:
Holding down your right mouse button while dragging and dropping makes it easier to see what you're doing.

Opening a Recently Opened Document

Ready to open a file you used yesterday? Chances are, you won't need to start clicking your way through an endless chain of folders to find and open it. Instead, head for the Documents list on the Start button menu. Click on Documents, shown in Figure 21-5, and Windows 95 will list the last 15 documents you've used.

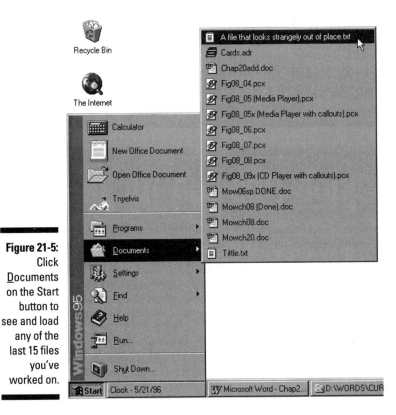

Figure 21-5:
Click
Documents
on the Start
button to
see and load
any of the
last 15 files
you've
worked on.

Click on the document's name, and Windows 95 loads that file into the program that created it, and then brings them both to the screen.

Sending to Simpler Times

Right-click on most icons, as shown in Figure 21-6, and a menu pops up, containing, among other entries, the words *Send To*. This seems easy enough to understand, given the items that pop up when you click on Send To command: With a single click you can send your object to your mail program, fax card, floppy disk, or if you're a laptop user, your Briefcase program.

But to really take advantage of the Send To command, you need to start adding your own items to the Send To menu. For example, wouldn't it be convenient to put Notepad on the list so that you could send any file to Notepad with a simple click? Or you could list a folder named Temporary on the Send To menu, making it easy to send files quickly to a folder for temporary storage.

Figure 21-6: Customize the Se<u>n</u>d To command to send files to your own favorite places.

Best of all, it's easy to add your own items to the Send To command; just follow these steps:

1. **Right click on the My Computer icon and choose <u>E</u>xplore from the pop-up menu.**

   The Explorer program appears on-screen.

2. **From drive C, double-click on your Windows folder.**

   The Windows folder opens, displaying its contents.

3. **Double-click on the SendTo folder that's in your Windows folder.**

   The SendTo folder opens, displaying a shortcut for every item that appears on your SendTo menu (see Figure 21-7).

Figure 21-7: The shortcuts listed in your SendTo folder are shown as menu items in the Send To area that appears when you right-click on an object on your desktop.

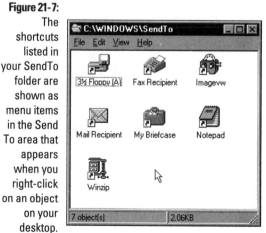

4. **Drag and drop shortcuts into the SendTo folder for items you want to appear on the menu.**

For example, drag and drop a shortcut for Notepad into the SendTo folder, as well as a shortcut for any often-used folders or programs.

5. **Close the Explorer program and any open folders.**

Any shortcut you place in the SendTo folder shows up in the Send To menu that appears when you right-click an object.

Getting Rid of the Seedy Stuff

Sometimes Windows 95 goes overboard with its level of friendliness, especially when you insert a compact disc into your CD-ROM drive. If you've slipped in an audio CD, for example, Windows 95 automatically starts blaring the first song on the album. Or if the CD contains a Windows 95 program, Windows looks for a special "AutoPlay" program on the CD and starts loading that, as well.

If you just want to grab a file off the CD, however, this friendliness turns into an obstacle: You have to wait until the CD's "automatic" program runs before you can shut it down and use Explorer to fetch your file.

To disable this CD friendliness, follow this trick: Hold down the Shift key while inserting the CD into your CD-ROM drive. That keeps Windows 95 from playing your audio CD or looking for the CD's AutoPlay program.

To permanently keep Windows 95 from automatically fiddling with your CDs, follow these steps:

1. **Click the My Computer icon with your right mouse button and choose Properties from the menu.**

2. **Click the Device Manager tab and find the CDROM drive entry.**

3. **Double-click on the CDROM drive entry to open it up and click on the CD-ROM driver that appears directly below it.**

4. **Click the Properties button at the bottom of the page and, when the new Properties page appears, click the Settings tab.**

5. **Click in the Auto insert notification box to remove the check mark.**

This disables the AutoPlay feature. To restore the feature, simply reverse the process and put the check mark back in the box.

Chapter 22

The Secret Credits Screen

*W*hen artists finish a painting, they place their names in the bottom corner. But when a programmer finishes a program, where does the name go? Many companies won't let their programmers stick their names on their programs.

So because programmers are such a secretive, sneaky bunch, they often hide their names in the program itself. These hidden initials, sometimes called *Easter eggs*, have been popping up for nearly 20 years.

Computer history buffs point back to the late 70s; back then savvy players of Atari's 2600 game console discovered a secret room with the programmer's initials hidden in the ADVENTURE game cartridge.

Today, programmers are hiding a lot more than their initials. Here are some of the goodies you'll uncover in Windows 95 — as well as the secret keystrokes you'll need to discover them.

Uncovering the Hidden Credits Screen in Windows 95

The folks at Microsoft certainly couldn't be stopped from hiding their names in Windows 95. (In fact, they've hidden their names in earlier versions, as well.) Here's how to see the Windows 95 Team's lively song and dance:

1. **Click on a blank portion of your desktop with your right mouse button.**

2. **Choose Folder from the New menu.**

3. **Name the folder** and now, the moment you've all been waiting for.

   Just type in those words, exactly as you see them.

4. **Click on the folder with your right mouse button and choose Rename.**

5. **Rename the folder** we proudly present for your viewing pleasure.

6. **Click on the folder with your right mouse button again and choose Rename.**

7. **Rename the folder** The Microsoft Windows 95 Product Team!

8. **Double-click on the folder to open it.**

Sit back and watch as the show begins, seen in Figure 22-1. (And listen, too, if you have a sound card.) And prepare to sit for a long time. A l-o-t of people worked on Windows 95, and they seem to have listed all of them. (In fact, you may have to push your mouse around a few times during the display to keep your screen saver from kicking in!)

If the trick doesn't work, you've probably spelled something wrong or capitalized a letter somewhere where you weren't supposed to. Keep trying, using the exact order spelled out above.

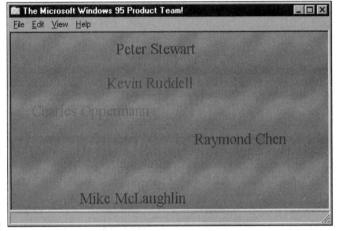

Figure 22-1:
Windows 95 comes with its own multimedia secret credits screen.

Still using Windows 3.1?

Don't be ashamed to admit it. In fact, Windows 3.1 comes with its own secret credits screen, described next. Tell your friends, although it's pretty much old news by now.

1. **Hold down Ctrl+Shift throughout the next two steps.**

2. **Click on Program Manager's Help menu and choose About Program Manager.**

3. **When the box pops up, double-click on the Windows icon.**

   The icon is in the box's upper-left corner.

4. **Click on OK.**

5. **Repeat Steps 2 through 4.**

   The Windows icon turns into a waving flag.

6. **Repeat Steps 2 through 4 again.**

   This time, you've hit it big time, and the show begins.

   ✔ See the man pointing at the chalkboard? As you keep trying the trick, over and over, you spot four different guys.

   ✔ The guy with the glasses is Microsoft's CEO, Bill Gates.

   ✔ The bald guy is Microsoft's Steve Ballmer.

   ✔ The bearded guy is Microsoft's Brad Silverberg.

   ✔ The bear is The Bear, Windows 3.1 team mascot.

   ✔ Yet another secret: The Windows 3.1 credits screen isn't limited to Program Manager. It works in just about any program that comes with Windows 3.1: Cardfile, Calendar, Paintbrush, Clock, and others.

And now for Windows 3.0 . . .

Still using Windows 3.0? (I won't say anything if you won't.) All this fancy credits stuff won't work. But this trick will:

1. **Hold down F3 and type** WIN3.

2. **Release F3 and press Backspace.**

   Surprise — new wallpaper!

Appendix A

Should I Upgrade to Windows NT 4.0?

• •

*T*hose of you who read Chapter 4 in this book know that Microsoft perpetually releases new versions of Windows. (And why not, seeing as how each new release brings oodles of cash into the corporate coffers?)

The newest release is Windows NT 4.0 — a move up from its predecessor, Windows NT 3.51. Although Microsoft made people wait a few years before they could upgrade from Windows 3.11 to Windows 95, Windows NT 4.0 appeared on the scene relatively quickly after Windows 95 hit the shelves.

That leaves a big question: Who should upgrade to Windows NT 4.0? When you're through reading this appendix, you'll be able to make an informed decision.

What Hardware Does Windows NT 4.0 Need?

Each new release of Windows requires a more powerful computer, and Windows NT 4.0 requires a machine with the following guts:

Table A-1	Windows NT Hardware Requirements
What Microsoft Says	*What Microsoft Means*
A 486 or Pentium	A fast Pentium, Pentium Pro, or ultra-fancy RISC computer, explained later.
VGA	Super VGA
Hard drive with 123MB free	2 gigabyte hard drive

(continued)

Table A-1 *(continued)*

What Microsoft Says	*What Microsoft Means*
High-density 3.5-inch floppy drive	High-density 3.5-inch floppy drive
CD-ROM drive	Fast CD-ROM drive
12MB of memory	16MB to 32MB of memory
Optional mouse	Mandatory mouse
Optional networking	Mandatory networking

The chart needs a little bit of explanation. First, Windows NT is a real hog. Unlike Windows 95, which can be squeezed onto a 60MB hard drive with just enough room leftover for Microsoft Word (seriously — I did it this evening), Windows NT needs 123MB just for itself. That's a *lot* of overhead.

Next, Windows NT can't be installed from 5 $1/4$-inch disks; you need a 3 $1/2$-inch disk drive. If, for some reason, you're running a stripped-down computer with no disk drives, you can install Windows NT from a CD-ROM drive. In fact, that's the easiest way to install the thing, since it's so huge. Windows NT can also be installed over a network if you don't have a CD-ROM drive on your computer.

Here's something new: Windows NT can run on more operating systems than just Intel's 486/Pentium/Pentium Pro-type computers. Windows NT can run on computers that use RISC (Reduced Instruction Set Computer) technology: The Windows NT operating system can work on a MIPS R4x00, Digital Alpha AXP, or Power PC. However, most of these computers cost megabucks in comparison to the plain-old desktop PCs, so you probably won't be picking one up at CompUSA.

The fact that Windows NT can run on so many different types of computers is a bonus: If you're moving from one company to another, you may still be able to work on the same Windows NT operating system, even though the new company uses a different type of computer than your old company uses.

What Can Windows NT 4.0 Do Best?

Windows NT, seen in Figure A-1, looks almost identical to Windows 95, seen in Figure A-2. But, beneath the skin, Windows NT is completely different. Windows 95 is more like a family car, designed for daily driving. Sure, it can be stretched for maximum performance. And if you stop by a garage sale and see a big piece of Rattan furniture you can't pass up, you can probably fit it into the back seat and get it home.

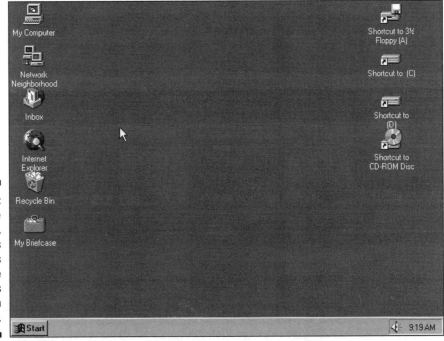

Figure A-1:
On the
surface,
Windows
NT looks
just like
Windows
95, seen in
Figure A-2.

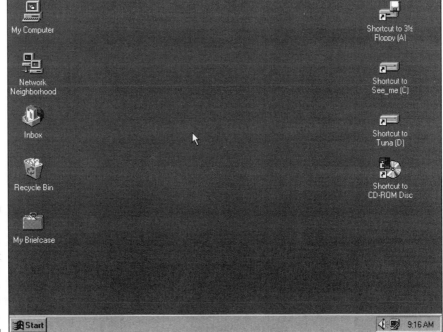

Figure A-2:
Windows 95
looks just
like
Windows
NT, seen in
Figure A-1.

On the other hand, Windows NT is like a powerful truck, built for heavy loads. It's as easy to drive as a family car (provided you don't have to get under the hood and try to adjust the transmission), but it has the power to carry large pieces of furniture on a daily basis without tearing the upholstery in the back seat.

To cut away from this goofy car analogy, Windows NT is basically made for networking in large environments, where large chunks of information need to be moved around reliably, securely, and at top speed. Windows NT lets you customize the network to a fine degree, allowing wide varieties of access.

Windows 95, too, offers networking capabilities. And, for a small office setting, it's probably all you need. (Chapter 16 shows you how to set up a network in Windows 95.)

But Windows 95 can't offer all the networking options needed by corporations that may string dozens of computers together.

What Can't Windows NT 4.0 Do So Well?

Windows NT may be powerful at networking, but that doesn't mean it's a winner in every category. Here's where Windows NT drops a few notches in esteem.

No plug and play

When you stick a new piece of hardware into your computer, Windows 95 makes an effort to recognize the incoming piece of gadgetry and automatically install the right piece of software to make it work. Known as *Plug and Play,* this new technology has smoothed wrinkled brows all over the world. For once, computers have made a giant step toward greater ease of use.

Windows NT 4.0 doesn't use the Plug and Play technology. Microsoft, already behind schedule in releasing Windows NT 4.0, had to leave the Plug and Play technology out in order to make its production deadline. Look for Plug and Play in the next release of Windows NT.

Lousy game support

Since Windows NT 4.0 is primarily used in a networking environment for large corporations, games weren't a high priority in system design. Don't be surprised if some of your favorite games won't run under Windows NT. (In fact, you won't even find support for many of your multimedia gadgets. No Virtual Reality helmets here, unfortunately.)

Why Windows 95 programs don't work well on Pentium Pros

Thinking about buying a Pentium Pro to run Windows NT? Great! Windows NT certainly flies on a Pentium Pro, as will all your Windows NT programs. But your old *Windows 95* programs will run more slowly on a Pentium Pro — perhaps even more slowly than if you'd kept them running on a regular Pentium.

See, Windows NT is a full-blooded 32-bit operating system, designed to take advantage of the latest 32-bit Pentium Pro technology. But Windows 95 still contains a few vestigial chunks of 16-bit code. And those chunks of 16-bit code are enough to keep Windows 95 programs from running at top speed on a Pentium Pro.

If you're running mostly Windows 95 programs, avoid the Pentium Pro and stick with a Pentium.

Large and hard to configure

Finally, Windows NT is huge, requiring more than 120MB of hard disk space just for itself. Also, since it offers so many options for networking, Windows NT is much harder to configure. You'll probably have trouble when plugging new parts into your computer or trying to get your latest piece of software to run correctly.

So, Should I Upgrade to Windows NT 4.0?

If you're in a corporation running large networks where dozens of people log on daily, Windows NT may be what you've been waiting for. First off, it's probably more robust than any previous version of Windows: It won't crash so darn often. If you've been using Windows NT 3.51, you'll find Windows NT 4.0 easier to use — since it now uses the Windows 95 interface, it's finally been brought up to speed in the Windows world.

But unless you're running a large network, you probably won't find much advantage in upgrading to Windows NT 4.0.

First, the operating system takes up too much space on the hard drive. Second, Windows NT may be great for the network crowd, but it's terrible for gaming. The lack of Plug and Play support makes Windows NT harder to use.

The verdict? Windows NT 4.0 is not for home users, or even small-office users. Unless you're running a large network, stick with Windows 95.

Index

Title	Author	ISBN	Price
The Internet For Macs® For Dummies® 2nd Edition	by Charles Seiter	ISBN: 1-56884-371-2	$19.99 USA/$26.99 Canada
The Internet For Macs® For Dummies® Starter Kit	by Charles Seiter	ISBN: 1-56884-244-9	$29.99 USA/$39.99 Canada
The Internet For Macs® For Dummies® Starter Kit Bestseller Edition	by Charles Seiter	ISBN: 1-56884-245-7	$39.99 USA/$54.99 Canada
The Internet For Windows® For Dummies® Starter Kit	by John R. Levine & Margaret Levine Young	ISBN: 1-56884-237-6	$34.99 USA/$44.99 Canada
The Internet For Windows® For Dummies® Starter Kit, Bestseller Edition	by John R. Levine & Margaret Levine Young	ISBN: 1-56884-246-5	$39.99 USA/$54.99 Canada

MACINTOSH

Mac® Programming For Dummies®	by Dan Parks Sydow	ISBN: 1-56884-173-6	$19.95 USA/$26.95 Canada
Macintosh® System 7.5 For Dummies®	by Bob LeVitus	ISBN: 1-56884-197-3	$19.95 USA/$26.95 Canada
MORE Macs® For Dummies®	by David Pogue	ISBN: 1-56884-087-X	$19.95 USA/$26.95 Canada
PageMaker 5 For Macs® For Dummies®	by Galen Gruman & Deke McClelland	ISBN: 1-56884-178-7	$19.95 USA/$26.95 Canada
QuarkXPress 3.3 For Dummies®	by Galen Gruman & Barbara Assadi	ISBN: 1-56884-217-1	$19.95 USA/$26.99 Canada
Upgrading and Fixing Macs® For Dummies®	by Kearney Rietmann & Frank Higgins	ISBN: 1-56884-189-2	$19.95 USA/$26.95 Canada

MULTIMEDIA

Multimedia & CD-ROMs For Dummies® 2nd Edition	by Andy Rathbone	ISBN: 1-56884-907-9	$19.99 USA/$26.99 Canada
Multimedia & CD-ROMs For Dummies® Interactive Multimedia Value Pack, 2nd Edition	by Andy Rathbone	ISBN: 1-56884-909-5	$29.99 USA/$39.99 Canada

OPERATING SYSTEMS:

DOS

MORE DOS For Dummies®	by Dan Gookin	ISBN: 1-56884-046-2	$19.95 USA/$26.95 Canada
OS/2® Warp For Dummies® 2nd Edition	by Andy Rathbone	ISBN: 1-56884-205-8	$19.99 USA/$26.99 Canada

UNIX

MORE UNIX® For Dummies®	by John R. Levine & Margaret Levine Young	ISBN: 1-56884-361-5	$19.99 USA/$26.99 Canada
UNIX® For Dummies®	by John R. Levine & Margaret Levine Young	ISBN: 1-878058-58-4	$19.95 USA/$26.95 Canada

WINDOWS

MORE Windows® For Dummies® 2nd Edition	by Andy Rathbone	ISBN: 1-56884-048-9	$19.95 USA/$26.95 Canada
Windows® 95 For Dummies®	by Andy Rathbone	ISBN: 1-56884-240-6	$19.99 USA/$26.99 Canada

PCS/HARDWARE

Illustrated Computer Dictionary For Dummies® 2nd Edition	by Dan Gookin & Wallace Wang	ISBN: 1-56884-218-X	$12.95 USA/$16.95 Canada
Upgrading and Fixing PCs For Dummies® 2nd Edition	by Andy Rathbone	ISBN: 1-56884-903-6	$19.99 USA/$26.99 Canada

PRESENTATION/AUTOCAD

AutoCAD For Dummies®	by Bud Smith	ISBN: 1-56884-191-4	$19.95 USA/$26.95 Canada
PowerPoint 4 For Windows® For Dummies®	by Doug Lowe	ISBN: 1-56884-161-2	$16.99 USA/$22.99 Canada

PROGRAMMING

Borland C++ For Dummies®	by Michael Hyman	ISBN: 1-56884-162-0	$19.95 USA/$26.95 Canada
C For Dummies® Volume 1	by Dan Gookin	ISBN: 1-878058-78-9	$19.95 USA/$26.95 Canada
C++ For Dummies®	by Stephen R. Davis	ISBN: 1-56884-163-9	$19.95 USA/$26.95 Canada
Delphi Programming For Dummies®	by Neil Rubenking	ISBN: 1-56884-200-7	$19.99 USA/$26.99 Canada
Mac® Programming For Dummies®	by Dan Parks Sydow	ISBN: 1-56884-173-6	$19.95 USA/$26.95 Canada
PowerBuilder 4 Programming For Dummies®	by Ted Coombs & Jason Coombs	ISBN: 1-56884-325-9	$19.99 USA/$26.99 Canada
QBasic Programming For Dummies®	by Douglas Hergert	ISBN: 1-56884-093-4	$19.95 USA/$26.95 Canada
Visual Basic 3 For Dummies®	by Wallace Wang	ISBN: 1-56884-076-4	$19.95 USA/$26.95 Canada
Visual Basic "X" For Dummies®	by Wallace Wang	ISBN: 1-56884-230-9	$19.99 USA/$26.99 Canada
Visual C++ 2 For Dummies®	by Michael Hyman & Bob Arnson	ISBN: 1-56884-328-3	$19.99 USA/$26.99 Canada
Windows® 95 Programming For Dummies®	by S. Randy Davis	ISBN: 1-56884-327-5	$19.99 USA/$26.99 Canada

SPREADSHEET

1-2-3 For Dummies®	by Greg Harvey	ISBN: 1-878058-60-6	$16.95 USA/$22.95 Canada
1-2-3 For Windows® 5 For Dummies® 2nd Edition	by John Walkenbach	ISBN: 1-56884-216-3	$16.95 USA/$22.95 Canada
Excel 5 For Macs® For Dummies®	by Greg Harvey	ISBN: 1-56884-186-8	$19.95 USA/$26.95 Canada
Excel For Dummies® 2nd Edition	by Greg Harvey	ISBN: 1-56884-050-0	$16.95 USA/$22.95 Canada
MORE 1-2-3 For DOS For Dummies®	by John Weingarten	ISBN: 1-56884-224-4	$19.99 USA/$26.99 Canada
MORE Excel 5 For Windows® For Dummies®	by Greg Harvey	ISBN: 1-56884-207-4	$19.95 USA/$26.99 Canada
Quattro Pro 6 For Windows® For Dummies®	by John Walkenbach	ISBN: 1-56884-174-4	$19.95 USA/$26.95 Canada
Quattro Pro For DOS For Dummies®	by John Walkenbach	ISBN: 1-56884-023-3	$16.95 USA/$22.95 Canada

UTILITIES

Title	Author	ISBN	Price
Norton Utilities 8 For Dummies®	by Beth Slick	ISBN: 1-56884-166-3	$19.95 USA/$26.95 Canada

VCRS/CAMCORDERS

Title	Author	ISBN	Price
VCRs & Camcorders For Dummies™	by Gordon McComb & Andy Rathbone	ISBN: 1-56884-229-5	$14.99 USA/$20.99 Canada

WORD PROCESSING

Title	Author	ISBN	Price
Ami Pro For Dummies®	by Jim Meade	ISBN: 1-56884-049-7	$19.95 USA/$26.95 Canada
MORE Word For Windows® 6 For Dummies®	by Doug Lowe	ISBN: 1-56884-165-5	$19.95 USA/$26.95 Canada
MORE WordPerfect® 6 For Windows® For Dummies®	by Margaret Levine Young & David C. Kay	ISBN: 1-56884-206-6	$19.95 USA/$26.95 Canada
MORE WordPerfect® 6 For DOS For Dummies®	by Wallace Wang, edited by Dan Gookin	ISBN: 1-56884-047-0	$19.95 USA/$26.95 Canada
Word 6 For Macs® For Dummies®	by Dan Gookin	ISBN: 1-56884-190-6	$19.95 USA/$26.95 Canada
Word For Windows® 6 For Dummies®	by Dan Gookin	ISBN: 1-56884-075-6	$16.95 USA/$22.95 Canada
Word For Windows® For Dummies®	by Dan Gookin & Ray Werner	ISBN: 1-878058-86-X	$16.95 USA/$22.95 Canada
WordPerfect® 6 For DOS For Dummies®	by Dan Gookin	ISBN: 1-878058-77-0	$16.95 USA/$22.95 Canada
WordPerfect® 6.1 For Windows® For Dummies® 2nd Edition	by Margaret Levine Young & David Kay	ISBN: 1-56884-243-0	$16.95 USA/$22.95 Canada
WordPerfect® For Dummies®	by Dan Gookin	ISBN: 1-878058-52-5	$16.95 USA/$22.95 Canada

Scholastic requests & educational orders please Educational Sales at 1. 800. 434. 2086

FOR MORE INFO OR TO ORDER, PLEASE CALL ▶ 800. 762. 2974

For volume discounts & special orders please call Corporate Sales, at 415. 655. 3000

7/29/96

IDG BOOKS WORLDWIDE™

Order Center: **(800) 762-2974** *(8 a.m.–6 p.m., EST, weekdays)*

Quantity	ISBN	Title	Price	Total

Shipping & Handling Charges

	Description	First book	Each additional book	Total
Domestic	Normal	$4.50	$1.50	$
	Two Day Air	$8.50	$2.50	$
	Overnight	$18.00	$3.00	$
International	Surface	$8.00	$8.00	$
	Airmail	$16.00	$16.00	$
	DHL Air	$17.00	$17.00	$

*For large quantities call for shipping & handling charges.
**Prices are subject to change without notice.

Ship to:

Name _____

Company _____

Address _____

City/State/Zip _____

Daytime Phone _____

Payment: ☐ Check to IDG Books Worldwide (US Funds Only)

☐ VISA   ☐ MasterCard   ☐ American Express

Card # _____ Expires _____

Signature _____

Subtotal _____

CA residents add
applicable sales tax _____

IN, MA, and MD
residents add
5% sales tax _____

IL residents add
6.25% sales tax _____

RI residents add
7% sales tax _____

TX residents add
8.25% sales tax _____

Shipping _____

Total _____

Please send this order form to:
IDG Books Worldwide, Inc.
Attn: Order Entry Dept.
7260 Shadeland Station, Suite 100
Indianapolis, IN 46256

Allow up to 3 weeks for delivery.
Thank you!

IDG BOOKS WORLDWIDE REGISTRATION CARD

Visit our Web site at http://www.idgbooks.com

ISBN Number: 1-56884-607-X

Title of this book: MORE Windows® 95 For Dummies®

My overall rating of this book: ❏ Very good [1] ❏ Good [2] ❏ Satisfactory [3] ❏ Fair [4] ❏ Poor [5]

How I first heard about this book:

❏ Found in bookstore; name: [6] _____

❏ Advertisement: [8] _____

❏ Word of mouth; heard about book from friend, co-worker, etc.: [10] _____

❏ Book review: [7] _____

❏ Catalog: [9] _____

❏ Other: [11] _____

What I liked most about this book:

_____

_____

_____

What I would change, add, delete, etc., in future editions of this book:

_____

_____

Other comments:

_____

Number of computer books I purchase in a year: ❏ 1 [12] ❏ 2-5 [13] ❏ 6-10 [14] ❏ More than 10 [15]

I would characterize my computer skills as: ❏ Beginner [16] ❏ Intermediate [17] ❏ Advanced [18] ❏ Professional [19]

I use ❏ DOS [20] ❏ Windows [21] ❏ OS/2 [22] ❏ Unix [23] ❏ Macintosh [24] ❏ Other: [25] _____

(please specify)

I would be interested in new books on the following subjects:

(please check all that apply, and use the spaces provided to identify specific software)

❏ Word processing: [26] _____

❏ Data bases: [28] _____

❏ File Utilities: [30] _____

❏ Networking: [32] _____

❏ Other: [34] _____

❏ Spreadsheets: [27] _____

❏ Desktop publishing: [29] _____

❏ Money management: [31] _____

❏ Programming languages: [33] _____

I use a PC at (please check all that apply): ❏ home [35] ❏ work [36] ❏ school [37] ❏ other: [38] _____

The disks I prefer to use are ❏ 5.25 [39] ❏ 3.5 [40] ❏ other: [41] _____

I have a CD ROM: ❏ yes [42] ❏ no [43]

I plan to buy or upgrade computer hardware this year: ❏ yes [44] ❏ no [45]

I plan to buy or upgrade computer software this year: ❏ yes [46] ❏ no [47]

Name: _____ Business title: [48] _____ Type of Business: [49] _____

Address (❏ home [50] ❏ work [51]/Company name: _____)

Street/Suite# _____

City [52]/State [53]/Zip code [54]: _____ Country [55] _____

❏ **I liked this book!** You may quote me by name in future IDG Books Worldwide promotional materials.

My daytime phone number is _____

IDG BOOKS WORLDWIDE

THE WORLD OF COMPUTER KNOWLEDGE®

 # YES!

Please keep me informed about IDG Books Worldwide's
World of Computer Knowledge. Send me your latest catalog.